# DEVIL
## AMONG US

# DEVIL
## AMONG US

BY MIKE McINTYRE

GREAT PLAINS
PUBLICATIONS

Copyright © 2008 Mike McIntyre

Great Plains Publications
420 – 70 Arthur Street
Winnipeg, MB  R3B 1G7
www.greatplains.mb.ca

Great Plains Publications gratefully acknowledges the financial
support provided for its publishing program by the Government
of Canada through the Book Publishing Industry Development
Program (BPIDP); the Canada Council for the Arts; as well as
the Manitoba Department of Culture, Heritage and Tourism; and
the Manitoba Arts Council.

Design & Typography by Relish Design Studio Ltd.
Printed in Canada by Friesens

Library and Archives Canada Cataloguing in Publication

McIntyre, Mike
    Devil among us : how Canada failed to stop a pedophile /
Mike McIntyre.

ISBN 978-1-894283-80-9

    1. Whitmore, Peter, 1971-.  2. Child molesters--Canada--
Biography.
3. Kidnapping--Canada.  4. Criminal justice, Administration of--
Canada.
5. Child sexual abuse--Canada--Case studies.  I. Title.
HV6570.4.C3M35 2008              364.15'36
  C2008-902491-5

*To Chassity – who knows me better
than I know myself.*

# INTRODUCTION

This book is based entirely on actual events. The dialogue contained in the text is real. Some of the content may be disturbing for young and/or sensitive readers. Discretion is advised.

All material is factual and has been derived from the following sources: extensive interviews with the families of both Manitoba and Saskatchewan victims; interviews with police officers, lawyers, victims advocates, legal experts and other justice officials; dozens of interviews with key witnesses, community residents and politicians; sworn testimony from numerous court proceedings; official court records and transcripts; police reports; psychiatric reports; risk assessments; parole documents; previously published stories; extensive online and newspaper archive research; and first-hand knowledge of covering the Whitmore case. The names of all victims and their families have been changed to protect their privacy and in conjunction with existing court orders.

This is my fourth true crime book and, without a doubt, my most difficult and important to date. As a father of two young children, the Peter Whitmore case struck a raw nerve with me. Whitmore truly could be the poster boy for Canada's revolving door justice system and his case demanded further examination and explanation. I believe the end result is an eye-opening look at a system which clearly struggles to deal with the most dangerous among us and, too often, simply pays lip service to the protection of our most innocent and vulnerable citizens.

It was a long and difficult journey, one that I could not have completed without the help of many people. Special acknowledgment to the families of the two victims in Winnipeg and Saskatchewan, who I got to know personally and whose strength and courage is a true inspiration. You are always in my thoughts and I am grateful for entrusting me to tell your stories.

I would also like to thank Bernard Tremblay and the RCMP, Dan Brodsky, Roz Prober, Vivian Song, Jana Pruden, Barb Pacholik, John Gormley, the residents of Whitewood, Bruce Owen, Jason Bell and all my colleagues at the Winnipeg Free Press; and Gregg Shilliday and the staff at Great Plains Publications for always believing in me.

Finally, none of this would be possible without the love and support of my family including my wife, Chassity; son, Parker; and daughter, Isabella. They are the greatest inspiration anyone could ask for.

www.mikeoncrime.com

# PROLOGUE

## PETERBOROUGH, ONTARIO
September 19, 1980

To: Dr. C, The Medical Center

*My apologies for the delay in sending you a note regarding this boy's assessment. His school report, to me, was somewhat delayed, and as usual, summer holidays always seem to catch me somewhat delayed, come September.*

*I saw Peter and 'Mom' on several occasions and as well, did receive a fairly extensive report regarding his academic behaviour and needs as the Psych Services in Toronto saw fit. As you know, Peter is currently attending a regular classroom in Omemee, and living in a fairly busy family. His placement there has been arranged privately by his guardian, and contact with his natural mother has been maintained fairly regularly.*

*Clinically, of course, Peter very definitely presents as a very vulnerable child in need of support, not only in the academic area, but also in the social and emotional one. He handled himself fairly age appropriately, from time to time, but required frequent re-assurance and support to allow him to complete the tasks requested of him.*

*Behaviourally, there was some limit testing which he easily responded to. He spoke very warmly of his natural mother, and has convinced himself that fairly soon, in the near future, he would be residing with her.*

*In talking with Mrs. Budd, the current foster mother, Peter has exhibited a considerable amount of frustration in adapting to normal family routine. Most of his frustration is expressed in aggressive activity which now the family anticipates and has been able to intervene quite often, earlier, and help Peter express himself more appropriately. Certainly Mrs. Budd's attitude and her current management techniques leave little to critique. I feel that Peter will thrive considerably providing the family can survive his emotional demands. I discussed this with them, the fact that Peter's behaviour can be a very emotionally draining one, and therefore, the family must take precautions to build up some protections for itself so as not to have the placement deteriorate.*

*I suggested to 'Mom' that the school can request psychological educational assessment by a consultant that the county quite often uses. For further support, I also directed Mrs. Budd to explore the possibility of Peter's involvement at Youth of Otonabee, although he may be somewhat young for that kind of group activity.*

*At the moment I know of no groups at the Mental Health Clinic. At this stage, I see no need for psychotherapy, but rather his emotional needs can be more appropriately met and potential conflicts resolved by a living, modeling situation.*

*The Ritalin he is currently taking would seem to very definitely help to contain some of his difficulties with distractibility and poor concentration, and I would think, that we should probably not alter his drug regimentation since he seems to be suffering very little from side effects.*

*Diagnostically, of course, Peter is very difficult to categorize other than that he is experiencing very definitely a behavioural reaction of childhood, primarily with a perception problem, but also, showing many of the hallmarks of early maternal deprivation with the resultant poor self-esteem...and need for attention at all costs.*

*Hoping this will be of help to you in your continuing involvement with this family and Peter.*

# CHAPTER ONE

## WHITEWOOD, SASKATCHEWAN
### SUMMER 2006

Every small town has one – a popular gathering point where people meet regularly to discuss whatever happens to be on their mind that day. The weather. Gas prices. Sports scores. Report cards. Gossip. It's where the heart of the community beats strongest.

Whitewood was no different. And one of the best places to take the town's pulse is at the Can-Am Restaurant. Located at the intersection of two major arteries – the Trans-Canada Highway and Highway 9 – the truck stop diner is usually jumping at all hours of the day and night.

And it's not just the 1,000 local residents who keep it going.

Whitewood is known as the Crossroads Community – their local slogan is "where the world truly travels by our door every day." The south-eastern Saskatchewan farming community is a traditional rest stop for weary travellers – westbound drivers still face another 90 minutes to Regina, those heading east are still a good two hours from Brandon, Manitoba.

As such, it's the perfect place for a quick pit stop. Hungry truckers know they'll always be greeted with a smiling face, a good meal and even better conversation.

Yet on this warm mid-summer day, strangers walking into the eatery were met by some unusual sights and sounds.

Oh, the food was still as good as ever – particularly the generous servings of homemade pie, always warm and flaky. But it was obvious to any outsider that something was troubling Whitewood.

Locals sat quietly in booths and at tables, their conversations considerably muted. Some exchanged nervous glances towards the front door. Others quickly darted their eyes away.

In town, the reaction was much the same. The streets were virtually empty, with discarded bicycles sitting on front lawns next to soccer balls and skipping ropes. Children were nowhere to be found.

Windows were closed, despite a refreshing breeze. Blinds were drawn, despite the ample sunshine beaming down from above. And doors were shut and locked, a rarity indeed.

It was clear Whitewood had rolled up its welcome mat.

"It's scary. I lock my door now," a middle-aged woman told a journalist while peering out from behind her door.

"It's got to take a sick mind to do this. My God, what a story," another long-time Whitewood resident added a few doors down.

"This isn't supposed to happen in a place like this," said a third local.

It had only been a few hours since they'd heard the news. But most residents were clearly still in a state of disbelief. The story had been all over the news that morning, a tale so shocking that even the town's veteran mayor was at a loss for words.

"You can never tell what is coming down the highway... and probably we don't want to know," said a clearly distraught Malcolm Green.

Their trust had been violated. Their innocence had been stolen.

• • • • •

JULY 30, 2006

It was late in the evening by the time Kevin White got around to checking his phone messages following a relaxing weekend at his cottage.

The RCMP had called with an urgent request for the owner of the Whitewood Chrysler dealership – who also heads up the local Citizens on Patrol group. A 10-year-old local boy had failed to return home that afternoon after going for a bike ride. There was serious concern he'd been abducted.

Police were now calling White, having heard reports from several locals that a mysterious stranger seen driving around town had come to get some work down on his van days earlier. Police desperately needed to get some information on the customer. White instantly recalled his strange encounter with the man.

It had been two days earlier – about 7:45 a.m. Friday morning – when White pulled into the parking lot. His attention was quickly drawn to a van bearing Alberta plates. It hadn't been there the previous evening when he'd locked up.

White passed by the van without stopping as he went inside the dealership. He hadn't even sat down at his desk when there was a series of loud knocks. White didn't recognize the two faces standing at the front door.

One was a white male, perhaps in his early 30s, with dark brown hair, a few days worth of facial hair, maybe 5'10, and 190 pounds. At this side was a tall, lanky boy, aboriginal, seemingly in his early teens. White went outside to see what they needed. The older man began talking.

"We've got some tire trouble," he said, pointing to the parked van White had observed on his way in. "It's flat."

White walked over for a closer look.

"We slept in the van last night," the man continued. He then introduced himself. "Robert Summer," he said, extending a hand.

Summer said they'd driven over something the previous night, punctured the tire and then pulled into the dealership, waiting for it to open in the morning.

White asked the man where they were headed.

"Moosomin," said Summer. The small town was about 50 kilometres east of Whitewood down the Trans-Canada. "My wife lives there."

The young boy stood silently by his side. White looked over his way, prompting Summer to continue talking. "My son," he explained.

White nodded, and then got down on his knees to take a closer look at the deflated tire. "You're from Alberta, eh?" said White, now just making friendly chat with his customer.

"Yeah, St. Albert. That's where all the big money is," Summer agreed with a chuckle.

White got up and began heading inside, Summer and his son following him. White wasn't sure if he had the right replacement.

"I only have $300 on me," Summer said. He began questioning how much a new tire would cost, seemingly concerned about the expense.

White thought it somewhat odd for a man who'd just bragged about coming from oil-rich Alberta. White found a used tire in the back, which seemed to please the man. He quickly made the repair while his office manager – who had since arrived for work – began writing up the invoice. The total was $113.

Summer briefly went outside to the van to get his money, leaving his son alone with White. The boy looked around the inside of the shop but said nothing. Summer returned, paid cash – and then inquired about another vehicle he'd seen parked in the lot.

"I'll give you $300 for it," he said, surprising White with the out-of-the-blue offer. He said he was thinking about getting it so his son could drive. White wondered to himself if the boy was even old enough to drive.

White said he'd want at least $500 for the clunker.

"All I've got is $300," said Summer.

• • • • •

White hadn't thought much more about the early-morning visit – until now. Since White was out of town, he told police he'd get his office manager to help them. White immediately dialled Lynnette Luypaert at home and explained the situation.

Luypaert rushed over to the store, where she was met by police. She dug through the files and quickly found the invoice she'd written up for Robert Summer.

Police were especially interested in the licence plate and vehicle identification numbers of the van in question. Both had been recorded.

Police took a copy of the invoice and immediately plugged the numbers into their computer system. There was an instant hit.

And it was the worst news possible.

• • • • •

Larry Munroe kept looking at the front door, believing his son would walk through it any moment. He refused to think anything else.

"He'll try and run," a defiant Larry told the RCMP officers who had gathered inside their living room. "He won't fall prey to that scum."

Larry was a proud, strong man – qualities he'd instilled in 10-year-old Adam. He truly believed his son would find a way out of this mess.

The Munroes may have been self-described "simple farm folks," but they were no simpletons. They were fighters, survivors.

*God help whoever did this to us*, Larry thought to himself. *They don't know who they're dealing with.*

Paula Munroe wished she could share in her husband's optimism. Instead, horrible thoughts were racing through her mind about what could be happening that very moment to her baby boy.

A mother's first instinct was to protect her child at all costs. Yet Paula was now struggling with the reality there was nothing – absolutely nothing – that she could do for Adam at this very moment.

Adding to her grief was the overpowering feeling of guilt. Paula blamed herself for Adam's disappearance and took no solace in the re-assuring words from her husband or police.

The tears came flooding down her cheeks. The colour drained from her face. The past 24 hours were now a blur of memories and emotions as the family struggled to understand what had happened.

Police were patient, but also persistent. They needed as much detail as possible, as quickly as possible. Time was of the essence.

• • • • •

Larry took police back to the previous evening, when the stranger had shown up on the family's sprawling, 360-acre property just outside Whitewood.

The man was driving a van with Alberta plates. With him was a young native boy.

The pair had actually visited the Munroe farm six days earlier, on Saturday July 23. On that day, they came by looking to sell a DVD player, apparently needing money for gas.

The Munroes had declined the offer but Adam had given the man and the boy a dozen fresh eggs. The visit was brief and non-eventful.

Now the pair was back – only this time they were paying a social visit. Paula was home at the time with her three children as Larry was in town running some errands.

The man introduced himself as Robert Summer. The teenage boy was his nephew, Kyle. Summer gave a little more background, telling Paula how his wife had died of cancer two years earlier. Now he was looking for a fresh start on life, having just re-located from Alberta.

Summer said he was a carpenter by trade and had just bought an old home in the area, which he was planning to restore. He thought it might be nice to introduce his son to some new kids in the area and asked Paula if she'd mind letting Kyle play with Adam for a bit that evening.

Paula agreed, knowing Adam was always happy to have a new friend to show around.

Adam agreed to give Kyle a tour of the farm, then showed off some of his wacky inventions he'd made. Even though he was only in grade four, Adam told everyone his dream was to be a scientist when he grew up. There certainly was no limit to his energy and creativity.

His latest creation was a coffee machine made out of a cardboard box, tape, foil and Styrofoam cups. Then there was his toy robot. Adam also had a way with animals of any kind, such as the injured crow he'd helped nurse back to health the previous year.

The family had called her "Russell Crow," a nod to the popular actor. Adam also adored his pet rats – always a hit with visitors.

Summer was on his way out of the Munroes' driveway when he stopped, then returned to the house. He told Paula he'd just punctured his tire. Larry had just returned home about the same time, got introduced to the visitor and quickly offered to help.

This was hardly an unusual situation for the Munroes. Since their farm was located just off a major highway – and clearly visible from the road – motorists would often come by with various requests. The need for gas. Directions. The use of a telephone. A quick repair.

The Munroes were always happy to help. That's how it is done on the Prairies, neighbours helping neighbours. And since they'd moved from Alberta four years earlier, folks in Whitewood had gone out of their way to welcome them to the community.

Whether it was breakfast at the Can-Am or a trip to the grocery store, Larry and Paula never went far without running into a familiar smiling face. They tried to return the good will, employing several local youths at their farm to help with some of the chores.

Larry and Paula regularly opened their doors to visits as well, as families and kids loved seeing the baby pigs, sheep, cows and chickens up close. The couple also farmed out their animals for birthday parties and petting zoos for festivals and carnivals in the area.

Life was good in Whitewood. Adam and his two sisters – Sarah, 12, and Brittany, 9 – had adapted to the move nicely and were fitting in well at the local school.

But none of that mattered now. Adam was missing and their world was falling apart. It all seemed like a nightmare – but the officers sitting in their home were a cruel reminder of how real this was.

Larry told police how Summer said he'd just had the same tire patched a day earlier at the local Chrysler dealership, which was now closed. Larry knew just the person who could help get Summer on his way. He called Willy Cowan at home, and the local auto body shop owner agreed to meet the men at his shop.

It was just after 7 p.m. Saturday when Larry arrived with his guest. Cowan and Summer were introduced, and then made small talk as the repair was quickly made. Summer mentioned his son was going to a school up the highway, near a reserve, and was enjoying life in Saskatchewan.

Larry and Summer returned to the farm within the hour. Kyle and Adam were still playing, but Summer told his nephew it was time to go. Perhaps they could return another day, he said. The Munroes said that would be nice.

They didn't have to wait long – Summer returned Sunday morning. He told Paula he'd noticed the sign on their main gate off the highway, advertising eggs for sale, and was interested in picking up a dozen or two.

Summer also suggested to Paula that perhaps the two boys could play together again that day. He mentioned having some errands to run and thought it might be a good way to pass the day.

Paula agreed, knowing her son would enjoy the company. And with Larry working on the road driving his truck that day, she thought it would help keep the kids occupied while she tended to various chores around the farm.

Adam was excited about the chance to show Kyle a "haunted house" in the area. The old vacant property – located about a mile southwest of the Munroe farm – was the stuff of local legend for kids in Whitewood.

Summer offered to drive the boys to the area for a closer look, but Adam said he wanted to go for a bike ride instead.

It was just after 11 a.m. when the two boys headed out. Adam took his bike, while Kyle grabbed an older spare one lying around the farm.

Paula told her son not to be too long, that she wanted him home for lunch. Adam promised they wouldn't go far and would be home soon.

Paula watched as the boys pedalled away, marvelling at her son's social skills and ability to make new friends so quickly.

She resumed working around the property, her two daughters helping as well. It wasn't hard to lose track of time on the farm, where the real clock that matters is the bright one in the sky. With so many daily tasks to complete, daylight is both a friend and foe.

Yet Paula started to get concerned as the noon-hour came and went and Adam still hadn't returned.

She called her husband, explaining what had happened. Paula said she was going to take the girls and go take a quick walk through the area, figuring she'd find them playing in a field nearby, catching frogs or God knows what else, oblivious to the clock.

Now it was Paula who was struggling with the realities of time. Although it had been just a few hours earlier, that long, lonely walk seemed like a lifetime ago.

Her anger with Adam for not coming home on time had been replaced with worry and regret. The safe, comfortable confines of her community now seemed foreign.

She went over to a neighbour's, hoping that maybe Adam had popped in for a visit. He was good friends with Whitney Shepherd, 9, but the little girl told Paula she hadn't seen him.

"If you do see Adam tell your mom and get her to phone the police, okay," Paula said before leaving.

Paula continued her search and told police how her heart sank when she spotted something familiar in a vacant garage near the house the boys had been headed towards.

It was Adam's bike. But there was no sign of her son. Beside it lay the bike Kyle had been riding. He, too, was gone.

Paula had called Larry immediately, telling him something was very wrong. It was all starting to come together now.

"Rob Summer and Kyle have him," she screamed into the phone. "They took him."

Larry was having a hard time believing his wife's shocking claims. He felt he was a good judge of character and couldn't believe the man he'd just helped the previous night could have done something to his son.

Larry said he was on his way home. Paula immediately called police, reporting her son missing. And the excruciating waiting game began.

As police now sat in their home late in the evening taking notes, the Munroes were still very much in the dark about what was happening. Their fears grew when officers pulled out a picture and asked them if they recognized the man.

It was Robert Summer.

"Who is he? What has he done?" Paula demanded. She knew the photo was a mug shot – which indicated the man was known to police.

Police didn't want to get into details but told the family they would do everything possible to find their son.

The Munroes also had major questions about Kyle. Who was this boy? Was he truly the man's son? Had he helped lure Adam into a trap? Or was he a victim, too?

The police left, promising to stay in touch and to pass on more information as quickly as they could. They told the Munroes to stay close to the phone, to stay strong and not give up hope.

But these were just words, empty words to a family reeling from the news that a man they'd let into their lives – and their home – had now taken something so precious.

They had so many questions, so many horrible scenarios going through their heads. What did this man want with Adam? What was he doing to him? Why had he picked them?

Until now, the only invaders the Munroes had to worry about were the coyotes and foxes trying to get at their barnyard animals.

But then along came the mysterious Summer with a story that preyed on their trust and now may cost them their son.

# CHAPTER TWO

## ARLINGTON, TEXAS

It started as a quick visit to a loved one's house – and ended in a horrific discovery that would forever change the way police do business.

Donna Hagerman was driving through her old neighbourhood in Arlington, Texas, on the afternoon of Saturday Jan. 12, 1996. Her two children – Amber, 9, and Ricky, 5 – were in the backseat.

Donna thought the kids might like to say hi to grandma and grandpa so she pulled into the driveway of the Highland Drive home where she had been raised. Jimmie Whitson was working on a car in the front yard, while Glenda was inside the home.

Amber and Ricky made a beeline for the two bicycles their grandpa kept in the front yard, just for them. The children asked if they could go for a ride around the neighbourhood. Donna agreed, but told her kids to take a quick spin around the block, the come straight back.

Amber and Ricky headed to the parking lot of what used to be a Winn-Dixie grocery store. It was a popular gathering point for neighbourhood kids who would set up ramps to ride their bikes.

According to police and media reports, both Amber and Ricky took a turn on the ramp. Ricky then told his sister they'd better get going. Amber insisted on another ride.

Ricky headed back, without his sister. Upon arrival, his mother and grandpa told him to return to the parking lot to get Amber. Ricky pedalled away, but returned moments later. He was still alone.

Amber was gone, he said.

Jimmie Whitson got in his truck and went straight to the old grocery store to find his granddaughter. He arrived to find a police car sitting in the parking lot.

An officer explained they'd just received a 911 call – an area resident had just watched a young girl being pulled into a black, late-model pickup truck. She was kicking and screaming.

All that had been left behind was a bicycle.

Jimmie instantly recognized it as the one Amber had just been riding. Family members say it took all of eight minutes from the time Amber left for her bike ride until she was grabbed off the street by a stranger.

Police learned that a truck matching the description of the abductor had been seen driving around the area earlier that day. Police believed a predator was at work.

Police and the FBI quickly formed a task force to investigate the kidnapping and made repeated pleas to the public for information. Her picture was soon on every newspaper and television station in the state.

"Please don't hurt my baby," Donna Hagerman pleaded publicly. "She's just an innocent child. Please, please bring her home safe. Please."

The desperate search ended four days later with a grisly discovery. A man walking his dog found the nude body of a little girl in a creek, just outside an apartment block in Arlington.

It was Amber. Her throat had been slit. An autopsy later revealed she was likely alive for at least two full days before she was killed.

The task force had few leads to work with but developed a potential profile of her killer. They surmised the man was probably in his mid-20's, lived nearby and may have recently had some stress in life that caused him to last out against an innocent victim.

Thousands of tips began pouring in, but none proved fruitful. More than a year after it was formed, the task force was disbanded and the case grew cold.

However, Amber's name would live on forever.

In July 1997, police and the media in Dallas, Texas developed a voluntary partnership designed to improve the flow of public information in future child abduction cases where there is believed to be "imminent danger."

The idea was to get word of a missing child out as quickly as possible – in the same way urgent weather alerts were already being broadcast.

Finding a name for the project was easy – they would call it an Amber Alert.

It didn't take long for word to spread and other major American cities to get on board. The U.S. Justice Department got involved and began to oversee all programs, both city and state-wide. All 50 U.S. states now have Amber Alert plans in place.

The U.S. government says more than 150 children have been found, at least in part to their cases being the subject of Amber Alerts.

The warnings are now distributed by every means possible – radio stations (both commercial and satellite), television, e-mail, text message and electronic roadside signs, where possible. Some states have even used video lottery terminals to reach the public.

The police agency probing a disappearance ultimately makes the call whether to issue an Amber Alert. The U.S. justice department has established several criteria for when to issue an alert, including:

- law enforcement must be certain that an abduction has taken place
- the child must be at risk of serious injury or death
- there must be sufficient descriptive information of child, captor, or captor's vehicle to issue an alert
- the child must be 17 years old or younger

However, police have made exceptions to these guidelines, especially in cases of parental abductions where Amber Alerts have been issued despite a low risk of imminent harm to the child. Vulnerable adults – such as those suffering from developmental problems or mental illness – have also been included in warnings.

Not everyone agrees Amber Alerts are an effective tool for police.

James Alan Fox, an American expert on kidnapping and murder, wrote in the *New York Times* that the system has the potential to "stir up mayhem such as vigilante hysteria and dangerous car chases." He also claimed too many alerts could result in a "cry wolf" syndrome where most of the public simply tune out.

Canada was slow to react and didn't get on board with Amber Alert until 2002, when Alberta launched the country's first program. Several provinces soon followed – Ontario, Quebec, Manitoba, New Brunswick, Prince Edward Island and Newfoundland in 2003, British Columbia and Nova Scotia in 2004. Saskatchewan finally launched its program on July 15, 2004.

The RCMP is immediately notified whenever an Amber Alert is issued given their role as a national police force. Border officials are also contacted.

It was pure coincidence that the official launch of Amber Alert in Saskatchewan came exactly 10 days after a five-year-old child disappeared under mysterious circumstances.

Tamra Jewel Keepness was last seen in her Regina home around 11 p.m. on Monday July 5. It wasn't until the following afternoon that family members apparently noticed her missing.

Her disappearance sparked one of the largest searches in Regina history and yielded more than 1,500 tips – but remains unsolved to this day.

Police believe Tamra was the victim of foul play and continue to investigate. Family members have repeatedly said they believed she was randomly snatched from her bedroom, but police don't think that was the case. They believe Tamra's abductor was known to her and have remained focused on her family.

At the time Amber Alert was introduced, the massive search for Tamra was winding down. Saskatchewan justice officials said her case wouldn't have met the criteria they'd established.

"An Amber Alert wouldn't have added anything to the media assistance and the broadcasters and the information that went to the public in that case," Chief Terry Coleman of the Saskatchewan Association of Chiefs told local media at the time.

Media outlets did receive an urgent bulletin that Tamra was reported missing, including a description of the girl. Even the U.S. television show America's Most Wanted got involved by posing information on the case on its website. A $25,000 reward was also announced.

In Saskatchewan, all police agencies and media outlets that are members of the Saskatchewan Association of Broadcasters are part of the Amber Plan along with Child Find Saskatchewan, Saskatchewan Justice, Canadian Border Services and SaskTel.

The plan works as follows:

- The police agency investigating the case will immediately provide a prepared text to the RCMP Division Operational Communication Centre.
- The Amber Alert notification would include the victim's name, age and physical description including clothing; a recent photograph of the victim, along with the time and location where they were last seen.
- Police should also describe the vehicle that was involved in the abduction, last known direction of travel and possible destination, plus any description of the suspect.
- The public would be given a standard toll-free number to call, and police were to remind citizens not to try and be heroes by taking down the suspect themselves.

- The RCMP Division Operational Communication Centre would receive Amber Alert notification forms and complete a fan out on the abduction to member media outlets, all Saskatchewan Police Services, RCMP Detachments and Canadian Border Services Agency units.
- A special tone would be provided to media outlets to signify an Amber Alert. The tone may be followed by a crawl for television or a voice message for radio.

The RCMP Division Operational Communication Centre was tasked with notifying all broadcasters when an Amber Alert is cancelled and the reason for cancellation.

Broadcasters were to alert the public as soon as possible. The policy recommended that media outlets broadcast the alert four times per hour in the first four hours, twice per hour for the next five hours and with each regularly scheduled news broadcast for the remaining 15 hours.

In extended situations, individual media outlets will decide how often information will be broadcast. Broadcasters will also broadcast Amber Alert cancellations.

• • • • •

For all the planning that had gone into Saskatchewan's Amber Alert protocol, more than two full years would pass until the system would get its first test.

But that would all change with the sudden disappearance of Adam Munroe. RCMP realized how critical the situation was and that the Whitewood boy was in grave danger.

It was late Sunday night when police had the paperwork ready and the full Saskatchewan public began learning about what had happened in their own backyard. But there was yet another twist to this disturbing case.

The mysterious stranger had stolen two kids, not one.

# CHAPTER THREE

## WINNIPEG, MANITOBA

Kyle Mason was no stranger to going missing – or putting his family through hell.

Loved ones certainly hadn't forgotten October 2004, when the 12-year-old bolted from his teaching assistant at Churchill High School. The family made a public plea through the media for his safe return.

"We love him and I want him to come home," the boy's grandmother, Carol Mason, said through tears.

Kyle's behaviour had been erratic in the weeks preceding his disappearing act. There were numerous arguments and blow-ups with family members that usually ended with him running from the house.

Once he was found with his older brother and once he spent the night at the home of a stranger after making up a story about being kicked out of home.

Family members launched a desperate search for Kyle, including driving around the streets at all hours of the day and night.

"I've been living in my car," his stepfather, Al Baxter, said. "We just want the boy to come home."

The family pointed to a recent *Winnipeg Free Press* story about a child molester police were searching for.

"A runaway is at risk from these people," Kyle's grandmother said.

She said her grandson probably had a false sense of safety after spending a few nights away from home without anything terrible happening.

Winnipeg police said they would keep an eye out for the boy, but were not actively looking because of his history of running away. If he was younger than 12, different rules would apply.

Kyle eventually came home – four days later. He wouldn't say much about where he'd been or what he'd done while away, but explained that he didn't like the restrictions he faced at home or school and wanted some freedom, albeit temporarily.

Kyle pulled a disappearing act of a different kind the following year, when his curiosity got the best of him while exploring one of Winnipeg's riverbanks.

He got too close to the water and slipped in the mud, his feet and legs becoming stuck. Firefighters were eventually called out to rescue him from the sludge.

There had been other close calls with Kyle, who seemed to be a magnet for trouble. Yet despite this background, Kyle's family were absolutely convinced this time that something truly terrible had happened to him.

• • • • •

It had all began to unravel on Friday July 21 – the day Al Baxter brought home the stranger.

Baxter worked in construction and had been toiling away at a roadside project in Headingley, just on the western out-skirts of Winnipeg. A new hire had showed a few days earlier. His name was Robert Summer.

Ken Melnyk, general manager of Con-Pro Industries, had approved Summer's hiring. Summer had told the on-site supervisor he desperately needed money.

Summer was quickly put to work alongside about a dozen other employees, including Baxter. The two men spent some time talking that day and realized they had something in common.

Summer said he was from Newfoundland, a member of the Coast Guard who had been out in Calgary working with his brother while on a four-month leave. Now he wanted to make it back home to visit his estranged wife and two children.

Baxter's common-law wife, Jennifer Mason, had been born and raised on the east coast. Baxter shared this detail with Summer, along with other information about his family. He talked about some of the trouble back home, including his troubled stepson, Kyle, and his penchant for running away.

Summer mentioned needing to find a temporary place to stay – he was currently living out of his van – and wondered if Baxter had any ideas. Baxter said he might – but that they needed to check with his wife first.

Following work that day, Baxter invited Summer back to his place. Mason and her four children were home at the time and introduced to Summer. Baxter suggested to Mason that they could maybe help Summer out.

"I feel so sorry for him," Baxter told Mason in a private con-versation. Summer was sitting in their basement at the time.

"I'm not sure that's what I want to do," said Mason.

She had some concerns, especially about bringing an outsider into a home that was already filled with tension.

Summer eventually came upstairs and interjected, telling Mason he didn't want to be a burden. He suggested they go out for dinner – his treat – and talk about it further. They ended up at a local Chinese food restaurant.

Mason eventually agreed to compromise, telling Summer he could stay as long as he wasn't alone in the house with the children.

She explained that a caregiver came in several times a week to provide assistance and that Summer would have to make sure he left the house whenever she or Baxter weren't home.

Kyle interrupted the conversation. "Hey dad, I know you just got paid today. Gimme $20," he said.

"No," said Baxter.

"Awww, c'mon, give it to him," Summer said, jokingly.

Baxter didn't seem to find it funny. "No, we don't give him money anymore. He just uses it to buy pot," said Baxter.

Summer said he understood. "I worked in social services for four years. I've dealt a lot with getting kids off drugs," he said.

Baxter and Mason were all ears. But Summer was clearly having second thoughts about the potential living arrangements.

"You guys have a lot going on in your lives, a lot of chaos," said Summer. "I'm not really sure I should stay."

Mason insisted he should. Although leery at first, she was feeling comfortable with Summer after further discussions – especially as he spoke about his life in Newfoundland. He seemed like a friendly, charismatic fellow – and his background with the Coast Guard had curried some favour.

Summer said he wanted to thank them. "I'll show you I'm a good guy. Let's go buy some groceries," he said as they left the restaurant.

Mason and Baxter said that wasn't necessary.

"You know us Easterners, we're giving like that," Summer said with a smile.

They all headed to a neighbourhood Safeway store where Summer agreed to pick up the $150 tab. He said he didn't want to be a burden on them and would certainly do more than his fair share around the home in exchange for their gratitude, including paying rent.

Summer then surprised Mason with yet another offer. He wanted to take Kyle camping.

"Just for a couple weeks, to get him away from some of the bad influences," Summer explained.

Mason quickly rejected the offer, somewhat taken aback.

They returned home, with Mason heading straight to the kitchen to put the groceries away and tidy up. Baxter and Summer stayed outside in the backyard.

The men eventually came inside – and Summer told Mason they had come up with a plan.

"Me and Al are going to take a trip," he said.

"What?" asked Mason.

Summer explained that he had arranged to buy a truck in Regina and needed to pick it up. He said the only hitch was what to do with the van he was currently driving.

Summer had come up with a brilliant idea. "I'll give you guys the van," he told Mason. "Al's been a good buddy to me."

There was one small catch – Baxter needed to come along for the ride to Saskatchewan. Once there, Summer would get his new vehicle and Baxter could have the van. For free.

MIKE MCINTYRE

Baxter was certainly impressed. The family was of limited means and could use any help they could get.

Summer brought Kyle back into the mix, now suggesting that perhaps the boy could come along with the men for the ride. Summer said it would probably do Kyle some good to get away from the big city for a few days.

"Mom, can I go, can I go?" asked Kyle, who was standing nearby and heard the whole conversation.

Mason agreed a change of scenery might be a good thing but was still nervous. Her concerns were softened by the fact Baxter would be going as well and could keep a close eye on Kyle.

She reluctantly agreed, and Summer suggested they leave immediately. He said they could get to Regina by morning, and be home the next night.

• • • • •

It was about 9:30 p.m. when Summer, Baxter and Kyle pulled out of the driveway and were on their way.

They hadn't got out of the city yet when Summer suggested they stop somewhere to clean out the van. He told Baxter he didn't want to leave him something so dirty and dusty.

They ended up pulling over in Headingley, at the construction site where they'd met, and gave the van a good once-over. Several papers and food items were tossed in the trash.

Baxter called Mason around 11 p.m., telling her they had stopped but were about to get on their way. He said he would call her in the morning from Regina.

• • • • •

# DEVIL AMONG US

## BRANDON, MANITOBA

Baxter slowly opened his eyes, taking a few seconds to get re-acquainted with his surroundings. The clock on the van showed it was after 1 a.m. He had slept most of the two-hour drive from Winnipeg and now looked around to see they were parked at the Brandon bus station.

Summer was still behind the wheel, with Kyle seated in the backseat. Summer had a look of concern on his face.

"There's a problem with the van," he told Baxter.

Summer said the vehicle had been stalling and probably wasn't going to make it to Regina. Then he dropped another bombshell.

"When we cleaned the van out last night we threw out a bag. It had $2,000 in it," said Summer.

Baxter couldn't believe it. He hadn't seen the money, but Summer insisted it must have got mixed up with some of the garbage from the floor.

Summer had an idea. He wanted Baxter to hop on the Greyhound and go back to the construction site to get the money. The bag of money would hopefully still be in the garbage, he said. Summer said he would stay behind in Brandon to go get the van fixed. Since they didn't have an appointment, it was probably going to take the whole day anyway.

Summer also suggested Kyle stay behind. He said the pair had been talking while Baxter slept and Kyle really wanted to go camping. Summer said he would pay for Baxter's bus ticket, plus a one-way plane ticket from Winnipeg to Brandon so Baxter could get back as soon as possible. He could get back by the end of the day, the trio could camp for the night, and then carry on to Regina the following morning.

Baxter was uneasy about the plan but knew he was still getting a good deal out of this – a new van, at least to him. And he agreed some time spent in the great outdoors might do wonders for Kyle's behaviour. He talked to Kyle, who was very excited about the chance for adventure. Baxter agreed to go.

Summer got him the bus ticket and Baxter was on his way just before 7 a.m. He told Kyle he'd see him real soon.

● ● ● ● ●

## WINNIPEG, MANITOBA

Jennifer Mason was furious with her common-law husband. Despite her earlier protests, he had left her son alone with a virtual stranger. And in Brandon, too.

Baxter had returned to the construction site but had no luck finding the money that Summer described. He'd poured through the garbage – finding other items he did recognize from the van – but no bag filled with cash.

"You brought a strange man into your house and let him around the girls," Mason's mother told her in a phone chat that morning. "And how convenient the van broke down," she added.

Mason was starting to wonder if Summer had deliberately misled the family. Yet she held off on calling the police, somewhat leery based on her previous dealings over Kyle's exploits. Mason knew her complaints might be met with resistance from officers once they looked up the family's history. Still, she was very concerned.

"How could you leave my son with a stranger," she yelled at Baxter when he returned home that afternoon.

Mason started doing some digging on her own, calling several repair shops in Brandon asking if a man and teen boy had come in with a broken van bearing Alberta plates. Nobody had seen them.

Mason also called the Coast Guard, wanting to follow up on Summer's claims of working for them. It took some effort but she eventually got the answer she feared – they'd never heard of Robert Summer.

• • • • •

It was early Sunday morning when the phone rang. Robert Summer was on the other end.

"Is Al there?" he asked.

"Where the fuck are you?" a furious Mason shouted into the phone.

"Calm down," said Summer.

"Where's Kyle," Mason demanded.

"He's right here," said Summer.

Summer assured her everything was just fine, that there was no need to worry. He said they had some problems finding someone to fix the van at a good price and were now searching for a "backyard mechanic."

Summer said Kyle was having a good time and had enjoyed camping out the previous night. Mason repeatedly asked Summer exactly where they were. Summer would only say just outside Brandon but gave no specifics.

Mason ordered him to put Kyle on the phone. "Where are you," she asked her son.

"I dunno," Kyle said.

"Kyle, look around, can you see anything? Any streets, any signs?" his mother pleaded.

"I don't see anything," he said.

Summer was now back on the line. "Quit freaking out. I'm gonna bring him back tonight."

That wasn't good enough for Mason. "I never told you you could take him. You don't have my permission," she said.

Summer said everything would be fine – then abruptly hung up the phone.

Mason knew what she had to do next.

•••••

The next few hours seemed like an eternity. Mason was still livid with Baxter for putting Kyle in this position. And she was sick with worry, despite Summer's claims that all was well.

She didn't believe this was another case of Kyle simply being rebellious. He was in trouble. And she had now brought the police in.

That night, Mason sat alone on her front steps, clutching a pillow and blanket. She was fighting sleep, her eyes tired and heavy but opening at the sound of every passing vehicle. She was waiting for Summer and her son to return.

But it never happened.

•••••

Mason and several other family members drove out to Brandon the following day, intent on finding Kyle themselves.

She didn't believe police were taking her report seriously – especially given Kyle's prior history – and couldn't sit around doing nothing.

"Why would your husband leave your son with this stranger?" the confused call-taker had asked Mason. She tried to explain the situation but found herself tripping over her own words, her anger growing by the minute.

"He was left behind with a parent," police said in explaining why they couldn't do much for her.

Mason reminded officers that she was the legal guardian – and she hadn't given Summer the okay to disappear with her boy.

"They're probably just on an adventure," one officer told Mason. "Maybe (Kyle) is having the time of his life."

• • • • •

While in western Manitoba, Mason stopped at several area campgrounds, checked numerous gas stations and visited every mechanic she could find. She was carrying a photo of Whitmore.

"This man's got my son," she explained.

• • • • •

It had been Wednesday July 26 when Winnipeg police released a public alert through their daily news release. Although investigators were somewhat skeptical, there was enough reason for concern given the passage of time and his mother's emotional pleas for help.

Police released a brief news bulletin which ran the following day in the *Winnipeg Free Press*.

*Kyle Mason, 14, was last seen Saturday around 6:45 a.m. at the bus depot in Brandon. The youth, who is from Winnipeg, contacted his family from a pay phone near Brandon the following day but did not provide further details.*

*Police believe he may be traveling with a Caucasian male who is between 40 to 50 years of age, with curly blonde hair and blue eyes, is 5-11 and weighs between 180 and 200 pounds.*

*Sgt. Kelly Dennison said the older man is an acquaintance of the family but could not provide further details.*

*It's believed the two are riding in an older model, light blue van with brown panels along the side and Alberta license plates.*

*Mason is 5-6 and 151 pounds with short brown hair and green eyes.*

• • • • •

Several more days had passed and still no word about Kyle's whereabouts. Jennifer Mason wasn't going to stand pat. She took it upon herself to begin calling media outlets in town, practically begging for more news coverage of her son's disappearance. This time wasn't like all the others, she said. Kyle must be in danger.

Mason was also playing amateur detective – including collecting cigarette butts from her backyard that she believed had touched Summer's lips. She gave them to police, asking for a DNA analysis.

Mason had recovered a piece of packaging that fell from Summer's van and landed in her yard. It apparently had contained some type of chain. She also told police about a tattoo she remembered seeing on Summer – the name Josh, surrounded by a heart, on his arm.

Mason had also gone online, checking various websites for high-risk criminals who might be at large. She didn't come across any matches. She and several family members also made up their own missing posters which they spread around the Brandon area.

Finally, she learned the Winnipeg Safeway store they'd gone shopping at days earlier was equipped with surveillance cameras.

"They probably have him on video," Mason told police, who promised to look into it and get back to her.

Mason was doing everything humanly possible to find her son and felt like she had finally – finally – convinced police that sometime terrible had happened.

Unfortunately for Mason, she was right. And Kyle's story was about to go national.

# CHAPTER FOUR

## WHITEWOOD, SASKATCHEWAN
JULY 31, 2006

It had been the longest night of their lives.

Larry and Paula Munroe were trying to remain strong, especially for their two young daughters. But the darkness outside their window had only brought a sense of dread; every second spent wondering where Adam was.

Was he trying to escape? Calling out for his mom and dad? Was he hurt? Was he dead? The terrible thoughts kept coming, try as they might to think positively.

It was now morning but there were still so many questions, so few answers. It had been more than 18 hours since Adam left for the bike ride. Yet it seemed like he'd been gone forever.

Police had told the Munroes that an extraordinary step was being taken in their efforts to find Adam as quickly as possible. Saskatchewan's first-ever Amber Alert was issued, meaning news of the abduction was being broadcast in every corner of the province, and no doubt through much of the country.

The Munroes were also surprised to hear that Robert Summer's "son" was in fact a 14-year-old Winnipeg boy named Kyle Mason. Like Adam, Kyle was a victim as well.

Few details were provided, but the Munroes were told that Summer had tricked Kyle's family a week earlier.

Larry and Paula could not accept this. Kyle had been alone in their home, with Summer nowhere in sight, and yet he hadn't uttered a single word to them about being kidnapped.

Kyle had plenty of opportunity to tell them the truth, to ask for help, to warn them about Summer – and yet he had stayed silent.

The Munroes looked at Kyle as a predator as well. He must have known what was going to happen when they left for that bike ride. He must have been involved.

Police had one last update for the Munroes. The name Robert Summer was bogus. No such person existed.

Fortunately, police had been able to use the vehicle identification number seized from the car repair shop – combined with eyewitness identification from the family of both missing boys – to find the predator's true identity.

His real name was Peter Whitmore.

To the Munroes, it meant nothing. They had never heard of this man before. They knew nothing about him. That was all about to change.

As they continued to stay close to the phone, waiting for updates from police or even a call from Adam, Larry and Paula turned on the television.

They wanted to see how much, if any, media coverage of Adam's case was happening.

Larry stopped on CTV, where national morning show "Canada AM" was airing. It wasn't long before the story came up.

*Adam is four and a half feet tall, 70 pounds, with red hair and brown eyes. He was last seen wearing black track pants with a red and white stripe and running shoes. Kyle is 5-6 tall and 151 pounds with short brown hair and green eyes. Whitmore is six feet tall, white, with a heavy build, brown hair and blue eyes. Whitmore may be driving a 1988 blue Dodge Caravan with wood panelling and an Alberta plate."*

Then came the bombshell – the man who had stolen their son about to be on their television set.

• • • • •

The interview had been conducted nearly six years earlier under exceptional circumstances.

Just days after being released from prison, Peter Whitmore had been driven out of his west-end Toronto neighbourhood by a group of concerned citizens who didn't want the repeat sex offender anywhere near their children.

Whitmore, then 29, had been exposed by some of the 1,500 area residents who jammed a 700 seat auditorium to protest his release into their community.

Many were able to find out his exact address and Whitmore fled, believing his life was in jeopardy. Residents spoke loudly and clearly. Some wanted him to wear a tracking device. Some wanted around-the-clock police surveillance. Others just wanted him dead.

With his lawyer, Dan Brodsky, at his side, Whitmore walked into the CTV studios on Friday Oct. 20, 2000 in an attempt to placate the angry mob.

Valerie Pringle, then the host of national morning show "Canada AM," conducted the interview.

PRINGLE: A convicted child molester was forced to flee his Toronto home after local residents discovered where he was living although they knew he was in the neighbourhood. Peter Whitmore is a repeat offender. He was released from prison last week after serving five years for kidnapping and raping an eight-year-old girl. With us now: Peter Whitmore, also his lawyer Daniel Brodsky. Good morning. Where do you go now?

WHITMORE: I'm not sure.

PRINGLE: Who decides that?

WHITMORE: I'm not sure who's going to decide where I go. Probably –

PRINGLE: Do you decide or is it done in collaboration with the police?

WHITMORE: It will be done in collaboration with the police and my lawyer.

BRODSKY: What we've got is we've got some short-term placement. We're working on a long-term plan but for the time being we've got him a place to be that's safe, we think, for a little while. But we need to put a long-term plan in place. And all we're doing is working on it right now. Given what's happened, it is really hard for that to take place.

PRINGLE: Given what's happened, do you think there will be any community that will accept you living there?

WHITMORE: I'm hoping there will be but it's hard to say right now if anyone is going to accept where I go.

PRINGLE: Do you understand that any community would want you?

WHITMORE: I'm not sure if any community would want me.

PRINGLE: I think people are really troubled by the fact that you refused treatment in prison. Why did you do that?

WHITMORE: I never actually refused treatment in prison –

PRINGLE: What did you do?

WHITMORE: We had a program called Regional Pacific Centre in Kingston. The director was pulled out for charges – outside. So the program was shut down for three years.

PRINGLE: So you are saying nothing was offered to you?

WHITMORE: No, because when I did have something offered the doctor – LaFontaine – was charged with assaulting four different inmates. And so I am unable to take the programs and complete them because of different things.

PRINGLE: Because I believe the understanding is that you have refused treatment and are not currently undergoing treatment for your problem. And do you see it as a problem? Do you think you're sick?

WHITMORE: Yes, I see a problem and I'm currently looking for treatment – available options.

BRODSKY: The difficulty my client faces is that there is no pill, there's no surgery, there is no drug that you can take that is going to help with the problem. So what we're doing is looking at different options. Mr. Whitmore is keeping an open mind about it. He is committed to treatment but what we want to know is what's out there for him, because there is no magic –

PRINGLE: In all this time in prison that he's had, and since, you haven't received treatment?

WHITMORE: No.

PRINGLE: Not since your first conviction.

WHITMORE: That's correct.

PRINGLE: So that's a long time to be looking for treatment.

BRODSKY: No, what my client is saying – actually, he should say himself, if he wants to – is ask him what type of treatment is available for him in prison. Because I think what you'll find is there wasn't a lot available to him.

WHITMORE: In the provincial system there is no treatment for sex offenders. That was right at my first sentence and this current one just past.

PRINGLE: Are you concerned that you will re-offend?

WHITMORE: No.

PRINGLE: Do you have any control over your impulses?

WHITMORE: I have control over what I do. And I'm not concerned I'm going to re-offend. I am looking for treatment at the time, though, to help alleviate any problems that may arise.

PRINGLE: You have been described as unrepentant. And you were described that way after the rape and confinement of an eight-year-old girl, which is what you went to prison for.

WHITMORE: That's right. I feel bad for what happened. I can't change the past but I can change the future, and not do it again.

PRINGLE: Do you think that's possible?

WHITMORE: Yes.

PRINGLE: You have also been described as cunning and manipulative in terms of gaining access to kids.

BRODSKY: That's a description, but the fact of the matter is what you got right now is a fellow who if he were to offend violently again the Attorney-General would most certainly consent to the institution-of-dangerous-offender proceedings. And no matter what he has before him – the potential of a lifetime of imprisonment, and with that strong disincentive and a commitment to seeking treatment – you really do have the potential. It's very difficult to treat pedophilia. But there have been some remarkable successes. He's motivated to take treatment and he knows that if he were to fail and offend violently again he could spend the rest of his life in jail.

PRINGLE: How do you feel about going back to jail?

WHITMORE: I'm not interested in going back to any sort of prison.

PRINGLE: What you want to do with your life? Can you work? Do you have family support?

WHITMORE: I'm unemployable right now – um, I missed the last question.

PRINGLE: Do you have family support? Do you have people –

WHITMORE: I have one family member for support, and that's it right now.

BRODSKY: Not even somebody who lives in the province he's living in. Like, he had some support but as a result of all of the events that took place yesterday that's now evaporated. And so he has virtually nothing. He really is looking for a community or a person or someone who can offer a suggestion. The difficulty for him is there is nothing out there. No matter where he goes the community is going to be uncomfortable. He's got certain conditions –

PRINGLE: And understandably?

WHITMORE: But if people want me to – I want to take treatment. And it's going to be very hard to take treatment if I'm moving from town to town because of media or people not wanting me.

PRINGLE: Do you think the public should be notified when you move or notified of your whereabouts?

WHITMORE: My whereabouts, but not my exact address. I mean I'm trying to reintegrate back into the community and trying to change my life by taking treatment and other programs, and I find it hard to do when I'm chased out of different communities.

BRODSKY: We have taken the position that targeted institutions should know. The people who run schools, playgrounds etc. where my client is not allowed to be – and not allowed to be for the rest of his life – should be notified, but -

PRINGLE: And that would help you?

WHITMORE: That would help me and it would help the community as well.

PRINGLE: But if everybody knows where you live then you're a hunted man.

WHITMORE: That's right; I'd be a marked target.

PRINGLE: Can people trust you?

WHITMORE: I believe so, but I have to have some sort of, um, new record to prove that.

BRODSKY: He needs a place to live because in order to put money in the bank you have to have a place to live and you have to be able to put it there. He needs to get a track record;

he needs a place to go where he can sit, where he can get a job. He doesn't want to be receiving social assistance. He wants to be able to go get a job and try to re-integrate into society and become a productive member. But he needs to be given a chance to do that. And so far he's not been able to find anybody who will give him a chance.

WHITMORE: The community can trust me. I have 24-hour police surveillance on me, and has been since I've been released from prison, and probably will be for quite some time.

BRODSKY: Both for his protection and the community's.

PRINGLE: What happens if you go near kids?

WHITMORE: In what regard?

PRINGLE: Well, in terms of being able to control yourself.

WHITMORE: I have no problems walking past anybody. Um, –

PRINGLE: Do you have anything to say to the kids who you've victimized already?

WHITMORE: I've attempted treatment, I am taking treatment. And I can apologize but that's really not going to help anybody – by saying I apologize. I have to show that I'm actually doing something to change it so no one else gets hurt in the process – or any future people.

PRINGLE: So why did you agree to come on television?

WHITMORE: Just to let people know that I feel that with all the media presence and everybody else that I could be a target unless everyone knows what I'm going to do. And that's why I'm here, just to let people know what I'm going to do – or attempt to do.

•  •  •  •  •

Larry and Paula Munroe felt like their hearts had just been ripped out of their chests. The man who had their son was a monster.

The television report had only brought on a slew of new emotions and questions, including why police hadn't told them about Whitmore's past.

There was a building rage within the family, especially Larry. He couldn't understand how the man he just watched on television from six years earlier could have slithered into their lives. Why was he even out of prison given his apparent history of attacking children?

Paula's guilt was overpowering. She had let this man into her home. She had let Adam go for the bike ride. She had found his discarded bike.

# CHAPTER FIVE

## CHILLIWACK, BRITISH COLUMBIA

Laural Mathew was stunned at the news. The RCMP corporal had been overseeing Peter Whitmore for much of the past year while he was living in the community.

Since his last release from jail in June 2005, Whitmore had been under a court-ordered peace bond which limited his movements in Chilliwack.

Whitmore had moved in with his aunt, Lynn Hopkins, at her apartment on Yale Road. Despite her nephew's past troubles, Hopkins had agreed to show her support by opening her doors. She promised to watch Whitmore closely and report any problems to police.

Whitmore's conditions included a nightly curfew and order to report regularly to local RCMP. He also had to stay at least 400 metres away from places children were known to gather – such as parks, playgrounds and swimming pools. Whitmore was also prohibited from being alone with any child.

Mathew had extensive contact with Whitmore and his disturbing case file. She had spent countless hours discussing his troubled past, shaky present and uncertain future. And while she had always expected the worst, Mathew had been pleasantly surprised by Whitmore's apparent compliance.

Yet things took a sudden turn weeks earlier when Whitmore's year-long peace bond expired – and he suddenly left Chilliwack, headed for Alberta. Whitmore was apparently going to the town of Morinville to spend time with his brother. Mathew had been told that RCMP in that jurisdiction would be applying for a new court order with similar conditions.

Still, Mathew was concerned that a change of scenery and routine might not be the best move for a man who clearly needed stability in his life. Now, it appeared, the worst possible scenario was unfolding.

Mathew was a blur of emotions, filled with so many questions about how this could have happened. But Mathew knew those answers would have to wait. For now, the main priority was the safety of the two boys Whitmore had apparently abducted.

Mathew was being asked to play a potentially pivotal role in the manhunt. RCMP felt her recent history with Whitmore made her the ideal candidate to reach out to him.

"We thought she had a good relationship with him so her voice, if he heard it, might prompt him to drop the kids off in a safe place," Const. Steve Hiscoe told reporters who had gathered in Chilliwack to pursue the local angle to the national story.

With time of the essence, Mathew quickly gathered her thoughts and put herself in front of a video camera – armed with a heartfelt message she hoped would somehow reach Whitmore.

"Peter, I worked with you for a year here in Chilliwack and I got to know you pretty well. You were doing so well while you were here and I know that you have been going through some stress lately and you've obviously been put on edge, but Peter this needs to come to an end," she said.

"The best thing for you to do – right now – is to find a way to do what you've always done before and release the children. It's time to do that now Peter. All you have to do is drop them off at any safe place where they can be found. If you need someone to help you, call a lawyer or a family member or me. I gave your aunt all of my contact information – you can call her and either she or you can get in touch with me any time, day or night. What we want for you and the kids is to be OK. Peter, you've got to do this now."

•••••

## WHITEWOOD, SASKATCHEWAN

Dozens of tips and sightings were pouring in as a result of the Amber Alert – but police had found nothing of substance. They believed Whitmore and the two missing boys were likely still in the area. It was clear from his dealings with people in Whitewood that he didn't have a lot of money.

It was possible Whitmore would try and dump his van, suspecting that police would be looking for it. That would leave Whitmore desperate – and perhaps even more dangerous.

"We do believe there is potential for harm," RCMP spokeswoman Heather Russell told reporters.

Since rural Saskatchewan was so vast, with many isolated locales that would provide good cover, RCMP had taken to the air to get a better view of the ground. Police across the country – but especially in neighbouring provinces Manitoba and Alberta – were urged to be extra vigilant.

North Dakota border officials were notified in case Whitmore tried to run south. Air, rail and bus companies had also been alerted.

Police were counting on the community to play a pivotal role, knowing the case would outrage citizens and cause many to take actions. Police urged everyone to search their properties, especially any outlying sheds or barns that could be used as a hideout.

The community reacted quickly.

"We know the police have done an extensive air and land search. But people who've lived here all their lives know there are places to hide," Mayor Malcolm Green said as he faced a plethora of news cameras for a second straight day.

"We want to blanket the area. I believe they're still here. For our own peace of mind we want to be sure."

Green said now was not the time for assigning blame, especially to the families of the two victims. "This is how these guys operate. They are very manipulative. This guy is so good at what he does; you can't fault any of the parents. These are darn good people," he said.

But Green did have serious concerns about Whitmore's prior criminal history. "We're mad this has hit home. We need a better system to track these kinds of guys. This guy had freedom of movement," he said.

Green predicted a happy ending to the case. "I think (the boys) are okay. This guy always gets caught."

Many citizens had already come forward with detailed maps of the area, which included abandoned barns and huts which might make for good cover. He said residents were meeting to discuss their plans for a co-ordinated ground search.

They would then blitz the south-eastern Saskatchewan area, bringing as many different towns and rural municipalities in as possible. At least two or three people would be on every search team, with the thinking that there was safety in numbers.

Many residents were still stinging at the deception used by Whitmore and how he'd preyed on everyone's trust.

"Larry Munroe is as friendly as they come. He'd give you the shirt off his back," said one local resident who had come to know the family well since they moved to Saskatchewan.

The community was also hoping the power of prayer might make a difference as several residents had set up a prayer circle through a local church. Many of these same people were wondering "what if" – just a week earlier, 27 kids had gathered in Whitewood for a vacation Bible school. Whitmore was likely driving around the community, looking for victims, the entire time.

Kevin White and Lynnette Luypaert were shocked to learn the customer they'd helped that previous Friday morning was a dangerous pedophile. But they were at least relieved the information taken down on the vehicle had helped quickly identify Whitmore.

"It shows the benefit of living in a small town. Everyone knows one another," said Luypaert.

Green had spoken briefly with Larry Munroe to offer his support, and urged reporters to leave the family alone while they searched for their son.

"As you can appreciate, they're going through a very difficult time, but Adam's father wants to say, 'I'm thinking of you, bud,' and that the family is very concerned for his safety. He also wants to let Adam know that they're working very hard to bring him home."

Meanwhile, the Munroes had put a sign on their front gate clearly stating "No Media" as television news trucks began swarming the community and staking out their farm.

• • • • •

Kyle Mason's family was speaking out from Winnipeg.

"We're falling apart here. There's not a moment that goes by Kyle's not on our mind. We hope the Creator is watching over him and the other boy," his grandmother, Carol Mason, told the *Winnipeg Free Press*. "We hope no harm has been done to them."

She believed her grandson was being held against his will by Whitmore – despite the fact it appears he had at least several chances to escape if he wanted to. "He is probably petrified by this guy and doesn't know what will happen to him," she said.

Mason also had questions about why Whitmore was free to roam about the country. "Why didn't they keep this guy on some kind of extended parole? It doesn't make any sense," she said.

Other family members, including Kyle's mother and stepfather, were holed up in their home. Numerous reporters and cameras were parked outside their front yard, under the watchful eye of city police. They had also taken their phone off the hook, tired of being inundated with calls for comment. They knew police would come and get them the moment there was news.

Dan Brodsky was also speaking out, joining Mathew in calling for his client to surrender.

"Peter, if you're watching this broadcast, go and turn yourself in," the Toronto-based Brodsky said in a live interview on CBC Newsworld. "Put the kids on a bus."

Brodsky said there were "a lot of very scared people" and that Whitmore should walk into the nearest police station for his own safety. He also vowed to get Whitmore legal help.

Brodsky was stunned to learn Whitmore had not been under any type of court order at the time of the abductions. Section 810 of the Criminal Code allows courts to impose limits on ex-convicts who have served out their full sentences. The most recent order against Whitmore – called a peace bond – had apparently expired on June 15, 2006. Brodsky wanted to know why it wasn't renewed.

Brodsky said he'd heard that police in Alberta had made arrangements with Whitmore to voluntarily get a new order since he'd just come into their territory from B.C. to spend time with his brother.

RCMP had apparently set up a time for Whitmore to report to court to have the new peace bond implemented.

"The last time I spoke to Peter, it was coming up to a year – there hadn't been any breaches," Brodsky said in an interview with CTV News. "Everybody was happy with his progress; he was living with his aunt. I anticipated that the order would continue and there would be no problems."

Brodsky said blame rested with whoever allowed the peace bond to expire. "The legislation that was used to supervise him was working. He was living in B.C. It was over a year that he had been out, not committing offences," he said.

"These are not complicated conditions, and we learned with Peter and other people like Peter that they need to be supervised. They don't need maximum security, but they need maximum supervision – and that requires people on the back end to understand who they're dealing with and to do their jobs."

Canada's justice minister, Conservative MP Vic Toews, was also been asked to weigh in on the breaking news story. Toews told CBC his government was calling for tougher sentences for pedophiles such as Whitmore. He didn't want to specifically discuss Whitmore's case while the search was ongoing but said flimsy sentences such as probation and conditional penalties must end.

Brodsky fired back during his interview, saying the real problem is the lack of communication between police agencies.

"The authorities in Alberta allowed the order to lapse. After it lapsed — this is astonishing — but after it lapsed they went to Peter and said, 'Hey Peter, we know that you have your complete freedom now and you can do whatever you want; you're completely finished with the justice system. But if you stay here, we're going to take your freedom away again next week. And you'll consent to those conditions won't you?'" he said.

Whitmore wasn't seen again.

· · · · ·

The political posturing was of little concern to the residents of Whitewood and the families of both missing boys. With each passing hour, the situation became grimmer.

As the manhunt intensified – with citizens preparing to take to the farms and fields en masse – a local business in Whitewood had used their outdoor sign to send a powerful message that perfectly summed up the mood in the community.

"Shoot the pedophile."

# CHAPTER SIX

Jake Goldenflame has learned to accept a cold, ugly truth about himself. He is a pedophile. Always has been, always will be.

Boys, especially young teens, remain the object of his deviant desires. The sexual urges have subsided a bit with age, but not entirely. Now in his early 70s, Goldenflame says the thought of being alone with a 14 or 15-year-old boy still gets his heart racing.

He knows he can never be "cured." And any child sex offender who claims they have been is lying, he says.

"We're not going to recover, because we never had anything (to fix). This is our sexual orientation. It's not a matter of whether we can make it go away. We can't make it go away," says Goldenflame.

He cites the famous findings of Alfred Kinsey, who is generally regarded as the father of sexology. Kinsey spent his career studying the science of human sexuality. His Kinsey Reports – *Sexual Behavior in the Human Male* (1948) and *Sexual Behavior in the Human Female* (1953) – are the bestselling scientific books in history and continue to be relevant today, more than 50 years after Kinsey's death.

"Kinsey basically wrote there are as many types of sexual attractions as there are colours of the rainbow," says Goldenflame.

Despite his candid admissions, Goldenflame swears he hasn't touched a child for more than two decades. And he claims to have found the key to living a successful life in the community. There's no disputing some of his more recent triumphs. He's become a darling of the talk show circuit, including appearances on Oprah Winfrey and CNN. He's authored a critically acclaimed book – Overcoming Sexual Terrorism – in which he maps out his mistakes and charts a course for other offenders to follow.

Goldenflame has become a vocal critic of weak sex offender legislation and lobbied for tougher penalties, including the creation of "Megan's Law" in California. He set up his own website, www.calsexoffenders.net, which gives advice to convicted pedophiles about how to stay out of trouble and remain in the community. He has travelled around the world to speak at various conferences, forums and even prisons. He also received a law degree from People's College of Law in Los Angeles in 1985 and a Master's Degree in American Studies from the University of Southern California in 1972.

Still, Goldenflame will forever be labeled a sex offender. And he knows there are many just waiting for him to fail, people who think it's only a matter of time before he goes back to his old ways and preys on children – if he hasn't done so already.

"I hear that criticism all the time, that it hasn't been so many years since I've offended, that's it's just been that many years since I've been caught," says Goldenflame.

Goldenflame, who lives in California, admits he spent much of his adult life abusing young boys while struggling through two failed marriages. He says his offending behaviour stemmed from his own brush with a sex offender at the age of 13. The older man picked him up off the streets and molested him.

His most shocking attacks occurred on his own daughter, beginning at the age of three and continuing for two years. The girl finally disclosed the abuse and Goldenflame was arrested and charged. Goldenflame still struggles to explain why he targeted his own daughter. He was sentenced to 10 years in prison in 1986. Goldenflame swears it was the best thing that ever happened to him.

"When the law finally took hold of me and said they were gonna lock me up for years, I could finally get the help I needed," he says.

Oprah Winfrey once asked Goldenflame how he felt when his daughter spoke up about what he'd done.

"Tremendous relief that it was finally out, that I no longer had to carry this tremendous burden of guilt and shame and self-loathing, that finally it was out and I could do something about it," he told an international television audience.

Goldenflame says he took every available program while behind bars – including group therapy, one-on-one sex offender counselling, victim empathy and anger management. He was released in 1991 after serving just half his sentence based on progress he made in jail in lowering his risk to re-offend.

"Looking back 25, 30 years when I was at my worst, I remember knowing I needed counselling, that I needed professional help. But I had been afraid to get it because of my fear they would call me crazy and lock me up," he says.

Goldenflame said he also found a "higher power" while behind bars. "To me the heart of the whole thing is that while I was in prison, I was one of those who established a spiritual relationship, a spiritual connection," he says.

"I have now come to believe we can attract a certain spiritual presence in our life if we live a certain kind of life. That means keeping it clean, orderly, respectful, be willing to bow down to a power greater than you."

He recalls visiting with a prison chaplain and being profoundly affected by one of the psalms the man was reading.

"He said 'The fear of the Lord is the beginning of wisdom'. To me, that's what it's all about. If you stray from that path, you're going to lose the benefit of having that presence in your life. I live in that fear. I would rather lose anything else than lose that presence," says Goldenflame.

He's also learned to avoid hiding from the truth. "I tried that and it doesn't work," he says.

In 1998, Goldenflame took formal vows as a Buddhist, charged with assisting all those injured by sexual abuse. He has also apologized to his now-adult daughter and worked with other victims of abuse who are trying to recover.

Goldenflame says he's developed a simple formula for resisting temptation and maintaining his freedom. "What you need to do is face the fact and take responsibility for it. To take charge and say 'This is the way I am, I accept that, although I don't like it. But what's the responsible way to live?'" he says.

For Goldenflame, that means avoiding teen boys at all costs. "I don't go to the types of places where I would be congregating with adolescent boys. I just stay away from those kinds of settings. That's just a part of my life. And as a result I live an incident-free life," he says.

"Either you're going to accept what you've got and you're going to live responsibility on the basis of it or you're not. And if you're going to live responsibly you're going to avoid temptation."

Goldenflame has also developed an appreciation that the boys he molested were indeed victims. "The American Bar Association did a study on brain development. It found that the human brain isn't fully developed until about 25 years. And the faculty that gives you the ability to appreciate long-range consequences comes last," he says.

"That made me realize that if you can't appreciate long-term consequences of various actions until you're 25 years old, what right does someone have coming to you at 15 years old with a sexual solicitation?"

One of Goldenflame's most championed projects is the passage of "Megan's Law," which lets the public know details about registered sex offenders in their neighbourhood. Decisions are made state level about what information will be released, but common details include the abuser's name, picture, general address and criminal history.

The law was enacted in 1994, and requires people convicted of sex crimes to notify police about where they are living after being released from jail. These conditions can be applied for a fixed period of time, or permanently in the case of dangerous, high-risk offenders.

The law was named after Megan Kanka, who was kidnapped, raped and murdered by a convicted sex offender who lived across the street. She was only seven years old. Jesse Timmendequas was convicted of the crime and is now serving life in prison without parole.

Richard and Maureen Kanka said they had no idea a predator lived in their neighbourhood and were in the dark about

Timmendequas' background. They vowed to fight for tougher legislation and started a petition which resulted in more than 400,000 signatures within days.

"Every parent should have the right to know if a dangerous sexual predator moves into their neighborhood," the couple told local media.

New Jersey became the first state to enact Megan's Law just months later.

Not everyone believes the public notification process is a good one. Some justice officials fear the exposure only forces sexual offenders to go into hiding, thus making them potentially more dangerous.

There have been cases of vigilantism, where angry citizens have physically attacked sex offenders living in their neighbourhood. There are also concerns that the process hinders rehabilitation.

Goldenflame firmly believes the rewards outweigh the risks. He became the first offender to register under Megan's Law in California and now preaches the virtues to other offenders.

"It's like I tell guys in prison all the time. All society is asking us is the same thing they ask of everyone else. To use self-restraint and stay away from kids," he says.

He says keeping a sex offender away from high-risk areas where children gather is akin to "keeping an alcoholic out of a bar."

Goldenflame does worry that legislation may become so restrictive that some pedophiles may actually get more aggressive – even killing their child victims – in an attempt to avoid getting caught.

To that extent, he's expressed concerns about "Jessica's Law," a 2005 bill in Florida that has been adapted by most other U.S. states. The provisions include lowering the criteria for the types of offenders who would be required to register and mandatory minimum sentences of 25 years in prison and lifetime electronic monitoring for adults convicted of molesting a child under the age of 12 through global positioning systems on their ankles.

Sexual battery or rape means an automatic life sentence with no chance of parole, or even the death penalty.

The bill was introduced – and quickly passed – by Florida Republican congresswoman Ginny Brown-Waite after nine-year-old Jessica Lunsford was raped and murdered in February 2005 by convicted sex offender John Couey.

Goldenflame wrote a letter to the Attorney General of California in 2006, saying the public safety of his state could face "devastating consequences" if Jessica's Law was allowed to pass. One of his major concerns is the requirement that sex offenders of all stripes must live at least 2,000 feet away from any school, park or playground – no matter how many years ago their conviction occurred.

"Criminal defendants will not plead guilty to any offense where registration is required, escaping punishment and registration while remaining within the towns and cities on lesser offenses. Some registrants will undoubtedly become so discouraged by this measure that they will relapse and commit new crimes. Others have already threatened to do so, out of vengeance," Goldenflame warned.

He said tens of thousands of low-risk California sex offenders who are currently living peaceful, law-abiding lives would be rendered "homeless" by having their names and addresses exposed.

"Women and children in rural areas, where police resources are fewer, will be placed at much greater risk of harm as all of the cities' former offenders come to reside near them, making the countryside into a place of terror. Nearby towns will experience similar concerns when wandering bands approach them every sunset, while some registrants may secretly defy the measure and continue to live in the cities by stealth. What name will they go by, when they can no longer be found? What are they likely to do if discovered? Will any engage in acts of domestic terrorism? Some have former military training which, if misused, could harm entire cities," Goldenflame wrote.

Goldenflame cited U.S. justice statistics which have shown that less than four per cent of the 90,000 plus registered sex offenders in California were arrested for another sex crime within three years of release. And he noted the vast majority of sexual offenders attack someone known to them – such as a child or relative – and that stranger abductions such as Jessica Lunsford were rare.

Goldenflame didn't want people to think he's looking for sympathy for sex offenders. He just believes that painting every abuser with the same brush won't make society a safer place.

He says he always reports to enforcement whenever he travels out of state to speak, including providing copies of his itinerary so they always know where he'll be and what he's doing. He relishes the opportunity to "check in" because it reminds him of what he done and the importance of following a straight path in life.

"I admire the professionalism of police. They certainly haven't caused a problem for me. They're just doing their job," he says.

It's a job, he says, made all the more difficult by predators who want nothing to do with rehabilitation and will stop at nothing to claim their next victim.

People like Peter Whitmore.

# CHAPTER SEVEN

## TORONTO, ONTARIO
### SEPTEMBER 10, 1993

He was 18 years old, living on the streets of Toronto and struggling with a life that at times didn't seem worth living. Feelings of loneliness, rejection and isolation would quickly manifest into pain, anger and even rage.

He knew what it was like to be preyed upon, the memories still very raw of sexual abuse suffered years earlier.

There was no way to erase the past. But the future was still to be written. He wanted to be in control. He wanted to be the boss.

He would become the predator.

• • • • •

"Guilty."

With that simple word – uttered after each and every charge was read aloud in court – Peter Whitmore had just admitted something very ugly about himself.

He was a sex offender. Four years worth of crimes had finally caught up with him.

The Crown attorney provided a brief outline of the facts. He explained how Whitmore, having just reached the age of majority in 1989, began targeting his first victim on the streets of Toronto. The prosecutor was careful to stress that this was Whitmore's first "known" victim, a reference which not-so-subtly hinted at further crimes for which he hadn't been caught.

The boy, just 11 years old, shared many of the same traits as Whitmore. A broken family, lengthy parade of foster homes and diminished feelings of self-esteem.

In many ways, he was the perfect target. And Whitmore had known exactly what to say to reel him in.

Their relationship would continue for many months, with Whitmore determined to continue the vicious cycle of abuse he first experienced at the age of two.

He began paying the boy small amounts of money in exchange for oral sex, fondling and masturbation. Whitmore was the master manipulator, telling the boy they were doing nothing wrong while offering himself up as a confidant and a friend.

The Crown suspected Whitmore had found other young boys to abuse during this time, but could only rely on the evidence they had.

Whitmore's behaviour began to escalate in March 1993. He went to the Douglas Snow Aquatic Centre in North York, knowing it would be filled with children. He brought an accomplice with him this time, a teenage boy he'd met on the streets.

Together they began scouting out potential victims, finally settling on an 11-year-old boy who had been dropped off by his family to swim. Whitmore had come up with a ruse, approaching the boy and asking him if he wanted to make some easy money.

He said he needed some help delivering a package to a nearby apartment block. Whitmore promised they wouldn't be long and would return to the pool right away. He lied. They arrived at the block, where Whitmore and his teen accomplice got the boy into a basement storage room.

They spent the next several hours sexually assaulting the boy, including oral sex and masturbation that brought the boy to ejaculation on three occasions. Whitmore also tried anal intercourse but eventually gave up.

The boy's frantic parents had gone to police when their son didn't return home that night, prompting a missing person bulletin to be issued to officers across the province of Ontario. Whitmore finally allowed the boy to leave the following morning, but told him not to tell anyone what had happened.

Whitmore wasn't finished.

He and his accomplice approached another 11-year-old boy on the streets of Toronto just days later. Whitmore didn't even try the bogus cover story this time. He told the boy he wanted to have oral sex with him and offered $100. He suggested they go to the same apartment storage room where he'd taken his previous victim.

The boy refused and ran away. Whitmore wasn't deterred. Now working alone, he targeted a 12-year-old boy later that same month and lured him to the storage room on the guise of a delivery job.

Whitmore told the victim they would do a walk-through of the job as a sort of "test" to see if he was a good fit. Once he had him alone, Whitmore grabbed the boy's crotch and tried to take down his pants. The boy was scared – yet alert enough to flee before anything more could happen.

His final victim was a 13-year-old paperboy who was offered $700 per week by Whitmore to be his personal sex servant. Whitmore said he wanted frequent oral sex. The boy reluctantly agreed and arranged a follow-up meeting with Whitmore.

Fortunately the police got to him first. The boy – and all the previous victims – told loved ones about what happened with Whitmore. Police were contacted and began putting the complaints together, realizing they had a serial offender in their midst.

Whitmore didn't try to hide his identity, a move that would prove fatal. Police interviewed victims and witnesses at the swimming pool and apartment complex and were quickly able to put a name to the face.

Whitmore's arrest in Sault Ste. Marie days later represented a new chapter in his criminal career. He'd been in legal trouble before, but nothing of this nature. His crimes were property in nature – thefts and fraud – and spanned several Canadian cities which seemed to indicate he was a man who liked to move around.

Further investigation would reveal just how willing he was to travel to search out new victims.

• • • • •

## LOCKHART, TEXAS

It's known as the BBQ capital of Texas – a mighty claim indeed for a state that takes great pride in grilled meat. The 12,000 residents of Lockhart were also big on hospitality, welcoming newcomers with open arms.

The city's website greets visitors with the following message:

# DEVIL AMONG US

*You'll find hundreds of thriving small businesses, a rich history and warm friendly people when you get to Lockhart. We've endured boom and bust to become a lively and energetic community with its eyes on the future. Lockhart has always been a favorite in Central Texas. With the steady growth of our region we stand ready to welcome even more families and businesses looking for an escape from the hassles of big city life. Beautiful historic homes line our city's entrance from the West. Quiet older neighborhoods and bustling subdivisions blend harmoniously to provide a wide selection of housing options.*

Much of the growth can be attributed to youth. According to the 2000 census, 26.5 % of the local population is comprised of children under the age of 18. As such, it was the perfect place to raise a family.

And for a predator to strike.

• • • • •

Peter Whitmore arrived in Lockhart in the fall of 1992, armed with sinister intentions and an elaborate cover story.

Whitmore was passing himself off as a private eye, with a specialty in tracking down lost and missing children.

He had set up his own company – called International Search and Rescue – and told locals he had been doing similar work in Canada under the name of National Search and Rescue.

Whitmore was eager to find work and approached staff members at the non-profit Heidi Search Centre in San Antonio, Texas to offer his "expertise."

Established in 1990, the centre was named after 11-year-old Heidi Seeman. The girl was abducted while walking home from visiting a friend, triggering a massive local search. A second child, 7-year-old Erica Marie Botello, was kidnapped several weeks later while the hunt for Heidi was ongoing.

Both cases would end in tragedy. Heidi's body was found days later in a rural area outside San Antonio. Erica's body was found in a storm drain less than one mile from where she lived.

According to the FBI, the search for Heidi was one of the largest and most expensive searches in U.S. history. More than 8,000 dedicated volunteers spent three weeks covering 1,200 miles and using over 50 miles of yellow ribbon as a symbol of the search.

According to figures provided by the Heidi Search Centre, they worked closely with the families of more than 2,300 missing children between 1990 and 2003. This includes 467 missing children, 1,664 runaways, 146 parental abductions and 35 stranger abductions. Of 2,328 cases, 93% ended with the child being returned home safely, four per cent ended with the child being found dead and three per cent remained active.

The agency offers services at no cost which includes both physical and emotional support. They rely heavily on financial help and volunteer assistance from those in the community and are grateful whenever new offers come their way. But staff has also learned to smell a rat.

Peter Whitmore may have looked like a professional – boxes of files he carried with him, a "security officer" badge he wore proudly – but there was something about this Canadian stranger that didn't sit right with folks at the Heidi Centre.

Whitmore claimed to be working on a historical case involving a missing child from a prominent Texas family and seemed eager to share information.

Instead, cautious Heidi officials contacted police in Lockhart with some pointed questions about the mystery man. It wasn't long before Whitmore was exposed as a fraud.

His paperwork was fake, his badge bogus, his credentials crooked. He had no private investigator's licence – which is required by law – and he was soon arrested and charged.

Police learned he had taken some files from the Heidi Centre regarding a well-known local case. He'd then contacted a family representative, claiming he might be able to help. His offer was rejected.

Whitmore then went to extraordinary lengths to dodge punishment. He shaved off clumps of his hair, telling anyone who'd listen that he had cancer and was undergoing chemotherapy.

Police didn't buy his feeble attempt at sympathy and began grilling Whitmore about his true intentions. There was immediate concern that children may have been at risk from Whitmore, but no complaints had come in to Lockhart officials. Whitmore did admit to having fantasies about young boys in the past but said it was no longer a problem.

Whitmore pleaded guilty just one day after his arrest to operating as a private eye without a licence. He was driven to San Antonio, turned over to the U.S. Immigration Service and immediately put on a plane with a one-way ticket back to Canada.

His time on foreign soil was over.

•  •  •  •  •

Police in Toronto now had a more complete picture of how Whitmore had been spending his time – and why there was a noticeable gap between his first sex attack in 1989 and the escalation of his behaviour in early 1993.

Whitmore was charged with numerous sex offences and didn't try to duck responsibility. In fact, he spoke openly with police about his crimes and even confessed to other victims who hadn't come forward.

Whitmore didn't know their names or any specific details and police could do little with the information.

He pleaded guilty to abduction of a person under the age of 14, three counts of sexual interference and two counts of invitation to sexual touching. Whitmore was sentenced to 16 months in jail, in addition to the six months of pre-trial custody he'd already served.

Mr. Justice C.J. Cannon also gave him a three-year probation order with several stringent conditions including sex offender counselling and having no contact with children under the age of 14. The hope was that this would be Whitmore's final contact with the justice system.

But the reality was that he was just getting started.

# CHAPTER EIGHT

JULY 29, 1994

Some use the time to brush up on their reading, improve their physical and mental fitness, take some programming, upgrade their education and maybe even find a cause or faith to get behind in a genuine effort to change.

Some are simply there for a good time – a chance to catch up with old friends and associates, share some stories from the streets and make grand plans for when they're back on the outside.

Some harbour a bitter anger, make life miserable for all around them and truly believe they've been wronged and society must pay for the injustice.

How a sentenced prisoner spends their time behind bars is often as unique as the individual offender. But their chances for success – or risk of failure – can be directly affected by the decisions they make while locked up.

Yet nearly every Canadian offender can rest easy at night knowing one thing. No matter how much effort they actually make towards improving their broken lives, no matter how much of a danger they might continue to pose, they *will* be released.

Some of the so-called "model inmates" might get out a little quicker. But what's a few extra months when you can spend that time doing whatever you damn well please?

According to Corrections Canada, sex offenders are more likely to return to prison for a sexual offence than the general prison population.

One study, conducted in the early 1990s, revealed that 13.9 per cent of all federal prison inmates are sexual offenders. In any year, two-thirds of convicted sexual offenders are in federal institutions, one-third are on some form of conditional release. Of those on release, 14.8 per cent were on day parole, 49.2 per cent were on full parole and 35.9 per cent were on mandatory supervision.

Another study from the 1980s showed that of sexual offenders released from federal institutions in Canada:

- 68.8 per cent of all sexual offenders and 48.8 per cent of repeat sex offenders did not return to jail.

- 6.2 per cent of all sexual offenders and 14.6 per cent of repeat offenders committed a new sexual offence.

- 5.9 per cent of all sexual offenders and 8.5 per cent of repeat offenders committed a new violent offence.

- 7.7 per cent of all sex offenders and 6.1 per cent of repeat offenders committed a new non-violent offence.

Peter Whitmore, still a young man, knew the system well. Although he'd pleaded guilty to his crimes, it was more about getting his case over with quickly, doing his time and then getting out.

He wasn't interested in changing. Not at all. Because Whitmore truly believed he wasn't doing anything wrong.

Jail hadn't been a picnic, because sex offenders are often given a rough ride behind bars. But Whitmore had kept his mouth shut, had stayed out of people's way and served his time as quietly as possible. And now, just 10 months after his sentence began, Whitmore was about to return to the streets.

He had completed two-thirds of the 16-month sentence, the magical mark for Canadian criminals. It was the time in an offender's sentence when they were virtually guaranteed release from custody, regardless of how they'd spent their time behind bars.

Only in the rarest of cases – where Corrections officials felt there would be an imminent risk of an offender committing a crime that resulted in "grievous bodily harm or death" to their victim – would their release be held up.

Nobody could say such a thing about Whitmore, at least not with any degree of certainty, so back into society he went. No matter that he'd done virtually nothing to work towards changing his behaviour. Or that he had no real support system in place upon release.

The day had arrived. Whitmore was a free man.

There were still some controls on his behaviour, thanks to the three-year probation order that forbid any contact with children under 14.

But it wouldn't take Whitmore long to prove those conditions weren't worth the paper they were written on.

• • • • •

## GUELPH, ONTARIO
## AUGUST 10, 1994

She arrived by cab over the noon-hour, a joyous sight for a family that had spent the past three days racked with worry and guilt. The eight-year-old girl climbed out of the back seat and walked into her crying mother's arms. Police were called immediately.

The confused cab driver quickly learned this was no ordinary fare. He had just delivered a missing girl back to her family. And investigators had plenty of questions. He took officers back to where it began, to the parking lot of the Canadian Tire store in the west end of Toronto.

The call had come in earlier that morning, from a man requesting a ride to Guelph, located about 100 kilometres west of Toronto.

Upon arrival at the store, the man explained that the girl would be travelling alone. He gave directions to the house in Guelph, where he said the girl's mother would be waiting.

"She'll pick up the fare," he said.

The cabbie thought something was up but hadn't asked any more questions. The girl seemed anxious to get going. And they had a long drive ahead of them. The girl was quiet throughout the drive but exploded with emotion upon seeing her family again.

Police explained they had to ask her some questions. It was very important that she remember as much as she could because they wanted to find the person who had done this to her. Of course, police knew exactly who was responsible.

Peter Whitmore had victimized another child.

• • • • •

# DEVIL AMONG US

"Every time we turn a corner, there's another corner," Detective Tom Archibald told the assembled gathering of media.

Police had gone public with their quest to find Whitmore, revealing some disturbing details about his latest crime. The investigation revealed Whitmore was going around the community passing out business cards for the U.S.-based Boys Town National Hotline for suicidal children.

He had approached several youths in the past week, offering his services as a counsellor. If they had a problem, Whitmore said he was there to listen. Whitmore was also touting himself as the head of "Children Protection Services" – a "babysitting" service for at-risk youths and young adults.

The business was just as bogus as the "National Search and Rescue" enterprise he'd launched in the U.S. – but it was every bit as devious. Whitmore was trying to gain access to children through any means possible.

Perhaps the most shocking discovery of all was the fact Whitmore had been planning his next move even while behind bars.

Police had traced back the events surrounding the disappearance of the young Guelph girl and learned the idea had been hatched by Whitmore while he was still housed at the Wellington Detention Centre.

Turns out Whitmore had befriended another inmate, Tony Salanis. Like Whitmore, the man was about to be released and mentioned wanting to seek access to his infant son. Salinas didn't think the boy's mother would allow it. The woman, who also had an eight-year-old daughter, had ended their relationship.

Whitmore offered to help – citing his credentials with Children Protection Services – and said he had plenty of experience in obtaining custody orders and "seizing" children on behalf of the parent. The two men agreed to meet up on the outside.

That happened shortly after Whitmore's release on July 29. Whitmore took Salinas to court, where he helped him obtain a temporary court order that allowed visitation.

Whitmore was no dummy and knew the system well. He played both sides of this dispute, meeting separately with the woman and her daughter to explain what was going on.

The woman was upset. Whitmore said he understood, explaining these types of custody cases take a toll on everyone. But he claimed he might have a solution.

Whitmore said it might be good to get the young girl out of such a poisonous atmosphere for a few days. Children are often hit the hardest by these types of disputes, he explained, and a break might be the best thing for her.

Whitmore told the woman he had plenty of experience working with fractured families. He spoke in a calm, measured tone that inspired a feeling of ease and comfort with the woman. She viewed him as trustworthy and reliable.

Whitmore sealed the deal by pointing out he was in a relationship with a woman, named Terry. She had cerebral palsy and was confined to a wheelchair. Whitmore assured the woman that Terry would also be helping care for the girl.

After consulting with her daughter, the woman agreed. And so on Sunday August 7 – exactly nine days after Whitmore had been let out of jail – he was now walking away with someone's daughter.

Whitmore promised the mother he would keep in constant touch. He assured her the little girl was in good hands.

• • • • •

They had gone directly to Whitmore's apartment in Scarborough, arriving shortly after midnight. Whitmore told the girl she could sleep on the couch. He didn't wait long to make his move.

While she was asleep, Whitmore stood over the girl, bent down and began kissing her. He backed off immediately when she woke up. She appeared scared. Whitmore said nothing. Terry was asleep in another room.

The situation took another grim turn on the morning of Tuesday August 9. The girl's mother had been speaking with Salinas about the ongoing custody situation.

That's when she learned the truth about the man who had her daughter. He might actually be a trained counsellor, she was told. But he's also a convicted child molester.

She immediately picked up the phone and dialled the number Whitmore had left. There was no answer.

She left a frantic phone message, telling him to call her immediately. She threatened to go to police but held off, hoping the situation would quickly resolve itself.

Whitmore returned the call late that afternoon. Both the woman and Salinas demanded he return the little girl. They told him to be at their home by 7 p.m. – or else.

The dinner hour passed and Whitmore was nowhere to be found. More calls to his apartment went unanswered. The next call was to police. They went to Whitmore's house, where Terry was now alone. She had no idea where he'd gone.

Whitmore was now on the run. He went to a sporting goods store and purchased a small tent. The girl was at his side, oblivious to the urgent drama that was unfolding around her.

Whitmore then headed to a campground on the outskirts of Toronto, knowing police would likely be searching his apartment. He thought isolated locale would provide the perfect cover. That night, Whitmore became more aggressive.

He forcibly kissed her on the lips, and then made her perform fellatio on him inside the tent. The now terrified girl spent the night alone in the woods with Whitmore.

By morning, Whitmore was ready to hit the road. He packed up the tent and got behind the wheel of his 1988 Chevy Cavalier.

He knew police would be swarming the province looking for him and decided he needed to get rid of the girl.

That's when he made the call for the cab and headed for Canadian Tire.

● ● ● ● ●

"You can never be too careful about who is taking care of your kids," Det. Tom Archibald said during the press conference announcing the search for Whitmore.

Police had obtained a Canada-wide warrant and were asking the public to keep their eyes open. Local media were all over the story – which included details about Whitmore's failed foray into the United States and his history of deception.

For one Ontario family, it was an all-too-familiar face appearing on their television screens. "It was like seeing a ghost," the mother of one of his previous victim's told the *Toronto Sun* in an interview.

The mother's son had helped put Whitmore behind bars just 11 months earlier – and she was stunned he was already back on the streets targeting other children already.

The wounds were still very fresh in her family. Whitmore had tried to lure her boy by offering him $100 for oral sex. He refused, but Whitmore would go on to attack other young victims before getting caught.

For yet another family, the nightmare was just beginning. The publicity surrounding Whitmore's latest crime had prompted a young boy to come forward with a terrible secret.

Whitmore had lived next-door to the now 11-year-old boy for a brief time in the summer of 1992. Although he was new to the Keswick neighbourhood, Whitmore had quickly made an impression.

He was friendly, outgoing and seem to have a natural charm with children. This rubbed off on many parents – including those of his young neighbour. Whitmore invited the boy to sleepover at his home – and the parents agreed.

Whitmore had wasted little time preying on the boy. He began fondling his genitals, and then said he would pay him $100 for fellatio. The boy said no, but Whitmore was persistent and persuasive.

He continued to wave dollars in front of the boy's face and molested him several times over the course of the night. The boy returned home the following morning but said nothing of the attacks. Until now.

His stunned parents picked up the phone and immediately called police.

●  ●  ●  ●  ●

## SHELBURNE, NOVA SCOTA
## AUGUST 12, 1994

Doug Stewart may have hung up his holster – but the retired police officer hadn't lost the natural instincts that all good cops have. And so it was that alarm bells began ringing as soon as he met the stranger for the first time.

The man had walked into Stewart's hotel, the Loyalist Inn, looking to rent a room. He claimed to be checking out the area after getting a job with the local armed forces base. He then pulled out a cheque book – bearing the name of an Arizona bank – and paid for his room.

Stewart wasn't convinced. He thought there was something fishy about the man's story and decided to play his hunch.

With the man now checked in, Stewart phoned the local RCMP detachment. He described the situation to police – mentioning his former career in law enforcement – and thought it might be wise to run the man's name through their computer system.

"What is it?" the voice at the other end of the line asked.

"Peter Whitmore," said Stewart.

• • • • •

It took only minutes for Shelburne police to realize they had a predator in their quiet coastal town. The Canadian Police Information Centre in Ottawa – known universally as CPIC – had quickly shown the existing warrant out for Whitmore's arrest.

Police rushed to the Loyalist Inn. Whitmore was in his room, alone, when he saw the cruiser cars pulling up to the hotel. He bolted out the front door, trying to flee.

He only made it a few metres. Whitmore was quickly down on the ground and in handcuffs.

Thanks to some great sleuthing by Stewart, one of the country's most sought-after fugitives was in custody.

He was taken to the local police detachment and placed in a holding cell. Toronto police were immediately notified of his arrest. The families of his two newest victims were notified, bringing a sense of relief. A news bulletin was released later in the day.

"We'd like to thank the press and the public," Staff Insp. Ed Ludlow told reporters. He said there had been at least 40 sightings and tips come into their office in the previous 48 hours.

"The publicity was a great help," he said.

• • • • •

Police weren't done with their investigation. With Whitmore back behind bars, investigators applied to the courts for a search warrant for his apartment.

They cited Whitmore's disturbing pattern of behaviour and the potential for more victims as grounds for the raid. A magistrate agreed.

Police had prepared for the worst upon entering Whitmore's home – and their concerns were proven to be valid. Officers found 15 separate binders inside the suite – nine containing pictures of young boys modelling clothing and swimsuits in catalogues, one containing young girls in similar poses, and two with a mix of boys and girls.

Police also seized three binders filled with travel brochures – more proof that Whitmore was a man who liked to stay on the move. There were also various documents for Children Protection Services including receipts for business supplies.

Further search of the apartment revealed even more disturbing material. Whitmore had an extensive collection of posters of a various child stars in popular movies and television shows. There was a book titled "TV – Free Activities You Can Do With Your Child" along with several self-help books for parents and their children.

Whitmore also had "The Doctor's Book of Home Remedies For Children" and another guide for non-prescription drugs.

In essence, Whitmore had all the tools of a professional pedophile. Now police hoped they'd be able to bring the hammer down on him.

# CHAPTER NINE

## SCARBOROUGH, ONTARIO
APRIL 5, 1995

Eight months after his arrest in Nova Scotia, Peter Whitmore was in court to admit to his crimes. After discussions with his lawyer, Whitmore was convinced that showing some "remorse" and not fighting the allegations was the best move he could make.

He pleaded guilty to two counts of sexual interference and invitation to sexual touching and was sentenced to five years in prison as part of a joint proposal from Crown and defence lawyers.

Crown attorney Julie Battersby outlined the disturbing facts, noting Whitmore gave a videotaped admission following his arrest on the east coast.

"Given their very young ages, clearly I really don't need to say anymore about that and how aggravating that is. I appreciate that's the nature of Mr. Whitmore's pedophilia, that he goes after – that's not good wording – that his preference is for young children, and clearly that in itself is an aggravating feature that he acted upon them in this case," said Battersby.

In legal terms, they call this a "quid pro quo." Each side had given something up – Whitmore had sacrificed his right to plead not guilty and force his victims to testify, while the Crown would shave some time off their preferred sentence to secure a conviction and spare the children from appearing in court.

The Crown was dropping the abduction charge, which Battersby explained was part of the negotiated plea-bargain. But Battersby said that doesn't make his crime any less serious.

"Mr. Whitmore was in the position of babysitter or care giver for the overnight sleep-over that he had (with the young male victim). Clearly that was a breach of trust situation. With respect to (the female victim), it was even more significant given that he was a caregiver for a period of about three days," said Battersby.

She questioned Whitmore's motives for setting up his child protection business, suggesting it was just a cover to gain access to other victims.

"Whatever his purpose might be, the very idea that he set up this business, knowing himself to be a homosexual pedophile, and knowing that it would provide him access to children is aggravating," said Battersby.

She said there would be plenty of treatment and programming available to Whitmore while behind bars.

"Hopefully he will engage in that treatment to assist him," she said.

Where the case really took a twist – and what would secure Whitmore's place in the annals of criminal justice – was what Judge Petra Newton did next.

She ordered Whitmore to stay away from children – not for a few months, or a few years. Forever.

Newton also banned him for life from going anywhere kids like to gather, including parks, playgrounds, swimming pools, community clubs or day-cares.

Whitmore – who was in agreement with the condition — would also be prohibited from ever trying to find a job where he might have contact with children under the age of 14.

The only exception would be to potentially have future contact with his own children.

"If and when he rehabilitates himself he may, at some point, be a person who has a family," said defence lawyer David Baylis.

He noted Whitmore no longer had contact with his only child, a son, from a previous relationship.

"At some point in this life he may re-establish contact with him, or he may have other children," said Bayliss.

Newton hadn't created a new law – but she was the first judge in the province to use existing legislation and make such an order. Under the Criminal Code, a judge can impose these kinds of restrictions on high-risk offenders. But normal durations were in the five to 10-year range.

Newton was convinced something more drastic was needed after hearing the facts of Whitmore's crimes.She was particularly swayed based on Whitmore's history of manipulating his victims – both parents and children – into believing he was an honest, trustworthy individual.

"Child sexual abuse requires severe censure by the court. The court must, through its sentencing process, express society's abhorrence of offences like you engaged in," Newton told Whitmore.

However, the judge found some positive things to say about Whitmore as well.

"It is clear that you have entered a guilty plea, that shows your remorse, it shows your potential for rehabilitation. It certainly has saved the time and expense of a trial. In my view that guilty plea is consistent with the statement that you gave to police upon your arrest, and the actions you exhibited upon your arrest. I am taking that into consideration as a positive feature in your particular case," she said.

"I find that your guilty plea does have a special significance as you did obviate the need for two very young victims to testify at both a preliminary hearing and at a trial; and relive and thereby exacerbate the trauma that surrounded these particular events. I am prepared to give you substantial credit for that."

Newton warned Whitmore that he faced a long, uphill climb to turn his troubled life around – and sent her own message to national parole officials before closing court.

"I strongly recommend sexual offender assessment and treatment as soon as possible, and I am certainly hopeful that will meet with the desired effect of such a recommendation," she said. "But I would also like to indicate that any application for parole is to be seriously questioned if you do not take the treatment that is required, and is very sorely needed in the court's view."

She gave Whitmore four months credit for his time already served in custody since his arrest, leaving him with 56 months left to serve.

Speaking outside court, Toronto police said they were pleased with the sentence – which wouldn't expire until December 1999 – and with the lifetime ban placed on

Whitmore. Privately, officers were hoping for something much more severe. Because they were convinced Whitmore was only going to use his time behind bars to regroup – not rehabilitate.

And that it wouldn't be long before the public was hearing his name yet again.

• • • • •

*"Twelve men broke loose in '73, from Millhaven maximum security."*

So begins the song "38 Years Old" by Canada's legendary The Tragically Hip. And while the group sings of a fictional escape, the truth is inmates probably have a better chance of making it big as a rock star than finding a way out of the maximum-security penitentiary.

Located in Bath, Ontario, Millhaven's 400 plus inmates include some of the country's most dangerous offenders. That includes sexual predators.

Millhaven has become one of the most popular facilities in Canada to send high-risk deviants, largely because of their comprehensive sex offender assessment program launched in 1993.

All prisoners with sex-related convictions are put through a three-step process upon entering the facility. Prison officials examine their criminal history in detail, conduct a detailed psychological assessment and then develop a treatment and risk management plan based on the findings.

It's a lengthy process that often includes interviews and statements from past victims and reading of court transcripts. One of the key elements, though, is really beyond the control of prison officials.

In a perfect world every offender would willingly sit down and launch into a detailed description of every facet of their life, including their crimes. Of course, in that same perfect world pedophiles wouldn't exist in the first place. The reality is many are unwilling to co-operate with the process. And those who do must be scrutinized closely for truth and accuracy.

Officials weren't sure what to expect from Peter Whitmore when he entered Millhaven to begin serving his first federal sentence.

Robert Keates, a case management officer, was tasked with Whitmore's file. His first assessment, written in May 1995 following a series of preliminary interviews with Whitmore, offered a grim prognosis for the future.

"Whitmore is viewed at this time as a high-risk offender. At 24, the subject finds himself serving his first federal term. His prior criminal history includes convictions of a similar nature and a portion of the current offences were committed approximately nine days following his release from a 16 month sentence," Keates wrote in his report.

"Whitmore acknowledges an attraction to young males and has in the past admitted to sexually assaulting numerous victims. His means of seeking out victims is of particular concern in that he appears highly manipulative. Of particular concern is (the victim's) young age, combined with his apparent modus operandi, which is to seek out victims or gain the confidence of them or their families through highly manipulative ways."

Keates wasn't the only one sounding the alarm. Even other inmates at Millhaven found reason to be concerned about Whitmore. On June 23, 1995, Whitmore was confronted by prison staff over rumours he'd been "muscling" his cellmate by threatening him and slapping him in the face.

Such conduct wasn't unusual behind bars, where the weak often struggle to survive. Pedophiles like Whitmore are usually at the bottom of the pecking order and routinely turn to violence to fight for their very existence.

Yet a complaint three days later certainly turned some heads. The same cellmate wanted to speak with prison staff about some disturbing things he'd witnessed from Whitmore.

"All I want him to do is get help. I know he needs help; he would stand six inches from the TV and stare at kids. He would even touch the screen where the kid's private parts were. I remember one time he told me women were nothing but trouble," the inmate said in a written report.

Whitmore denied the claims when confronted by prison officials. And while he continued to co-operate with the sex offender assessment, his seemingly candid answers were only raising more red flags.

Bruce Malcolm, director of sex offender assessments, met with Whitmore several times for the purpose of preparing a psychological report. He wrote up his findings in early August 1995.

"Whitmore does not view the children involved in his sexual offences, past or present, as victims. He views them all as willing participants, due to either genuinely liking him or because he paid for their sexual services. He advises that he does not consider performing fellatio on the victims as an intrusive sexual act; consequently he did not feel that the victims had been affected negatively by sexual activity. He concedes he has a problem, but perhaps he views it more as a legal problem, certainly not a moral one," Malcolm wrote in his report.

He noted Whitmore's bizarre explanation for sexually abusing the young boy – Whitmore claimed he was "going out with" the victim's 11-year-old brother when the victim "demanded" he perform oral sex on him or else he'd tell his mother Whitmore was having sex with his brother.

"Obviously he does not view this young boy as a victim," said Malcolm.

Despite his guilty plea, Whitmore was denying any sexual contact with the young girl he abducted. "Why would I? I like boys."

Whitmore claimed the girl became "easily confused" because of the tense situation involving her mother and step-father, who he claimed had sexually abused the girl.

On his first set of convictions, which involved the multiple male victims, Whitmore claimed the boys were already experienced sexually and that he "wasn't doing anything new" with them.

Whitmore said he didn't use physical force with the victims and they agreed to the sexual acts. "I didn't take them off the streets and rape them," Whitmore told Malcolm.

Whitmore also claimed the 11-year-old boy he abducted and held for nearly 24 hours seemed much older, at least 14.

"Boys from Bosnia look older," he said. Whitmore said he spent several hundred dollars on the boy during a "shopping spree" which came after their sexual encounter. Whitmore was also now admitting to other crimes for which he'd never been charged, providing graphic details about his desires and fantasies.

"He advises that he has had about ten or eleven what he considers to be 'relationships' with boys mainly under the age of 12. He indicates that he has tried to remain with a child after he was 12 years old but found it difficult. He states that he did manage to stay with one boy, from age 12 to 16. He relates that he has engaged in sexual acts with these boys, ranging from fondling, to fellatio, to acts of anal intercourse. Later in the interview he reported that he is more interested in being affectionate (hugging and kissing) with boys under the age of 12, and performing fellatio on those males who are aged 12 and over. He reports that he has had adult male sexual partners, but only due to his prostituting. He relates that he did not enjoy the sexual activity with adult males, but did so out of necessity. He states that it is more realistic for him to become attracted to young females (aged 12 to 16) and then make the leap from young females to adult females," Malcolm wrote.

"He indicates that in his leisure time he enjoys collecting photographs, apparently he had 50,000 photographs in his home when he was arrested. He suggests that very few of those pictures were of children. However, he advises that he was doing an experiment in which he was taking photos of many children from different ethnicities. He reports that he was very interested in seeing how different male children aged over the years, specifically between the ages of four and 17. It is noteworthy to mention that he states he reads certain literature that depicts an adult's experiences sexually assaulting children. He relates that he prefers 'true stories'," said Malcolm.

Whitmore even admitted he was still looking for other young companions, even while stuck in prison.

"Lately he has taken to writing numerous 'pen pals'. He obtained names of pen-pals from a list of individuals whom are 'gay.' He relates that he discovered, apparently by accident, that one of these males whom he writes has a sexual preference for young boys. He admits to having quite a curiosity about other males who sexually assault children. He contends that he is still 'learning' about himself, and that he feels that he can learn from others who have a similar preference. He indicates that although he has not 'acted on' sexually assaulting, rather aggressively, quite young children, he takes a certain amount of pleasure or enjoyment from reading about others who have," said Malcolm,

There was more. Whitmore continued with his wild claims – many of which had never surfaced before and likely could never be proven – about some of the things he'd done in the past to search for potential victims.

"It would seem that many of Whitmore's activities, whether for leisure or job related, revolve around access to young males. He states that he had been a Cub Scout leader, and claims to have never sexually assaulted any of the boys he came into contact with. He reports that prior to his arrest, he was writing 'nasty stories.' He indicates that he was writing child pornography stories. Also, he states that he was 'helping a friend' chose children for a movie. He contends that the movie was not of a pornographic nature. He relates that he has taken child psychology courses, to better understand children. He also reads books about children who have been sexually abused. He was unable to describe himself in general, but he advises that he 'likes to spend money' – specifically on other people (children)," said Malcolm.

Whitmore spoke at length about his family and childhood, offering a story that at times seemed to stray into the surreal. However, regardless of how much was fact versus fiction, Malcolm believed it offered significant insight into Whitmore's troubled mind.

He claimed his mother was admitted to a psychiatric facility shortly after his birth and that his father was never in the picture. Whitmore said he was "kidnapped" by his aunt's family but told Malcolm he was now questioning whether he was really related to any of the people who had raised him.

"He indicates that he began being suspicious at the age of 10 that those who said they were his parents were not," said Malcolm.

Whitmore mentioned having a sister and two older brothers from his "alleged" family.

"Whitmore describes a childhood history filled with sexual, emotional and physical abuse. He also depicts events which were traumatic, tragic, convoluted and rather confusing at times. He supports that until he was about 11 years old he lived a relatively happy childhood being raised by friends of his aunt. He advises that when he was about 11 years old his foster parents divorced. He describes them as having been good parents," said Malcolm.

Whitmore said he went to live with another foster family in Omemee, a small rural Ontario community best known as being the childhood home of legendary Canadian musician Neil Young.

Malcolm obtained a copy of a 1980 letter that had been sent to Dr. Donald Clark, who was working with Whitmore and his family at the time.

The letter – written by another doctor – detailed several ongoing issues and concerns with Whitmore's emotional stability at the time and how it was affecting several areas of his life including school.

It spoke of a fractured family that had clearly affected Whitmore, especially pertaining to his natural mother.

*"Peter very definitely presents as a very vulnerable child in need of support, not only in the academic area, but also in the social and emotional one. He handled himself fairly age appropriately, from time to time, but required frequent re-assurance and support to allow him to complete the tasks requested of him. Behaviourally, there was some limit testing which he easily responded to. He spoke very warmly of his natural mother, and has convinced himself that fairly soon, in the near future, he would be residing with her,"* the letter said.

*In talking with Mrs. Budd, the current foster mother, Peter has exhibited a considerable amount of frustration in adapting to normal family routine. Most of his frustration is expressed in aggressive activity which now the family anticipates and has been able to intervene quite often, earlier, and help Peter express himself more appropriately. Certainly Mrs. Budd's attitude and her currently management techniques leave little to critique. I feel that Peter will thrive considerably providing the family can survive his emotional demands. I discussed this with them, the fact that Peter's behaviour can be a very emotionally draining one, and therefore, the family must take precautions to build up some protections for itself so as not to have the placement deteriorate."*

Yet that's exactly what happened. Whitmore told Malcolm he returned to his mother, who had now divorced his alleged father and re-married, about a year later. His three siblings were also back home.

"He describes his step-father as having been an 'idiot' who had attempted to kill him. He indicates that the family was on a camping trip and his step-father tried to hang him. He contends that he suffered much abuse within the family and had to go into the care of the Children's Aid Society several times under the age of 16," wrote Malcolm.

Whitmore claimed his first sexual experience came while under government care. He was 14, and his partner was just 10.

"He states that he had already been having sexual fantasies of young males, but this was the first time he acted on those sexual thoughts," said Malcolm.

"He relates that he disliked living in the receiving home of the CAS. He indicates that various 'family' members put him in the hospital on at least four occasions due to the physical abuse. He reports that his mother began living with a man named Kevin when he was 14 or 15 years old. He described Kevin as an alcoholic and a 'druggie'. He indicates that his mother continued to ignore him and spend money. He states that he often had to 'eat out of a garbage can'. He relates that by the age of 16, he ran away and left home for good."

Whitmore's story didn't end there. In fact, it only got stranger.

"He states that when he left home he eventually ended up in California. He relates that he survived by doing some acting. Also, he engaged in prostitution. He indicates that he traveled a lot, moving frequently from town to town between the United States and Canada. At the age of 17, he indicates that he went to live with his 'father' in Alberta. Shortly after arrival, he stole his father's car and was charged accordingly by the police. He advises that he was sentenced to 30 days in a young offender facility," said Malcolm.

Court records confirmed Whitmore's arrest and sentencing, which marked his first official brush with the law.

Whitmore told Malcolm he was no stranger to these types of forensic reports, having gone through one at the tender age of 10. Whitmore was prescribed Ritalin to deal with his "hyper" behaviour.

"He indicates that he was hypnotized by a doctor because he was experiencing nightmares. He advises that he had recurring nightmares in which he was locked in a room in a burning house. He states that he also dreamt of being locked in a room with books, and no furniture, for extended periods of time," wrote Malcolm.

It was during hypnosis, Whitmore claimed, when he had a major flashback about a significant childhood event he'd managed to bury deep in his mind.

Whitmore claims one of his older brothers had raped him.

"He advises...he was about nine years old. He states that he cannot recall much of his childhood, especially the sexual abuse. He suggests that one of his brothers tried to kill him on a few occasions. He relates that when he was about 13 years old, his then 15-year-old brother shot him with a BB-gun. He states that his brother also tried to hang him on one occasion," said Malcolm.

Whitmore reported suffering other sexual assaults at the hands of adult males in his life but couldn't give any specifics because he'd "blocked" the memories.

"He reports that his sister is 'okay' in that she never did anything to him. He indicates that he has regular contact with her. He states that she will not discuss their childhood with him because she is in 'denial'," said Malcolm.

Whitmore discussed his education, or lack thereof. He'd only completed grade eight, telling Malcolm he often found himself being suspended or expelled for various behavioural problems.

"He reports that he has had long periods of unemployment and has supported himself through social assistance, occasional prostitution and frauds, although he suggests the frauds were committed more for the thrill of not getting caught," said Malcolm.

Whitmore said his troubled life had led him to consider suicide, with at least three or four half-hearted attempts since 1994. Even his alleged methods had Malcolm questioning the legitimacy of Whitmore's claims.

"He indicates that he generally makes an attempt while he is in custody, and before he is actually sentenced for a conviction. He relates that on one occasion, he scraped the paint off his cell wall, 'drank it' and also consumed 18 pencils," wrote Malcolm.

"He advises he thought he would perish of lead poisoning, but obviously did not. In the end, he states that it all just made him feel physically ill and just 'yucky'. He reports that in the other instances he did not really make an attempt, but gathered sheets in preparation of hanging himself. He states that he has not been experiencing any suicidal ideations presently."

Whitmore continued to tell stories straight out of a Hollywood movie plot – especially when discussing his apparent marriage to a Los Angeles police officer. Whitmore said he was only 16, while the woman was 22. He was struggling on the streets of California when their paths crossed.

"He indicates he got married to 'get away from everybody'. He states that their sexual activity was short-lived, however, a child was produced from such activity. Their son is presently 10 years old and living with 'some friends'," said Malcolm.

"Whitmore relates that he has regular contact with his son, who is apparently residing with a gay male couple. He claims that he has not had any sexual thoughts of his son, on the contrary, he seemed rather disgusted at the notion."

Malcolm asked what had become of his wife, and their marriage. Whitmore claimed they got along great because the woman – despite being a cop – "understood his problem of being sexually attracted to young males." Tragically, said Whitmore, she died in 1989 – after her car plunged over a cliff.

In his report, Malcolm noted several contradictions between what Whitmore told him and what he'd apparently said during previous interviews with medical officials.

The most notable was a prior claim from Whitmore that he'd fathered not one, but three children. One of the mothers, he claimed, was only 14 when she gave birth years earlier.

Whitmore wrapped up a truly memorable interview with Malcolm by claiming he was being treated unfairly by the justice system and given sentences that were too harsh, especially for his most recent crimes.

"He suggests there are sexual offenders, worse than he, that receive considerable less time for much more intrusive sexual acts," said Malcolm.

# CHAPTER TEN

Measuring a criminal's risk to re-offend is hardly a perfect science. Yet that hasn't stopped justice officials around the world from using a scientific approach to help with decisions of which inmates should be released, and when.

According to the National Parole Board, Canada began adapting a series of "risk prediction instruments" following earlier developments in other countries.

"During the 1960's and 70's in the United States and Britain, experimentation with risk prediction emerged in response to challenges that there were no clear criteria established to guide parole decision-making, and that the resulting decisions lacked consistency and equity," the board writes.

The NPB soon began their own research to find better tools to assist in their decision-making process. The move spawned a rapid growth in private industry devoted to creating risk assessment systems.

One of the most common tests, called the "Level of Supervision Inventory", was developed in Canada in the early 1990s by Dr. Don Adams and Dr. James Bonta. The test is fairly basic, consisting of 54 questions put to an inmate during a face-to-face interview.

Topics include their criminal history, education and employment, financial resources, family and marital background, living arrangements, leisure and recreation activities and history, friend and associates, alcohol and drug issues, emotional and personal issues and attitude.

Inmates are then given a score based on their responses – 37 of the questions will yield basic "yes" or "no" answers, while the others are graded on a sliding scale. Of course, the results can be hampered by a dishonest or uncooperative inmate.

Another popular risk assessment is called the "Psychopathy Checklist (PCL)", which was developed by Robert D. Hare in 1991. A psychologist grades an inmate in 20 different categories – assigning scores of either 0, 1 or 2. Topics include criminal history, lifestyle, attitude, impulse control, remorse, manipulation, callousness and charm.

The maximum PCL score any inmate could get is 40 – which would have them defined as a "classic or prototypical psychopath." A person with absolute no psychopathic traits would score zero. According to Hare, the average score for a person with no criminal background would be around five.

Peter Whitmore took the PCL test upon entry at Millhaven, scoring 30. That put him right at the starting point for a person defined as suffering from psychopathy. It also made him a likely candidate to re-offend.

A federal study of 81 male offenders provided some interesting insight to Canadian justice officials. The average PCL score was 22.1. The inmates were monitored for an average of 30 months. Officials found 57 per cent of them re-offended during that period.

However, those who scored about 30 on the PCL test had 80 per cent rate of recidivism. The number dropped to 59 per cent for those who scored between 17 and 30 and down to 40 per cent for those who scored 16 and under.

●　●　●　●　●

Peter Whitmore had worn out his welcome. He had become a disruptive force in Millhaven as other inmates continued to make complaints about his behaviour. Whitmore seemed intent on flexing his proverbial jailhouse muscles and his list of enemies was quickly growing.

Rather than risk a potential riot, prison officials decided it was best to move the problem out to a facility better-equipped to handle a criminal of his ilk. Whitmore was shipped to Kingston Penitentiary on November 27, 1995.

Originally opened in 1835 as the "Provincial Penitentiary of the Province of Upper Canada," Kingston is one of the oldest active prisons in the world. And one of the most notorious as well. Some inmates and justice officials have dubbed it "Alcatraz North", an ode to the long history of violent, dangerous criminals who have spent time there.

There is no double-bunking at Kingston, as every inmate gets their own individual cell. It's not a matter of making the criminal more comfortable – rather, it's an issue of security.

Kingston inmates are considered among the worst in the country – many have been kicked out of other prisons and required protective custody because of their crimes or gang ties. Despite taking precautions to maintain law and order, Kingston staff members are still frequently subjected to verbal and physical attacks.

It's not a pretty place – both for those required to live there and those who work there.

• • • • •

Different prison, same results.

Peter Whitmore continued to show little interest in dealing with the core issues that had landed him behind bars. He refused to participate in any of the sex offender programs offered by Kingston.

Whitmore did express mild interest in upgrading his education. He claimed to have finished Grade 12 – although officials were rather sceptical.

"He was admitted to the Seneca College program at the Kingston Penitentiary School on the strength of his verbal assurances...but when he proved unable to complete work at the college level, Whitmore was placed in the Adult Basic Education Program in order to upgrade his math," officials wrote in a 1996 report. Whitmore didn't seem to appreciate the demotion.

"Due to a lack of attendance on his part, Whitmore is now facing the prospect of being removed from the K.P. school altogether," his report stated.

And that's exactly what happened. And it wasn't long before Kingston officials grew tired of his act and removed him from the prison entirely. For the second time in a year, Whitmore was getting a new home.

This time it was Kent Institution, the country's only maximum-security prison in the Pacific region. Located in the city of Kent, British Columbia – about 150 kilometres east of Vancouver – the facility can hold up to 250 inmates who are deemed high-risk/high-need offenders. Kent also specializes in taking inmates who may be targeted because of their criminal history – specifically pedophiles like Whitmore – and added two segregation units in the early 1980s.

Whitmore wasted little time showing his new guardians why he was such a high risk. In early 1997, a routine search of his cell turned up several pictures of children which Whitmore had apparently cut out from various magazines and kept hidden inside books he'd borrowed from the prison library.

They appeared to have come from two sources – a children's exercise book which showed young girls in leotards and workout clothes, and a National Geographic magazine which had several images of young naked boys. The discovery prompted immediate action.

Whitmore was sent for a psychological evaluation with Dr. C. Smiley. Prison officials wanted to try and gain some better insight into his continuing conduct.

"This discovery of images was determined to be significant in light of the fact Mr. Whitmore is a convicted sex offender whose victims are children. The writer determined that Mr. Whitmore was probably using these pictures to generate sexual fantasies about children. This would indicate that he was at a high risk for maintaining/entering his crime cycle and for continuing to reinforce his inappropriate sexual responding to children," Smiley wrote in his report.

"Mr. Whitmore immediately adopted a defensive attitude and denied that the pictures were his. Mr. Whitmore appeared to be extremely agitated and angered by the allegations that the pictures were in fact his and that he was using the pictures for sexual gratification. Mr Whitmore acknowledged that he had other materials such as a Sears catalogue which contained pictures of young children in revealing attire (e.g. underwear, leotards, etc.). He stated that he used the catalogue only for ordering items and denied using the pictures for sexual gratification," said Smiley.

Smiley then made an interesting challenge to Whitmore.

"The writer proposed to Mr. Whitmore that perhaps he would be willing to demonstrate his motivation for change by removing all of the pages containing children from the catalogue (as it was determined that he had no intentions of ordering children's clothing). He angrily refused to do this stating that it would be 'destruction of property'," said Smiley.

"This poorly thought-out response demonstrated his determination and commitment to maintaining access to pictures of young children. Consequently, this incident has demonstrated that Mr. Whitmore's current motivation for treatment is poor," he concluded.

Smiley believed the best option was to move Whitmore yet again, this time to another specialized sex offender facility.

"Mr. Whitmore has yet to realize that the onus for change rests with him and that he is responsible for demonstrating to others that he is actively working towards eliminating any behaviour which contributes to his crime cycle (e.g., in this instance keeping and viewing pictures of children)," said Smiley.

"Further, in order to demonstrate sufficient motivation for change, it is imperative that he respond constructively to reasonable requests regarding any high-risk behaviours (e.g., re: Sears catalogue). Consequently, this incident has demonstrated that Mr. Whitmore's current motivation for treatment is poor."

Whitmore headed west to the Regional Health Centre in British Columbia, where he was enrolled in the Intensive Treatment Program for Sex Offenders. Once again, he showed a complete lack of interest in participating in treatment and programming.

His attitude was best demonstrated by a disturbing incident which occurred just days after his April 1997 arrival. The facility was holding an "Open House" where inmates would get a brief opportunity to socialize with family members. Whitmore got no visitors on this day – but he didn't seem to mind.

Staff members learned after the fact from other inmates that Whitmore had approached two young children who were there to see their father – at one point even embracing them in hugs. Interviews were conducted with the boys and an "Officer's Statement/Observation Report" was written and placed on Whitmore's file.

"It was brought to the attention of the writer...that Peter Whitmore befriended two young boys. He was excited by this and expressed his desire to meet them again and, in fact, he purchased a picture of this family from the patient they were visiting," program therapist Jacquelyn Darguay wrote.

She had also learned of a second attempt by Whitmore to gain access to illicit material involving two other inmates.

"He had approached a group member for a picture of his grandson and offered to send kiddie porn through the guise of a lawyer's letter to another group member. Finally, he had admitted using pictures from the library to fuel his fantasies," said Darguay.

The facility was through with Whitmore. He was moved back to Millhaven in June 1997 – 19 months after he was first booted out in a move that showed how little had been accomplished during that time and how frustrated justice officials were with his lack of progress and continued pattern of disturbing behaviour even while in custody.

Whitmore was back in the starting blocks, undergoing yet another detailed assessment regarding his psychological state, treatment options and risk assessment. He also began participating, albeit reluctantly, in group counselling sessions.

Jerome Fransblow, a clinical psychologist, was given the unenviable task of interviewing Whitmore. He tried to focus the discussion on the most recent incidents out west – but quickly found the subject to be a sore one.

"Mr. Whitmore again adamantly denied having hugged the children...and thus terminated his involvement with the program and left the interview," wrote Fransblow.

A night alone in his cell apparently had given Whitmore second thoughts. Although he stopped short of apologizing, Whitmore returned the following day and asked for another chance at treatment.

"The team reviewed his request and decided that it was not a good idea for him to return to the group he was involved with, due to the fact that he had minimized his offending and lied in group to such a high degree as to alienate the group he was involved with, to a point that the group would be seriously limited in their progress due to their feelings about him," wrote Fransblow.

Once again, Whitmore had earned the wrath of his fellow inmates.

"As such, the treatment team's recommendations at this time were that he returns for further treatment but in the next program. They also feel he continues to represent a serious risk to children and that detention referral should be considered," said Fransblow.

The detention referral was in regards to Whitmore's pending opportunity at parole. Whitmore had already passed the one-third mark of his sentence, which allows for an application to be made for early release to the National Parole Board.

He hadn't made a bid – likely realizing that his history of offending, lack of treatment and jailhouse incidents would mean an automatic rejection. Yet Whitmore had another date circled on his calendar that was quickly looming – May 15, 1998.

That's the day he'd hit the two-thirds mark on his sentence – and be eligible for statutory release. Whitmore knew he had a realistic shot at freedom and that only a strong recommendation from the Correctional Service of Canada could stop him. Fransblow suggested the CSC take the rare step in this case.

"In summary, Mr. Whitmore is a young man with serious credibility problems due to his lying, and who represents a significant risk to children as an untreated sex offender. He is currently displaying active signs of attraction to children, especially males within the institution," he concluded in his report.

Fransblow's findings got the ball rolling for other officials to follow suit. Whitmore was moved back to Kingston in the summer of 1997 and was assigned a new case-worker.

Scott Myhre had read the previous reports on Whitmore and saw nothing that changed his mind. He concluded that Whitmore remained a high-risk to re-offend and should not be released.

Among the findings of the latest Kingston report:

*"Hyper-alert. Superficially co-operative. Demanding of outside referrals. Speaks quickly. No psychomotor disturbance. No thought form disorder. Euthymic. Gives glib and superficial responses to a number of questions, such as: April 1992 offences were due to 'trial and error' and 'I always buy my friendships.' Grandiose re his criminal*

*activities. No suicidal/homicidal ideation. Quite bright, cognitively intact."*

The report also included a new revelation on the alleged "hugging" incident that occurred out west and which Whitmore had previously denied.

It had now been learned that Whitmore admitted the incident to another inmate, even saying he was "aroused" by having contact with the children. Prison officials believed he'd approached as many as four other inmates asking for pictures of their kids. Whitmore had now admitted to being a "chronic liar without credibility," according to the report.

It was clear how prison officials felt about letting Whitmore back into the community. Would the Parole Board follow the recommendations coming their way?

Or was Whitmore about to re-enter society?

# CHAPTER ELEVEN

## JANUARY 30, 1998

Denied.

Peter Whitmore's first appearance before the National Parole Board was short and sweet – at least for the victims of his crimes who couldn't understand why this predator even had a shot at early release.

Fortunately for them – and perhaps society in general – parole officials shared their concerns. With the Correctional Service of Canada recommending Whitmore not be granted statutory release, the board saw no reason to conclude otherwise.

A series of questions-and-answers with Whitmore reinforced their belief he was a serious danger.

"You are a 27-year-old first-time federal offender serving a four year, eight month sentence for invitation to sexual touching and sexual interference. The victims involved were both children, eight years of age. The incident involving the young girl occurred nine days after you were released from a 16-month term for similar offences. The offences in this case were abduction, invitation to sexual touching and sexual interference. Taken together, these offences demonstrate a pattern of persistent and inappropriate behaviour involving children," the parole board wrote in a summary of Whitmore's file.

"Both of these offences were considered to have caused serious and psychological harm and in sentencing, the judge banned you from places where children were to be found. Additionally, the sentencing judge recommended intensive sexual assessment and treatment and cautioned against conditional release in the absence of such treatment."

Whitmore's entire prison history had also been forwarded to parole officials, who expressed grave concern at his conduct behind bars and admissions he'd made to others.

"Your file indicates that you have admitted to having sexually assaulted other young males in several other cities. You claimed that these acts were becoming more progressive and that you were afraid that if it wasn't stopped, more serious harm could come to young people," the board wrote.

Whitmore was directly confronted with this issue – and he told parole officials he denied making the statements attributed to him.

"The board notes that while incarcerated, concern has been raised by professional staff of your practice of accumulating what they call child-related sexual material. In the interview today, an attempt was made to explore the potential link between this practice and your offence cycle. Although you appeared to understand the point that the board was making, you minimized your responsibility for possessing such material," the board wrote.

There was little positive to be said on Whitmore's behalf. But that didn't prevent parole officials from trying to find something.

"The board has examined the nature of your offences and has not found any evidence of brutality," they wrote.

No doubt the young victims and families who'd been hurt by Whitmore might have a different take on that.

The board also said there was no information to suggest Whitmore was currently planning any new sex crimes against children.

"Your persistent record of sexual behaviour would indicate a lack of awareness of the impact of your actions on your victims. You say that you are no longer indifferent to the consequences of your actions. Obviously the board has no demonstration of this newfound 'insight' in a community setting involving children, nor is it confirmed clinically by a treatment program outcome," the board wrote.

Parole officials pointed to Whitmore's poor results on several clinical tests and believed Whitmore was now just trying to say what they wanted to hear.

"Within the institution, both actuarially and clinically you are assessed as requiring intensive sexual treatment intervention. Although in two institutions you have been slated to begin this treatment, at this stage you remain untreated," the board wrote.

"Professional staff have questioned your motivation as a result of a practice they have observed of you acquiring inappropriate child sex-related material, and your participation in the group and practice of minimizing your offences was so disruptive to the group that it precluded continuing with the program," they continued.

"Because of your persistent record of sexual offence and lack of treatment in the institution, insufficient gains have been made to convince the board that there is available any supervision programs in the community which would be adequate to manage your risk if you were released into the community," the board wrote.

"Having considered all of the above, the board is satisfied that, if released, you are likely to commit a sexual offence against a child prior to expiration of your sentence and therefore orders you detained.

• • • • •

As 1998 moved forward – and Whitmore edged closer to the full expiration of his sentence – very little changed. The parole board's strong words had done nothing to convince Whitmore to re-evaluate his options. He was simply languishing in his cell, counting away the days until he knew there was no choice but to set him free.

By December 1998, Whitmore reluctantly agreed to participate in the high intensity sexual offender program being offered at the Ontario Regional Psychiatric Centre. Like his past "attempts" at therapy, Whitmore quickly lost interest and gave up. He took part in three group sessions before asking to be discharged.

Whitmore claimed he had concerns about staff members – citing a "lack of honesty" and what he believed were inadequate credentials – as his reasons for backing out.

Whitmore's act was wearing thin with police, who had been closely following his prisoner status and vowed not to be caught flat-footed when he was eventually released.

Det. Paul Lobsinger, a member of the Toronto Police Service, was tasked with gathering as much background information as possible on Whitmore. Police had a new tool in their arsenal and were preparing to use it for the first time against Whitmore.

But Lobsinger quickly discovered that Whitmore had been working hard behind the scenes to obtain a surprising weapon of his own.

And in the process had left behind some disturbing ammunition for police.

• • • • •

**AUGUST 17, 1999**

The package arrived at the offices of Toronto police, carrying with it an alarming message. Jill Clarke-Davis, the unit manager at Warkworth Institution, wanted to ensure officers knew that Whitmore would be getting out soon. And his chances of success in the community seemed slim.

"Reports indicate the subject has completed a variety of educational courses during his incarceration as well having completed the alternatives to violence volunteer program in 1996. Significantly, however, Whitmore has not yet addressed his need for intensive sexual behaviour treatment programming. He has been provided the opportunity on several occasions; however, he leaves the programming due to his being suspended for lying and/or lack of motivation," Clarke-Davis wrote in her report to police.

She gave a brief overview of what prison officials felt Whitmore's post-release plans included.

"Subject indicates that he is relocating to London to start over in a new and smaller city. He has not yet obtained residence or employment," she said.

Whitmore had also talked about heading back to British Columbia to live with his aunt and made claims about wanting to obtain support from some community agencies. He also spoke of a close relationship with a local pastor.

"(Prison officials) remain somewhat unconvinced his above noted gestures are genuine given his manipulative nature. Whitmore continues to show a lack of insight into his criminal behaviour. He continues to minimize the seriousness of his offences and/or deny them. He further asserts his interest in books, etc. containing pictures of children in various states of undress is strictly therapeutic. He shows no remorse and no victim empathy," said Clarke-Davis.

The letter ended with one final word of caution.

"Upon arrest, Whitmore is noted to have acknowledged assaulting other young males in various cities for several years. He is further noted to have indicated the acts were becoming more progressive in nature and 'that if things don't stop, more serious harm would come to these young persons'," said Clarke-Davis.

• • • • •

Timo Martin doesn't like to judge people. As a devout man of the cloth, Martin believes everyone will eventually answer to a much higher power than him. Yet as a human being, Martin couldn't help but form opinions on the people he met in life. And try as he might to think otherwise, Martin couldn't help but conclude that Peter Whitmore came across as a pretty nice guy.

Their paths had crossed, by chance, years earlier when Martin was ministering at the Toronto East Detention Centre. Whitmore had just been arrested and was awaiting trial. Martin spent some time alone with Whitmore, discussing his troubled path in life and what the future might hold. They re-united a couple years later when Whitmore had been transferred to Kingston Penitentiary, where Martin also visited frequently.

Martin, now retired, agreed to speak with Toronto police about some recent contact he'd been having with Whitmore. Det. Lobsinger documented Martin's story.

"Whitmore befriended him and when Whitmore was transferred to Kingston he visited him there. Mr. Martin has sent Whitmore a computer and printer, a television and set of headphones. It is believed that the television that he originally shipped Whitmore was used and that Whitmore refused to accept it and demanded a new one," Lobsinger wrote.

Police learned that Whitmore's aunt had been sending him some money in jail, which Whitmore then used to pay Martin for a new television.

"Mr. Martin has sent him money to buy things while in prison. He has told Whitmore he could live with him at his home. Mr. Martin tells police it should have been understood that it was only for the short term. Timo lives in a six bedroom house alone however he uses his house for religious and social meetings," said Lobsinger.

And that's where Whitmore's reasons for being so close to Martin became evident to police.

"These religious and social meetings consist of several groups of parents and their children. Whitmore is expecting that he is going to be working for Timo at his company however Timo says there is no room for his employment. Whitmore had six boxes and a green garbage bag shipped by courier to the company. He has mail delivered to the company. Whitmore has told Timo that he wants to get involved in the church and teach Sunday school," wrote Lobsinger.

Martin said Whitmore had made the claim in the past few weeks. And there was more.

"Whitmore has asked for Timo to send him pictures of the congregation and the children," said Lobsinger.

• • • • •

Whitmore's pending release had just taken on a whole new tone. Contrary to the recent findings from the parole board, it seems Whitmore was very much preparing for his criminal future.

Much like his last jail stint – in which he set up his bogus child protection business and actively began looking for victims before he was released – Whitmore appeared to be reaching into the same bag of tricks again. Only this time the police planned to be ready for him.

Martin concluded his interview with police with some final thoughts on Whitmore.

"Timo says that Whitmore is a friendly, likeable guy and gives the impression that he's a nice person. But he says he would not have the time to look after him because he travels a lot and that Whitmore would be alone in the house. He says that Whitmore is always after something and that he feels he's being used," wrote Lobsinger.

"It is the belief of the writer that Mr. Whitmore has a goal of offending against children and is determined to beat the social and judicial system that is currently in place to protect those very same children."

• • • • •

As Peter Whitmore was spending his final few nights behind bars, Toronto police were about to take a major step to protect the public.

The warning signs were everywhere to suggest Whitmore had no intentions of changing his lifestyle. And the thought of him being able to slink back into society and quietly stake out his next victims was enough to sicken even the most hardened child abuse investigator.

Police had already responded to enough calls involving Whitmore after the damage had already been done. They were determined to ensure history didn't repeat itself. And so on the eve of Whitmore's release, police put their plan into motion.

Officers went to court, detailed affidavits in hand, to convince a magistrate that Whitmore was a time bomb who could go off at any time. They noted that in a recent conversation with Whitmore, he claimed that his goal was to last "two weeks...I just have to last two weeks" once he was released. Police believed Whitmore was referring to how long he expected him to take before he re-offended against children

Using recent amendments to the Criminal Code, police said the only way to reduce the risk to children across the country was to impose conditions on his newfound freedom. Section 810 of the Code was originally drafted in 1892. Known more commonly as a "peace bond", the legislation was aimed at petty criminals with a history of committing property offences.

Once issued, the court order required the target to agree to a series of specific conditions and "keep the peace" while in the community. Any breaches would give police the authority for re-arrest and lead to additional charges and likely jail time.

It took just over a century before federal politicians apparently realized that there may be more dangerous criminals in society than the guy who enjoys breaking into homes or stealing your car. Like the guy who might try and steal your child.

So in 1993, amendments were made to the peace bond legislation and a new subsection – 810.1 – was created. The changes meant police now had the power to go after chronic, high-risk sex offenders who investigators fear may commit a new crime against a child under the age of 14 years – even when they are finished serving any remaining sentence and are not facing any new charges.

Police bear the onus of making their case before a provincial court judge. Simply referring to an offender's history likely wouldn't be enough. Additional information on treatment, risk assessment and jailhouse behaviour can vastly improve an application.

The Criminal Code states that an 810.1 order is designed to be "preventative and not punitive." The chance of success improves greatly when the offender agrees to the application. But many don't, believing they've "paid their debt" to society and should be free to do as they please once their full sentence expires.

In that case, the issue often becomes the subject of a hotly contested court hearing. Offenders can call evidence that paints a vastly different picture of their risk level.

After consulting with his lawyer, Whitmore agreed to be bound by specific conditions that restricted his movement and behaviour, especially in areas where children are known to be present such as playgrounds and schools. Of course, Whitmore was already under such an order stemming from his lifetime ban received in 1995.

Police had made a strong case, which included the disturbing revelations from Timo Martin. Whitmore would also be required to report his whereabouts to police – an important condition that investigators hoped would prevent him from just taking off. He had to report weekly to the sex crimes unit, in person, to ensure compliance.

The order was Canada-wide and would be in place for a full year. Police could return to court and seek an extension if Whitmore's risk remained high. And police agencies across the country would be able to access information on it through their internal computer systems.

However, Whitmore wasn't ready to concede all attempts by police to control him. Although he agreed that news of his peace bond could be spread to local Ontario schools, daycares and community clubs, Whitmore balked at the police request to issue a much broader "community notification."

Police believed the best way to ensure compliance was to make news of Whitmore's release as public as possible. They hoped an informed public would mean a protected public.

Whitmore disagreed. He argued in court that "widespread and indiscriminate publicity" might endanger his safety and damage his chances of re-entering society in a successful way.

An Ontario judge ruled in favour of the police bid, saying they couldn't be expected to notify "thousands of families individually." He said a widespread press release was the only way, marking the first time Toronto officers would take this route.

It wasn't perfect – but it was the best available tool police had at this time.

• • • • •

## DECEMBER 4, 1999

Peter Whitmore was gone.

Only hours after he'd been released from prison and tasted freedom for the first time years, the notorious sex offender vanished. Under terms of his peace bond, Whitmore was required to report to the Toronto police sex crimes unit that very day.

He didn't show up.

Although not entirely surprised by his non-compliance, police were stunned by how quickly Whitmore had expressed his utter contempt for the judicial system. An uncontrolled Whitmore was a dangerous Whitmore.

And the entire country was once again at risk.

# CHAPTER TWELVE

Timo Martin thought he was just doing someone a small favour. In reality, the Toronto pastor had literally given Peter Whitmore a vehicle to escape.

Officers with the sex crimes unit went to Martin almost immediately after Whitmore disappeared, hoping for some clues into his whereabouts. Martin admitted that Whitmore had come to see him following his release from jail.

Whitmore said he needed some help as he tried to adjust to his newfound freedom. He wanted Martin to help him rent a car. Whitmore said he just wanted to be able to drive around Toronto, to get re-acquainted with the city after so much time spent behind bars.

Martin reluctantly agreed, taking Whitmore to a car rental agency, paying for the vehicle and signing the paperwork.

He hoped Whitmore was serious about changing his life around – maybe even getting an honest paying job – and figured having a way to get around town would improve his chances.

Yet Whitmore apparently had more sinister plans.

• • • • •

A Canada-wide warrant was issued for Whitmore's arrest. News of the search quickly spread across the country, appearing in numerous newspapers, radio and television newscasts.

At least police had something to work with – the description of the rental vehicle Whitmore had sped away in. It was a green Toyota Echo with Ontario licence plate ABKK 954.

Police didn't know where Whitmore was headed, but thought he might go west to Alberta where a brother lived. Another possible destination was British Columbia, where his aunt lived. Or maybe Whitmore had headed south, back to Texas? Anything was possible at this point. Nothing was being ruled out.

Not surprisingly, his exit from jail and immediate vanishing act had created a public and political firestorm. His lawyer, Dan Brodsky, fanned the flames by blaming justice officials for "running him out of town" by issuing the public notification. He believed Whitmore panicked once he stepped out of jail and realized just how many eyes would be on him.

The Ontario government reacted by calling on Ottawa to introduce the country's national registry for sex offenders. Solicitor General David Tsubouchi said it would be an effective way for police across Canada to quickly share information about high-risk offenders. Tsubouchi said the Whitmore case showed peace bonds are simply not enough.

Under his government's proposal, all registered sex offenders would have to give their addresses to police for storage in the computer databank. Their information would then be kept on file for at least a decade and up to 25 years, depending on their criminal history.

Anyone convicted of a sex-related crime – from rape to child pornography – would be targeted. And there would be stiff penalties for breaching the registry requirements, including up to two years prison and a $25,000 fine.

Police liked what they were hearing. Det.-Insp. Kate Lines of the Ontario Provincial Police estimated that Ontario would add 2,000 names to the registry every year.

"If a child is abducted, the registry could potentially, within seconds or minutes, tell the police of every sex offender within a square mile," Lines told the *Ottawa Citizen*.

Not everyone was buying it.

Veteran defence lawyer Julian Falconer, who has acted on behalf of numerous sex offenders and is no stranger to challenges under the Charter of Rights and Freedoms, said such restrictive regulations might just drive more sex offenders into hiding. Just look at what happened with Whitmore, he said.

"The person you are most afraid of, the dangerous offender, will simply go underground," Falconer told the *Citizen*.

He noted that compliance in similar U.S. programs was only about 50 per cent, according to figures from the John Howard Society. Falconer said widespread public releases, such as the one done with Whitmore, could also backfire.

"If community passion is what we are going to rely upon (for justice), then ultimately we will run these people out into the Arctic," he told the *Citizen*.

Falconer also suggested that an offender who has served their sentence is entitled to privacy under the Charter – no matter how much of a risk they have been found to pose.

Justice officials were also forced to deal with questions about the way they'd handled Whitmore's previous sentencings. Specifically, why hadn't they made a dangerous offender application against Whitmore – a move that would jail him indefinitely.

Although he would still have a shot at parole after serving seven years, a dangerous offender label was the stiffest sanction available under Canadian law.

According to Corrections Canada, 279 criminals had been given the notorious designation since the legislation first passed in 1977. The majority were still behind bars. Nearly all were sex offenders. And 119 of them had been sentenced in Ontario.

Why couldn't Whitmore be number 120?

In an interview with the *Toronto Star*, senior Crown attorney Paul Culver said it wasn't as easy as it sounded.

"It's a pretty high threshold, so it almost never applies to a first-time offender, and only sometimes to a second offence," Culver said.

Of course, Whitmore was no rookie criminal. He already had two major sets of convictions under his belt. And his latest disappearing act appeared to be strike three.

While the public debate raged on, Toronto police were more focused on finding Whitmore before he had the chance to harm another child. But with each passing day, the situation was becoming more dire.

●　●　●　●　●

**PRESIDIO, CHIHUAHUA, MEXICO
JANUARY 11, 2000**

Peter Whitmore had come to this border town looking for a fresh start. And likely searching for a whole new pool of unsuspecting victims.

But his plans were quickly scuttled when he filed a refugee claim with Mexican officials. It was a clever attempt at a pre-emptive strike, as Whitmore knew that Canadian authorities would have a difficult time getting him back north if his bid was accepted.

Unfortunately for Whitmore, Mexican officials weren't about to play his game.

Instead of being accepted with open arms, Whitmore was slapped with handcuffs. His refugee claim was rejected and Whitmore was arrested for illegally entering the country and violating immigration laws.

Word of his capture quickly made its way to Canada – thanks to a heads-up from police in Texas – prompting a sigh of relief from nervous sex crimes investigators. The five-week manhunt was over.

Police had a hunch Whitmore was going south, but there had also been sightings reported in western Canada. One tipster was positive he'd seen Whitmore driving around the streets of Calgary just days earlier.

Police certainly had plenty of questions – and concerns – about where Whitmore had gone and how he'd spent his time. But their answers would have to wait at least a few days, until arrangements could be made to have Whitmore deported back to Canada.

But with Whitmore back in custody, the focus could now shift back to the much-maligned justice system. Whitmore had sent a very loud and clear message to the justice system by snubbing his nose at authority within hours of his release.

Now police hoped the system would send its own message to Whitmore.

• • • • •

"He feared for his life."

Toronto defence lawyer Dan Brodsky wanted Canadians to know that his notorious client, Peter Whitmore, had no choice. Staying in the country was not an option. He had to flee.

Brodsky, appearing at the sentencing hearing for Whitmore on his peace bond breach charge, told court that everyone must share in the blame for what happened.

He said Whitmore stepped out of jail for the first time of years – with no real support system in place – and found himself overwhelmed at the public furor over his release.

With no stable residence to call home, no job to report to, no money to his name, Whitmore did what came naturally. He ran.

With help from his friend, Timo Martin, Whitmore got into the rental car, pointed it south and kept driving. He didn't stop until his reached Mexico, which he hoped would be a "safe haven" that could truly give him a chance for a fresh start.

This was not about scoping out new victims, Brodsky insisted. It was about survival.

"He thought (the public alert about his release) was a licence to kill him," said Brodsky.

Brodsky also took aim the section 810.1 provisions, questioning how his client could be required to give a "fixed address" to police when no such one existed. Brodsky said it was "unconstitutional" – and that notifying the public about his client's release was a "recipe for disaster."

He even suggested Canadian authorities might have been better off just leaving Whitmore in Mexico.

"If he's such a danger to the citizens of Ontario, why worry if he's in Mexico," Brodsky said – apparently with a straight-face – In an interview with the *Toronto Sun* just days earlier.

Police and the Crown had a vastly different take on the issue.

They had uncovered evidence that Whitmore was planning to find a job in Mexico teaching English – work that would have put him directly in contact with young children. Following his arrest, Whitmore was found to be carrying a list of names of young students – most under the age of 14 – that he was apparently planning to tutor.

And while no direct evidence of sexual activity was uncovered, suspicious investigators knew that was no guarantee nothing had happened.

"There is no doubt that he ever intended on abiding by any of the conditions that were placed on him...Whitmore not only fled the province of Ontario but also traveled through the United States of America and made his way into Mexico. This is more than obvious that he never had intentions of returning to Canada much less the province of Ontario."

And so the Toronto police incident summary report began, a copy of which was given to the Crown.

"It is known by the investigating officers that while Whitmore was in Presidio County he attempted to 'trade' his rental vehicle for another vehicle that was more in tune with the countryside, (a Land Rover). He was also known to be in the company of young children while in Mexico and was known to be taking photographs of these children," said police.

"The accused was in the process of applying for refugee status in Mexico to avoid being deported back to Canada. It is not known what the basis of his claim that he was using but it was obviously a tactic to avoid prosecution for these offences."

Police said Whitmore's stunt had cost Timo Martin $6,250 to get the rental vehicle he'd signed for back to Toronto from Mexico.

"These costs include the rental of the vehicle, the cost of having two representatives go to Mexico to retrieve the vehicle and the cost of shipping the vehicle back to Toronto," said police.

"This accused, in attempting to mislead the police, left a trail of his travels to avoid arrest and prosecution on these charges. There is no doubt in the investigators minds that if this accused is released from custody...he will once again flee the province," said police.

Police had also discovered Texas justice officials wanted to get their hands on Whitmore – a warrant had now been issued for his arrest because he illegally entered the United States.

"Based on information received the authorities in Texas may be proceeding with making application to have the accused returned to them. If returned...this accused will serve at least four years and could very well serve six years," said police.

The Crown argued Whitmore was in no position to complain about the publicity surrounding his case, considering he was the author of his own fate by refusing to complete any treatment while in custody and exhibiting disturbing behaviour that warned of future attacks. The Crown also recited Whitmore's lengthy criminal history and high-risk of re-offending.

"This is a far more serious matter when the entire circumstances of this offender are looked at," Justice Sheppard said in handing down his decision. "The court must in this circumstance pay the greatest attention to...the denunciation of the unlawful conduct of Mr. Whitmore. This is because, of course, the entire ability to maintain a rule of law and in particular a rule of criminal law in the country must first and foremost be based on the enforceability of court orders and court directions. If the constitutionally protected judicial process can be ignored by any citizen and simply cast aside as either inconvenient or not worthy of compliance then of course the rule of law is undermined and we return simply to the anarchy of the street," said Sheppard.

"This is an individual who has a three page criminal record that, since 1993, is dominated by offences against children. He served the entirety of a penitentiary sentence between 1995 and 1999 because the National Parole Board denies his early release and his statutory release since he was diagnosed as a high-risk pedophile, untreated by any therapeutic program within the correctional system," he said.

Sheppard questioned Whitmore's motives, suggesting he had sinister plans for heading south.

"The court has not heard from Mr. Whitmore why he chose not to avail himself of any counselling or treatment programs. The inference has to be because Mr. Whitmore did not believe had a problem. It appears that that continues to be his view of himself," said Sheppard.

"Having been before this court on December 3...within hours Mr Whitmore chose to ignore the provisions of the recognizance. We have before this court lists of names, headed "English Class." These are all children of tender years, not all under 14 but the vast majority under the age of 14. This of course gives the court grave concern," said Sheppard.

"The inference the court draws from the totality of this reported evidence is that Mr. Whitmore intended to lose himself in Mexico for some indefinite period of time and put himself beyond the reach of the recognizance, beyond the reach of the Toronto Police Services. This section must carry a significant sanction when it is so flagrantly and deliberately breached, as it was with Whitmore's flight to Mexico and his failure to report to the police," he said.

Whitmore had already spent about a month behind bars since his return from Mexico. Sheppard said he was adding another 12 months in jail for the breach – and warned that any further violations would result in much stiffer sanctions.

Although the year-long sentence was lengthy when compared with others who had breached court orders, the court of public opinion had a much different take on the outcome.

Sheppard had refused the Crown's request for the maximum sentence allowed by law – two years in custody – and many citizens believed Whitmore had just been given yet another slap on the wrist and one more reason to continue his dangerous lifestyle without real fear of consequence.

• • • • •

**TORONTO, ONTARIO**
**OCTOBER 15, 2000**

Fool me once, shame on you. Fool me twice, shame on me.

That was the mindset of Toronto police sex crime investigators as Peter Whitmore was about to become a free man. Whitmore had served two-thirds of his year-long sentence and was preparing to walk out of jail.

Police wanted to make sure the public was prepared for Whitmore. Toronto police were considering an unprecedented step – releasing Whitmore's exact address.

They already had legal clearance to give his name, picture and background to the public once again, but police believed a more drastic move was called for given Whitmore's likelihood of re-offending.

"Mr. Whitmore has demonstrated by his previous conduct that he is a flight risk. The police need current and accurate information about Mr. Whitmore's whereabouts to ensure that he does not flee the jurisdiction with the intent of frustrating the order of the court," police wrote in their application seeking to obtain another section 810 peace bond. "The protection of the community necessitates the police being able to notify any other communities of the risk that Mr. Whitmore poses to children."

Det. Const. Brian Thomson, who worked in the behavioural assessment section, filed his own affidavit outlining Whitmore's previous flight to Mexico.

"I fear that Peter Whitmore still poses a threat to re-offend sexually against a child under the age of 14 years. I fear that upon his release from jail, Peter Whitmore will once again flee the jurisdiction of Toronto and fail to report to me his address or his location, as demonstrated by his actions in December 1999," wrote Thomson.

He said Whitmore had called him a few weeks prior, claiming he'd like to move to British Columbia to live with his aunt, Lynn Hopkins, upon his release. Thomson said he told

Whitmore he wanted him to remain in Ontario so police could closely monitor him.

His lawyer, Dan Brodsky, quickly sprung into action, doing the local and national media rounds and claiming such public disclosure might just get Whitmore killed.

"My client is terrified because he currently has an address but will be evicted should the address become public. He's concerned for his safety and the safety of the people he lives with," Brodsky told a gathering of reporters.

Police Sgt. Bruce Warren told the *National Post* that releasing Whitmore's address would be an unprecedented move by his department.

"In this case he's a repeat offender. While he was incarcerated [in prison previously], he refused to take any treatment for his problem. The Sexual Assault Squad deemed him to be a very good candidate to reoffend," said Warren.

Justice Victor Paisley green-lighted the new peace bond against Whitmore with all the same conditions, including reporting to police every Tuesday. Of course, that hadn't stopped him from fleeing the last time.

In an unusual condition, Whitmore was also required to report any romantic relationships to police. He then had to get "consent" if his partner had children under the age of 14.

Brodsky had tried to fight the public release, but his bid for an injunction against Toronto police was denied by Paisley.

The judge admitted the case raised a "serious constitutional issue" involving someone's privacy rights versus protection of the public. And while releasing information about Whitmore wouldn't necessarily reduce his risk of re-offending, he said there's also no evidence to suggest it would make the situation worse.

"On this motion, the applicant was not persuasive on the issue of whether he will suffer irreparable harm if the application is refused, on the record before me. The press release proposed appears to be factual and accurate. It does not disclose the residence of the applicant on its face. It is similar to press releases previously disclosed in relation to this applicant as referred to in the affidavit filed on his behalf, and no harm befell the applicant when that similar material was disclosed," Paisley wrote in his decision.

"There is, I am satisfied, some risk to any individual of vigilante action taken by unreasonable or irrational members of the public, but that is not the test. Reviewing the proposed press release, there is nothing in it and nothing suggested in it that, in itself, would arouse public anger. It appears to me that the risk that the applicant is concerned about is the possibility that there may be irresponsible media coverage relating to the applicant. But that is not the matter that is before me.

"On this material, I am satisfied that the proposed press release is a reasonable remedy authorized within the parameters of the regulation which is challenged. I consider as of some probative value the fact that in this very case as a result of publicity, another offence that the offender concedes he was involved in was discovered. Not all publicity is necessarily bad publicity as far as the public is concerned, and in that instance, the media coverage of this offender's actions apparently resulted in justice being done in relation to a separate issue, and I find it to be relevant and significant that in spite of the fact that a previous media release was issued by the Police Services Board in relation to this applicant and the media coverage that resulted, there is no suggestion that the accused was subjected to any threat, or any hint of a threat by anyone, as a result of that publicity.

"While I recognize the possibility that inflammatory coverage or even reasonably balanced coverage could result in vigilantism, I cannot assume that is going to occur. The onus is on the applicant; and in relation to a risk of serious harm, I wouldn't put that test as being very high. While the court will protect, and should protect, the interest of an individual who reasonably is concerned that he will be harmed on proper evidence, I don't see a reasonable risk that this applicant will be subjected to any realistic risk of harm on the record before me.

"I appreciate that a press release is a rather blunt instrument as a tool. It cannot target only those persons who have children who might be at risk, but it is the instrument that is available and I cannot, on the basis of the submissions I have heard, or the record before me, conclude that there is another instrument reasonably available that would serve the purpose of protecting the public. The protection of the public, particularly the children and the parents of children who might reasonable be at risk as a result of an unrehabilitated pedophile released to an unwary community, is obvious."

• • • • •

Brodsky suggested police should be focused on making Whitmore's transition back to society as smooth as possible.

"The best thing the police could do would be to get him a job, get him an apartment and protect his security because it will be impossible for him to do it on his own. He will constantly have to look over his shoulder and worry about vigilante justice," Brodsky told the *National Post*. "The more information that's given out, the worse it gets [for him]."

Brodsky filed an interesting affidavit from Dr. Hy Bloom, a forensic psychiatrist with a private practice in Toronto. Bloom's opinions were based on his reading of "scholarly literature" pertaining to the issue of community notification of sex offenders.

"Community notification of the release of sex offenders, on a large and systematic scale, is a relatively recent phenomenon. There is a regrettable lack of research findings into the effect of the practice, both on offenders and the community. I bring to the issue no in-depth study or personal research but rather my familiarity with the patterns and needs of sexual offenders and an ability to digest academic literature on the subject and evaluate its credibility and significance against the background of my own experience and training," Bloom began.

Bloom cited a 1998 study out of Wisconsin which looked at 30 sex offenders who had been released from jail and subject to community notifications. They were all deemed "Level 3" offenders, which is the highest risk category in the U.S.

"Many of the subjective reactions of the offenders were as might be expected. They report embarrassment, sometimes bitterness, and a sense that the notification process was irrelevant to the likelihood of their re-offending. The authors note that 'all but one of the interviewed subjects stated that the community notification process had adversely affected their transition from prison to the outside world. Most also spoke of how community notification had caused distress for families and loved ones, and alienation from former friends," said Bloom.

He said publicity through news coverage posed the biggest challenge to offenders. Surprisingly, only one person reported so-called vigilante activity from enraged citizens.

"For many, the news media was to blame for treating all sex offenders as though they were sexual predators and inaccurately reporting and sensationalizing their crimes," said Bloom.

One offender was quoted as follows: "If you have any familiarity with links and patterns of the cycle of sexual offence, much of it revolves around an individual being under pressure and his behaviour under pressure. Well, there is no more pressure than being exploited by the media, the people you work with, the people you live with, relatives, and so the pressure is constantly there," the man said.

Bloom said the authors of the study concluded that "public disclosure of the crime may undermine the therapy of offender and victim alike."

Bloom noted in his affidavit a similar, more comprehensive 1995 study done in Washington State – the first jurisdiction with a community notification statute – that followed released sex offenders for 54-months.

"The study identified no statistically significant difference in the arrest rates among Level 3 offenders subject to notification and a similar group not subject to notification over the 54 months. The authors did, however, detect one very significant finding – those recidivists subject to community notification were arrested for their new crimes much earlier than the comparison group," said Bloom.

"It is unfortunately difficult to interpret this finding. It might be argued that the pressures of community antagonism led to earlier re-offending; it might also be suggested that community notification led to faster identification and arrest of recidivists. Contrary, perhaps, to expectations, most recidivism was for non-sexual offences. In this most important area – actual reduction of crime – one might particularly welcome further, conclusive research," he said.

Bloom concluded by saying stability may be the key to successfully controlling and rehabilitating a high-risk offender.

"It serves to reduce stress, thereby lowering the risk for re-offending. Offenders with a secure residence, steady employment and personal support are much more likely to do well after release than those who struggle for the provision of personal necessities, without a network of encouragement and guidance," said Bloom.

He said the 1998 Wisconsin study found that housing and employment "have become nearly impossible for sex offenders" – and even more so when their release into the community is publicized.

"The notoriety created by the notification process has resulted in the inability or loss of residence and employment. Sex offenders continually worry about harassment, over having to move again, and about the possibility of placement in a correctional facility in lieu of residence in the community. They are deeply concerned also about the stress on their families and the loss of relationships resulting from community notification. This network of supportive relationships is critical reintegration," the authors wrote in their summary.

• • • • •

**TORONTO, ONTARIO**
**OCTOBER 16, 2000**

Police and justice officials had struck what they felt was a fair compromise.

Whitmore's exact address would remain private – in exchange for a general warning that he had moved into the Eglinton and Royal York area of the city.

"I think this is the best balance," Staff Inspector Ray Pilkington of the Toronto police sex crimes unit told reporters.

"I know this individual and his track record. If we released his address, he would go underground and disappear. At least this way I know where he is and can keep an eye on him. I think there is much less chance of him reoffending."

Pilkington said giving away Whitmore's exact address would likely create a mob-like atmosphere.

"This is much better than driving him out of town and passing the problem on to another community. I know people don't want him here but at least we will know what he is doing. This way we have some control," he said.

That wasn't good enough for many residents – especially since there were many daycares and schools in the area.

Many were vowing to do some amateur detective work, find where Whitmore was living and release it to the masses – including one angry city councillor. Mario Giansante, whose Kingsway Humber ward encompasses where Whitmore was now living, said the public deserves to know.

Whitmore's lawyers said justice officials had made the right call and pleaded for public calm.

Steve Skurka noted a recent story out of England in which several innocent people were attacked in the streets because they resembled pedophiles whose names and addresses had been published by a tabloid newspaper.

He cited other cases across Canada where similar vigilante attacks had occurred, including an Edmonton sex offender who was run out of town after residents camped on his doorstep and taunted him with slurs.

"(Whitmore's) certainly grateful that his address is not going to be known, although he is still fearful," Skurka told reporters.

"We are working to get him the treatment he needs and get him on the path of rehabilitation. I am very, very pleased with the decision. It's responsible action on behalf of the police. It's an attempt to calm the waters and avoid vigilante justice."

Yet the waters were anything but calm. Citizens began flooding local radio call-in shows, with many suggesting Whitmore lost his right to privacy years ago when he began preying on innocent children. Others suggested that maybe Whitmore should go live in the same neighbourhood as his lawyers.

Police could sense the panic and decided to call a community meeting to let residents share their concerns and voice their frustrations.

They released the following news bulletin on Oct. 17.

*"The Toronto Police sexual assault squad...have made arrangements for an information session to be held Wednesday October 18 at 7:30 p.m. at the Richview Collegiate located at 1738 Islington Avenue. This information session is for the immediate community who may be interested in discussing any safety issues*

*as a result of the release of convicted pedophile Mr. Peter Robert Whitmore. Mr. Whitmore has been released from custody after completing his sentence and is now bound by a series of conditions restricting his access to children. Mr. Whitmore has taken residence in the Royal York Road and Eglinton Avenue area. Members of the community are welcome to attend this information session from 7:30 p.m. to 9 p.m. to address any safety concerns they may have regarding Mr. Whitmore's release."*

Meanwhile, Whitmore was planning his next move.

# CHAPTER THIRTEEN

## OCTOBER 19, 2000

Peter Whitmore had been given an ultimatum. He had a 24-hour head start to flee the neighbourhood and find somewhere else to live before he would face the wrath of an angry public.

The message had been delivered loud and clear – by an angry mother of three who had stumbled across his new home. The woman had been reading about the Whitmore case and was stunned to learn the notorious pedophile was living in the upscale house next door.

Even more surprising was who had taken him in. Timo Martin, the Seventh Day Adventist pastor with a soft spot for criminals, had gone out on a limb once again in an attempt to help Whitmore.

Martin had laid out some strict rules; telling Whitmore he had to find a more permanent residence within a week and making him promise not to leave his Woodvalley Drive home.

He also got Whitmore to agree to some intensive one-on-one counselling sessions in which they would discuss his past, present and future. Whitmore was the first sex offender he'd ever counselled, but Martin saw some potential and refused to give up hope.

Whitmore admitted he was on borrowed time, that any future offending could land him behind bars for the rest of his life. He also claimed to be "scared" of children because of the risk they represent to his freedom.

And he promised to "never, never" commit another crime again. Martin wanted to believe him. But just like the last time, when he rented a car for Whitmore, his good intentions had backfired.

His neighbour clearly meant business, telling Martin to get rid of his houseguest immediately. Others on the street quickly followed suit, joining the chorus of concerns.

Although he hated to turn his back on Whitmore in his time of need, Martin saw the writing on the wall and agreed to the distraught woman's request. Whitmore said he knew it was the right thing to do, even telling Martin he wanted to go.

Martin contacted Dan Brodsky, Whitmore's lawyer, to tell him of the latest developments. Brodsky was saddened, but not surprised. He believed the community had given up on Whitmore before he even had a chance to prove himself. He saw that first-hand the previous night when he appeared before a gathering of concerned community residents at a "town hall" type meeting.

Brodsky had tried to explain that Whitmore had paid his debt to society and was truly trying to change his ways – but his pleas for calm were met with cries of "shame" and "what about our kids."

Residents had made it clear they would do everything possible to make Whitmore's life miserable. Some eventually did go to the media, blasting Martin for opening his door to Whitmore.

"It could be that he was trying to be a Good Samaritan but I don't think he was very wise," next-door neighbour Bill Graham told reporters.

"Our rights were betrayed," a female resident on the street said.

"He should have thought about his neighbours," said another woman.

Some even suggested Martin should be banned from working in the future with other ex-cons and even struggling immigrants. They didn't want him bringing those types of people into their community.

With residents now rolling out the unwelcome mat, Brodsky was forced to find another temporary home for his client. He settled on a downtown Toronto hotel. Police were notified of the move, as required by the court order. Two plainclothes officers came to Martin's home to escort Whitmore to his new locale, fearing there could be an uprising if he was spotted in the streets.

But Brodsky wasn't finished. His next move was to call some contacts he had in the Toronto media with an interesting offer.

How would they like to meet the monster?

• • • • •

"This is just a temporary place until we can come up with a long-term solution," Brodsky told a gathering of reporters who had responded to his interview request.

"The hunt is on again; nothing has been accomplished. We're expecting the downtown community to be searching for him soon."

Toronto police weren't very impressed by Whitmore's sudden change-of-address, believing the instability was a sign of bad things to come.

"I thought we had reached a workable balance, but now we have taken steps backwards. The problem is now being passed on to another community," Staff Inspector Roy Pilkington, of the Toronto police Sexual Assault Squad, told the *National Post*.

"There are no easy answers here. It's a real conundrum what to do with these people who are still considered high-risk. The law says he has paid his debt, but I don't know any community that would want a pedophile."

Brodsky said his client was considering moving back to British Columbia with his aunt, Lynn Hopkins.

Whitmore was in the room with Brodsky, surrounded by several reporters and photographers who had many questions for arguably the country's most controversial pedophile at that moment. Whitmore did and said all the right things, speaking in quiet, polite tones and showing glimpses of genuine charm. Christie Blatchford of the *National Post* later described Whitmore as follows:

"Of average height and weight, Whitmore is quite handsome, with a high clear brow and really warm eyes of a genuinely pretty blue and soft light brown hair that curls delicately here and there. His gaze is direct, and it says exactly what he says – Look at me. I am an open book. There is nothing to fear here."

Whitmore repeated the promise he'd made to Timo Martin, vowing not to re-offend. He went a step further, suggesting he might remain celibate the rest of his life.

"Certainly celibate from any children," he said.

Whitmore claimed he hadn't had any sexual thoughts about children for several years and that he planned to keep his distance.

"There will never be children in any house where I live," said Whitmore, adding the police are welcome to search his residence whenever they want.

Whitmore said he wanted to speak with the media to "to calm public fears and let people know what I'm doing." He vowed to seek treatment while in the community – the very kind he'd snubbed his nose at while behind bars.

"I know I'm not [going to reoffend] because if I do, I'm going to prison for the rest of my life. I don't want to harm anyone else. I've made that promise to myself," said Whitmore.

Although he said he wouldn't have any contact with children, Whitmore claimed he wouldn't have any sexual urges even if he did.

"I've walked the public street and I've seen 'em [children] and I feel nothing in regards to a sexual nature," he said.

Whitmore promised to call upon members of a local Mennonite support group that Brodsky had put him in touch with. The organization had previously offered to help Whitmore following his last release from jail, but he chose instead to run to Mexico.

Whitmore ended the interview by saying he didn't expect to even have the opportunity to re-offend, thanks to the vigilant Toronto Police Service.

"I have my surveillance. I'm not going to be able to gain access to any children," he said.

Whitmore said he'd like to eventually be able to walk down the street without being noticed and hoped to one day apply for a disability pension, claiming he's been suffering a form of leukemia for more than 20 years.

Reporters were sceptical, recalling Whitmore had previously told officials in Texas he had cancer and even going so far as to shave off clumps of his hair as part of his elaborate cover story. Whitmore had made similar comments to Canadian justice officials around the time of his last release from jail, implying that a section 810 peace bond wouldn't be needed since he'd probably die soon regardless.

Whitmore also tried to explain away some of his offences but quickly found himself eating his words. After claiming he would never abduct a child off the street, he said that his victims were children he had some kind of "relationship" with.

Heather Bird, a reporter with the *Toronto Sun*, reminded Whitmore that he'd only known the little girl he abducted in 1994 for a few hours.

"So four hours is a relationship, then?" Bird asked.

Whitmore tried to minimize his crime, claiming he "only" asked the girl for oral sex and went on the run with her because he believed her family members would come after him with a gun.

"Either way the child went home the next day in a cab," said Whitmore in a truly feeble attempt to cast himself in a positive light.

Whitmore also deflected blame for not getting treatment behind bars, claiming a variety of factors beyond his control made it difficult. Hostile inmates, staff members who refused him entry and cancelled programs were all cited as factors.

Whitmore raised some eyebrows when he suggested so-called "chemical castration" would be an option. The procedure involves taking powerful drugs which reduce an offender's sex drive. The treatment can't be ordered by the courts in Canada and is strictly voluntary.

Whitmore said he'd even be willing to "consider" wearing an electronic ankle bracelet if that's what justice officials felt was necessary to monitor his movement.

Unfortunately for the public, no such device was being utilized in Canada.

Blatchford wrapped up her story in the *Post* with the following:

"All of us there were adults. We never would have been in danger from him. We all knew going in precisely what he is, a thrice-convicted sex offender, a diagnosed homosexual pedophile, and a slick operator who often set up respectable fronts – usually companies that purported to track missing children – for his activities, once, remarkably, doing so from his jail cell.

"For myself, I remain repelled by the notion that a man in his position, who has served every last day of his time and has not re-offended, should be subjected to constant police surveillance and have his liberty so restricted and should be in hiding.

"The difference is that before I met him, I was furious about all this. And now that I have, I can barely rouse myself to care.

"I expected I might feel the need of a shower afterward. What is so frightening is that I didn't."

• • • • •

## OCTOBER 25, 2000

With money quickly running out and the public still out for blood, Whitmore's chances of success remained slim. However, the Mennonite Central Committee, a religious group which helps sex offenders upon their release from prison, had come forward after reading about Whitmore's plight in the media.

Assistant director Rick Bauman spoke out on Whitmore's behalf, saying the public is actually doing more harm than good by reacting so strongly to his release.

He said "isolating and harassing" Whitmore will only increase his risk of re-offending. As a result, the Kitchener-based organization had agreed to accept Whitmore in their "Circles of Support" program after consultation with Toronto police.

Dr. Robin Wilson, the program's chief psychologist, was tasked with doing a risk assessment. The result was one of the most comprehensive looks at Whitmore to date.

"File materials are universal in their assessment of Mr. Whitmore as being a high risk for future criminal involvement, particularly in regard to sexual offending," Wilson's report began.

"During our 90-minute interview, he was relatively candid about his history of interactions with minors, particularly (but not restricted to) boys aged 8 to 13. He denied any sexual indiscretions aside from those for which he was charged and convicted."

He said forensic testing on several levels showed Whitmore's degree of danger hadn't been reduced since similar testing was done behind bars.

"Perhaps the most compelling risk factor at hand is Mr. Whitmore's admitted sexual interest in young boys. While demonstrative of a good deal of self-awareness, it is important to recognize that this is a strong diagnostic indicator for pedophilia, which is a condition for which there is currently no available cure," said Wilson.

"Mr. Whitmore's present circumstances are particularly tense and stressful, which he readily admits. He has been rendered a pariah by the media and much of the community, to the extent that his whereabouts must be protected in order to prevent potential vigilantism. His situation is clearly unstable."

He said there were few options for dealing with Whitmore.

"Essentially, Mr. Whitmore is an untreated sexual offender. There are conflicting accounts as to reasons why he was unable to complete treatment during both his provincial and federal periods of incarceration. Mr Whitmore contends that he was willing to enter treatment, but that security concerns and resourcing difficulties prevented him from doing so. Regarding the former, it would appear that there were numerous incompatible relationships with other inmates which caused Mr. Whitmore some concern for his safety. In our present interview, he expressed considerable disdain for many of the CSC personnel who assessed and attempted to treat him while he was incarcerated. In particular, he expressed discomfort with being either assessed or offered treatment by persons who did not possess doctoral level training," Wilson wrote.

He said Whitmore was clearly "an engaging, intelligent and talkative man who seemed genuinely concerned about his present circumstances."

"However, his discussions were marked by a glibness and superficial charm. He also demonstrated a tendency to be self-serving in his assertions regarding his prior involvement with the system and his current circumstances. While the veracity of some of his statements would be difficult to ascertain, I was left with the general feeling that Mr. Whitmore tends to skirt or mold the truth to fit his needs. These features are consistent with previous diagnoses of anti-social personality disorder, and are also consistent with his admitted history of fraudulent and otherwise parasitic activities," said Wilson.

"There are many good reasons, clinical and actuarial, to consider Mr. Whitmore to be at considerable risk for future sexual offending. He has an anti-social and narcissistic personality structure, which tends to manifest itself in self-serving and manipulative use of others for his own personal gain. Further, he has a self-professed interest in young boys, which is likely the strongest available diagnostic indicator of homosexual pedophilia," wrote Wilson.

"Additionally, he has a relatively recent history of fleeing when faced with difficult circumstances. In closing, Mr. Whitmore is faced with many difficult circumstances in the community. He is clearly in need of compassionate community support, as might be afforded by the Mennonite Central Committee Circles of Support. However, it is likely that involvement in supportive and treatment services will prevent additional difficulties for Mr. Whitmore. Nonetheless, as it stands now, it would appear that he has few options other than to engage the process presented to him."

Whitmore agreed to attend some group meetings, which focus on establishing a strong support network for sex offenders who have recently been released from jail. But there was certainly some lingering doubt about how committed he truly would be.

"We believe it is better to be engaged and proactive, instead of disengaged and not acting at all," Bauman told reporters who questioned his group's involvement.

Dan Brodsky was continuing to speak out, saying Whitmore had reached a crisis stage. Although the healing circle was a good step, Whitmore was quickly running out of cash and would soon be forced to go on the move again. His next stop was the streets. And Brodsky warned that such a move would be bad news for everyone.

The MCC hoped they could somehow find Whitmore a job that would allow him to make some money and pay for a more stable place to sleep. But they knew their newest resident's resume would likely scare off most suitors.

Brodsky said a men's hostel was not a good option because Whitmore was wearing a proverbial "target" on his back based on his criminal history. Pedophiles were at the bottom of the criminal food chain, and other ex-cons would love nothing more than to feast on him.

"He's scared of any group situation. When he closes his eyes he has to worry about what might happen in his sleep," Brodsky told the *National Post*.

No doubt many of Whitmore's past victims could relate to sleepless nights and living in constant fear.

# CHAPTER FOURTEEN

**TORONTO, ONTARIO**
NOVEMBER 12, 2000

The man walked up to the front counter of the seedy hotel, located right next to the downtown bus terminal.

"Two nights, please," he said.

He counted out $160 cash and placed it on the table. The young boy, no older than 16, stood quietly at his side.

"My son isn't feeling very well," the man offered to the clerk. "We're going to take him to the doctor in the morning."

The clerk handed him the keys to room nine. The man and teen walked down the hall and disappeared into the room.

• • • • •

The call came into the Toronto Police Service just after 1 a.m.

"Peter Whitmore is inside a room with a young boy," the caller advised.

Police rushed to the Inn on Bay, fearing the worst and knowing every second counted. Officers stormed inside the motel and spoke with the front desk clerk. The man confirmed that a Peter Whitmore had just checked in, his "son" in tow. Whitmore had even shown photo identification.

Officers rushed to room nine, pounding on the door. Whitmore opened it seconds later. The young boy was seated inside. He was fully clothed and didn't appear to be in any distress.

"You're under arrest," the officers told Whitmore.

He briefly protested, claiming he hadn't done anything wrong. Police reminded him of the section 810 peace bond and lifetime court order which prevented him from having any contact with children.

Police took the young boy into custody as well, wanting to question him about what had happened. Back at the police station, the teen admitted that he was just 13 years old. And that he had run away from New Brunswick.

The boy explained that he'd just met Whitmore on the streets the previous day. The pair had struck up a friendly conversation, and Whitmore offered to show him around Toronto.

"Did he touch you in any way?" police asked in a videotaped interview.

"No, nothing happened," said the boy.

Police had their doubts. But perhaps they had caught Whitmore fast enough, preventing him from doing the inevitable. The fact Whitmore had given a bogus story to the clerk about the boy being his son suggested he was trying to deflect suspicions away from himself.

The interview continued for some time, with the teen continually denying any sexual contact. He described Whitmore as a nice man, nothing more. He said they had gone to the hotel just to get off the streets for a couple nights.

Regardless of his denials, police had enough evidence to charge Whitmore with breaching his court orders. Surely that would be enough to send him back to jail for a long time.

Child welfare officials were contacted about the boy and took him into custody, contacting his family back home on the coast and eventually returning him to New Brunswick.

• • • • •

Across Toronto the reaction was pretty much universal.

"Thank God he's back in jail."

There was also plenty of "We knew this would happen" going around town as news of Whitmore's arrest quickly spread.

There were also several disappointed people, including his lawyer, Pastor Timo Martin and members of the Mennonite Central Committee who believed they were actually making some progress.

Although Whitmore wasn't facing any new sex-related charges, everyone realized this was no minor slip-up. Media began asking some hard questions about how Whitmore could have breached so quickly, considering he was supposed to be under constant police supervision. Hadn't officers vowed not to let history repeat itself?

Police admitted they had scaled back their surveillance once Whitmore was accepted into the MCC program. Whitmore was a top priority – but he wasn't the only priority.

Because of limited resources, police had fallen into the unfortunate trap of relying on others – including Whitmore himself – to help keep the community safe. Obviously it hadn't worked.

When his funds had run dry for his downtown hotel, Whitmore had indeed moved to the streets as Brodsky warned.

He found refuge in a local drug "flophouse", the kind of place where dreams come to die.

Whitmore had managed to scrape together some money through borrowing and begging, which he used to pay for the hotel where he took the young street teen.

Christie Blatchford, continuing on the Whitmore saga in the pages of the *National Post*, eloquently wrote about his latest brush with the law and the sad message it conveys.

"Everyone tried. Dan Brodsky did what his father (prominent Winnipeg defence lawyer Greg Brodsky) had suggested and fought for the client, and also for the principle – here, that a free man, even a convicted sexual predator, having served his sentence, ought to at least be ably represented when the courts and the police are looking to restrict his movements and restrain his liberty.

"The Toronto police tried, not only by following him for so long as they could, but also by working with Mr. Brodsky, by having members of the sex assault squad talk to Whitmore and emphasize their desire to be reasonable, even by notifying the public in the first place that this dangerous man was out and about.

"The Mennonites tried; they always do. The flophouse owner probably tried, too. Perhaps even Whitmore tried.

"But the sex drive, however perverted, is a powerful thing, and so is the pedophile's ability to rationalize the rightness, the benign-ness, of what he does.

"As for that poor little bugger from the Maritimes, who was likely fleeing something bad, as almost invariably these children are, well, he ran straight into the arms of the nightmare he may have been too young, before Sunday, to have understood.

"Not anymore. And that's why the answer is, there is no answer."

•  •  •  •  •

Should Peter Whitmore be trading in his prison jumpsuit for a hospital gown? His lawyer, Dan Brodsky, certainly thought so. Following his client's latest major setback, Brodsky raised a few eyebrows when he suggested it might be time to try something different.

Living in the community clearly wasn't working. And jail obviously hadn't helped. Brodsky believed his client was a sick man. He likely wouldn't get much of an argument from any member of the public. So why not send him to the type of place where other sick people go?

Of course, Whitmore's illness was a little more complex – and most definitely lacking any kind of cure.

Brodsky approached Ontario justice officials, suggesting his client be immediately released from custody to get medical treatment. Not surprisingly, his request was met with an immediate "No."

So Brodsky, as he often did, took his pitch to the public.

"We know we have to wait a period of time in order to schedule a trial. The issue now is should he be in jail, or should he be in a hospital receiving treatment? I thought 'great', let's get him some treatment," Brodsky told reporters as he held court on the steps of Old City Hall in Toronto during Whitmore's first court appearance. "It does society no good having him sit in a cell waiting for his trial to come up."

However, Brodsky noted he'd spent several hours calling around to see what might be available in the province for

Whitmore – and learned that there was nothing. So now his client would sit in jail – again – with little prospect of rehabilitation.

Across Ontario – and no doubt much of Canada – those who heard and read Brodsky's comments were screaming back at their newspaper or television set. How dare he try and make Whitmore the victim here, many were likely shouting.

Whitmore had shown little interest in doing anything to improve his chances at a quality, law-abiding lifestyle. So why should anyone take him seriously when he now claims to want medical care – at taxpayer's expense, of course.

Brodsky raised the country's collective blood pressure a little more when he suggested Whitmore was going to fight his latest charges at trial. No matter that his lifetime court order was crystal clear – absolutely NO contact with children – and that he'd been caught red-handed in a hotel room with a 13-year-old boy.

"Mr. Whitmore's current instructions are that he wants to have a trial. He is not pleading guilty," Brodsky said defiantly.

"He has a defence which he proposes to raise. He has a story to tell and he'll tell it when he has an opportunity. He hopes that if the judge pays attention to his story he'll be released on an acquittal."

Brodsky put together some speaking notes on the Whitmore case, which he used as the basis for future presentations to colleagues in the justice community.

He wrote that "undisputed evidence indicates that a stable and supportive environment, including a residence and employment, is an important, if not the most important, component of the successful rehabilitation and reintegration of a sexual offender after release."

Brodsky recapped his client's background, including the 1999 peace bond that led to a full public release about Whitmore's presence in the community.

"The angry mobs gathered, there was a town hall meeting – it only served to notch up the community's outrage - the community was asked to be an extension of the police and to phone-in whenever you see the target. Peter Whitmore was run out of Etobicoke," said Brodsky.

Politicians gave speeches about him. His community supporters were terrorized – the retired minister was too scared to continue offering Mr. Whitmore a place to live and support. He ended up at my office followed by no less than 50 news reporters. He was placed in the trunk of a car and driven, ironically, to this hotel, where he lived until he could find a flophouse in downtown Toronto next to a nightclub. Within a month Peter Whitmore was back in jail – was anyone really surprised?"

Brodsky said "the public interest of media stories about Peter Whitmore's release and reintegration was illusory in retrospect. The negative consequences of that step were immediate and predictable. The intended positive consequences are uncertain and speculative. There is no perfect choice. But the widespread, indiscriminate communication of personal information about him did little good," he said.

"The balance of convenience favours a different approach next time. That is, permitting the more selective and valuable forms of community notification - targeted releases - which hold some promise of enhancing public security. Neighbours should have information, school principals, playground supervisors, etc., should have notice - but the mainstream dissemination of information was a failure in this case."

• • • • •

It seemed everyone wanted a piece of Peter Whitmore. His latest arrest unleashed a flood of finger-pointing and political posturing, with opposition parties looking to curry favour with an enraged public.

Stockwell Day, leader of the Canadian Alliance party, was first out of the gate. He went straight after Liberal Prime Minister Jean Chretien, accusing him of putting Canadian children at risk by "failing to protect them from pedophiles and sex offenders" like Whitmore.

Day claimed an Alliance government would get tough by building more jails and ensuring dangerous criminals are kept behind bars for their entire sentence. He said the number of inmates would eventually be reduced because criminals would be afraid to re-offend.

He detailed a revamped justice platform that included eliminating conditional sentences for serious crimes, putting those convicted of a second violent or sexual offence on lifetime parole and slapping dangerous offender labels on third-time offenders.

The Liberals reacted quickly, suggesting Day's "American-style" approach would actually increase crime.

"It is very strong on penalties and not very strong at all on reintegration into society," Chretien told reporters.

Joe Clark, leader of the Conservative party, also attacked the Canadian Alliance for trying to score cheap political points.

"This is photo-op politics at its most crass and it is unacceptable," Clark told a breakfast gathering of supporters in Ontario.

# CHAPTER FIFTEEN

With no defence for his actions, Peter Whitmore once again found himself backed up against a wall. He appeared in court on March 9, 2001, pleading guilty to his latest breach charge and receiving another 12 months in jail followed by three years of supervised probation.

Whitmore knew he was going back into custody, a realization that apparently had him throwing a bit of a pity party for himself.

His new case manager summarized Whitmore's return to the prison system in a report:

"Mr. Whitmore was initially very reluctant to participate in treatment. His first several weeks were spent in his bed area and his dorm. He would take bed rest at every opportunity," the case manager wrote.

"During this time Mr. Whitmore completed his assigned clean-up responsibilities. He did not associate very much with peers or staff and appeared to have in place treatment avoidant strategies."

However, Whitmore's behaviour seemed to change slightly for the better when he was confronted by staff in the spring of 2001 about his lack of participation.

"This appeared to motivate him to begin speaking with different peers," the report stated.

Whitmore took a brief step backwards when his request to get a job working in the library was rejected. Prison officials were well aware of his previous obsession with magazines and catalogues and wisely elected to keep him far away from any potential pictures.

Whitmore went so far as to submit a request to be moved to another facility.

"He was confronted about this behaviour and stated he had great difficulty saying what he wanted and how he was feeling. Within the discussion about the transfer he stated he did not really want to transfer, however felt very frustrated and hurt that he could not work in the library, since he felt he was doing a decent job and it made him feel good. Mr. Whitmore said he would submit a request for transfer every time he became upset about something," the report stated.

Whitmore did attend some jailhouse meetings and peer reviews but often remained silent and sitting on the sidelines. Paranoia appeared to be the main reason...

"Mr. Whitmore was burdened with not trusting anyone, staff or other residents. He believed people wanted to gather information that at some later time could be used against him, or could be used to hurt him."

Whitmore was also confronted about some of the wild stories he was telling about his life that stretched the boundaries of imagination. He admitted to exaggerating or outright lying about parts of his background.

Despite losing his bid to work in the library, Whitmore did manage to get his hands of some pictures of young boys. He was caught and given a "misconduct" which went on his permanent record – just the latest in a long list of such sanctions.

Whitmore agreed to sign a "treatment and behaviour contract" vowing to give a better effort, and prison officials noted positive changes as spring turned to summer and Whitmore's potential release date got closer.

"His contribution to groups began to improve. He was making a point of talking about what he was doing in his various groups and a little about what he was learning. He did not speak about his feelings. Mr. Whitmore appeared disconnected from his feelings. He is familiar with anger, anxiety and depression. When group discussions involved feelings, Mr. Whitmore would usually not participate."

There were occasional setbacks as Whitmore's behaviour continued to be somewhat erratic.

"Mr. Whitmore would engage in behaviour that would focus a lot of attention to him, and consume a lot of peer time and staff time," his report stated.

Whitmore got his second and third misconducts of this stint when he threatened a fellow inmate who confronted him about his behaviour. He was also placed briefly in segregation and put on notice that further screw-ups would have consequences.

"It is believed Mr. Whitmore learned a lot about himself and his offence behaviour while in treatment. He was committed to attending the programs he was in. He did the homework that was asked of him," said the report.

"He is in the early stages of treatment. His lack of recognizing and expressing feelings prohibited him from exploring empathy. Any victim impact work was done from an 'I think' perspective. It is believed that Whitmore has repressed a lot of his feelings, and this interferes with him being able to confront and change his core beliefs in a healthy manner. This is a process that would require time and trust."

Whitmore also participated in a "self-esteem training group" but struggled, claiming the work confused him.

Perhaps most importantly, he took part in a sexual offender workshop, one of the few times he stayed in an entire program without leaving.

"Here he worked to develop the cycle of his abuse and this was done at a beginning level. It did not manifest a great deal of insight. He did learn how easily his smaller actions would escalate into committing a crime."

Whitmore also attended the Relapse Prevention Group for sex offenders and came to two conclusions about himself, according to prison officials.

"He discovered that his two strongest seemingly unimportant decisions are driving aimlessly and going to an arcade. He identified his high-risk factors as collecting photos or cut-outs of young boys, buying friends and spending money foolishly," the review states.

$\bullet \quad \bullet \quad \bullet \quad \bullet \quad \bullet$

## NOVEMBER 10, 2001

Just when it seemed like Whitmore might be ready for a breakthrough....he was being sent back into the community. Having served two-thirds of his year-long penalty, Whitmore was eligible for early release.

The decision came despite strong concerns from prison officials that although Whitmore had been making progress, there was still plenty of work left to do.

"Mr. Whitmore was not (in treatment) long enough to have benefitted significantly from the treatment available. At the time of his discharge, he was only in the initial stages of identifying, accepting and exploring his issues," a November corrections report stated. "As such, he should not be considered to have completed the treatment program."

Most concerning, Whitmore was back on the streets without developing any kind of detailed relapse prevention plan or even having a structured release plan ready to go. It was a familiar scene to many, one that likely had a predictable ending.

"Mr. Whitmore was initially resistive to participating in treatment, yet as he developed relationships with staff and peers he became more conductive to this process. He acknowledged that when he came in, he came with an attitude. His overall participation and progress was at a beginning stage, lack of trust being a main issue in his therapy. He did manage to work through his attitude problem and become more serene. Mr. Whitmore indicated that he did feel a level of trust with some individuals," the report concluded.

Finally, Whitmore left prison officials with some parting thoughts as he walked out of jail to face an unknown future.

"Only I am responsible for my life. Only I am responsible for what I do or don't do," he said.

• • • • •

Peter Whitmore's aunt, Lynn Hopkins, had come out swinging. The retired school teacher was angry by the latest round of media reports about her nephew. And unlike the past, when she'd tried her best to ignore it, Hopkins decided this time the best offence was a good defence.

And so she put pen to paper, sending off a letter to the *Toronto Star* regarding a story they'd published days earlier about Whitmore's pending release. She painted a dramatically different picture of Whitmore than what had been told in court, psychiatric reports, parole reviews and jailhouse documents.

*In contrast to the picture painted by the Toronto press, my nephew Peter Whitmore is NOT public Enemy #1.*

*All those who really know him will tell you that.*

*I challenge the label as a pedophile based on a few non-violent incidents. What Peter has done was wrong but the punishment has far exceeded the crime, especially in view of Peter's background and immaturity at the time of the incidents.*

*Peter was taken from his mother when he was 2 weeks old. Some of his problems arise from a bad placement until age 2. He thrived in an excellent foster home from age 2-10. He suffered head injuries in a serious car accident at age 2 and another while a teenager.*

*From the start of Elementary school to Grade 9 when he dropped out of school for environmental reasons, he was always a special needs special education student. He survived his teenage years living on the streets. His main thrust has been trying to earn a living or to make money. Sex has NOT been a major concern to him. Experimentation and mistakes were made by him when he was the equivalent in maturity of a fourteen year old. As a former Ontario Elementary school teacher for many years I feel competent to make that assessment.*

*I have known Peter throughout his life. I have helped him when I could. Due to the other people in my life, I was unable to give him a home. When I can, I will. However, the constant harassment from the police and exaggeration and repetition in the media about Peter and, indirectly, of other family members naturally makes those who could help reluctant to step forward.*

*No one wants to be the centre of a negative media circus or public hanging. This has got to stop. Peter deserves a chance.*

*I want you to know that Peter was never a violent person as a child. Or as an adult. Another boy with him initiated the first incident. The inadequate parents in the second incident requested him to babysit the child. Peter did not abduct the child. He and his common law wife at the time babysat the child to earn money. Although the child stayed 4 days only one incident occurred. To spare the child's appearance in court Peter was persuaded to plead guilty to obtain "better treatment by the court"*

*Family members were not advised, as promised, of the final court date. Medical evidence would not have convicted him.*

*The five year sentence has stretched into 8 years with 3 more years of probation to come due to a break of probation given under a court order for NO further crime. Peter has no sexual offences since 1993 but the penalty goes on and on.*

*(To escape this horrendous media publicity, after his release from prison in 1999, all time served, Peter went to Mexico for a chance to have a normal life again. As is customary in our family, Peter did volunteer work there - driving ambulance and teaching English to mixed classes of parents and children eager to learn English. Peter never was with the children alone. Prison officials had advised him he wouldn't know for sure if he had a*

*problem with children until he had an established record of no offences against children while out of prison. Peter felt this would prove he did not. Instead this was used against him. A phony notice about him was sent to Mexico and Texas by Toronto Police.*

*Peter empathized with three boys he met (two others had gone out to eat) and having endured life on the streets, paid for their room and intended to return to his boarding place for the night. When you live downtown and you're lonely, you associate with street people for companionship. No charges were laid out but it was considered a breach of the probation.*

*I know of killers who got less punishment than Peter. Peter is a kind and gentle person. It is not in his normal personality to use force or violence. He does not drink alcohol or take non prescription drugs, or even use bad language. Peter has personality problems (fear, aloneness, presentation) which need to be addressed but I'm 99% certain he won't sexually reoffend.*

*Some of these problems are due to life in prison. However, during this years in prison, Peter has matured to the equivalent of early twenties age level. At the present time he loves to read novels and this has helped his development. He has finally accessed and completed the necessary sexual offender program.*

*Prison is a difficult and dangerous place. It qualifies a cruel and emotional punishment. At times it is abuse. I recognize its need in society but sometimes it is not the best answer*

*If Peter cannot live freely in the community, some community alternative housing or half-way house must be provided. Assistance in readjusting to society and fatherly advice and guidance would be helpful. Peter has accepted his punishment for his youthful errors in judgement and deserves a chance to have a life.*

*I've always been proud to be a Canadian. I have done many thousands of hours of volunteer work over the past 40 years. Others in my extended family have also served their communities excessively for years.*

*My father, Peter's grandfather, fought for 3.5 years in Europe in WW2 giving his life for our country in Italy in December 1943*

*It hurts and I find it hard to believe that my country can legally treat Peter and our family in this unjust manner.*

*Please stop the harassment by police and exaggeration and repetition and inaccuracies by the media and help Peter rebuild his life.*

*Thank you*

*Peter's Aunt*

*ADDITIONAL INFORMATION*

- *Peter's sexual charges occurred when his mental age (maturity) equivalent to 14 or 15 years. He has matured considerably when incarcerated.*
- *Head Injury from car accident at age 2 (Near Newmarket)*
- *Peter's biological mother was developmentally handicapped and patient at Royal Ottawa Hospital*
- *Peter was a Special Education student throughout school. Completed Grade 8. He has learned much from personal reading and life experiences. Moved often from 10 onwards, good home from age 2-10*

- *Non drinker*
- *No non-prescription drugs*
- *Constant fear for his life.*

• • • • •

**TORONTO, ONTARIO**
**DECEMBER 28, 2001**

Just over six weeks after he'd been released from jail, Peter Whitmore was back in court. Only this time it wasn't to face any new criminal allegations.

Police and justice officials were seeking to make history once again, asking a judge to slap Whitmore with an electronic monitoring device that would allow them to track his movements at all times. Specifically, they wanted to know every time Whitmore left his residence and hit the streets.

If successful, Whitmore would be the first person in Ontario to be outfitted with the tracking bracelet despite already serving his sentence. To date, only inmates out in the community on temporary releases were being monitored.

The Crown had sought a variation to Whitmore's ongoing probation, saying he was a perfect candidate given his long track record of offending.

They filed their bid the day before Whitmore's release.

"Mr. Whitmore is scheduled to be released from custody on November 10th, 2001, following eight months of incarceration and treatment. He has not made substantive improvement and continues to present a large risk to public safety and as a result, we need to know where he is all the time," the Crown wrote in court documents.

Whitmore was fighting the application, saying it would be an invasion of privacy. His lawyer, Dan Brodsky, called the move a "scathing indictment" of the entire justice system, claiming officials were now trying to cover for the fact they offered little in the way of effective treatment and programming to Whitmore while he was in custody.

Justice Patrick Sheppard had reserved his decision to this day after hearing two days worth of arguments which included evidence and testimony about Whitmore's time spent behind bars.

And while Whitmore had seemingly stayed out trouble in the weeks that had now passed since his release, justice officials believed it was only a matter of time before he slipped up.

They wanted to be able to stop him before anyone else got hurt.

"Continuous home monitoring, the court has been told, requires a subject to wear a bracelet which communicates with a sensor operating on electrical current plugged in to a wall outlet. The device will trigger an alarm, or register a change in status if the subject who is wearing the bracelet is approximately more than one hundred feet radius away from the device," Sheppard said as he began reading his decision.

"The monitoring device, if it is connected to a telephone line, can communicate that the subject is more than a hundred feet away to a Ministry operated computer in North Bay, Ontario. If there is no telephone line available, then the device can only store the information to be down-loaded by a person some hours or days after the event, requiring that individual to enter any building or location where the base monitoring device is located."

Sheppard was told by government officials that changes were coming in Ontario that would soon see these types of applications being brought regularly against people on probation, like Whitmore, or even those serving conditional jail sentences in the community.

"The government acknowledges that Mr. Whitmore would be, in some case, a test of this change of policy. However, as the court indicated in its questioning of the Ministry's official, continuous home monitoring will only tell the court where the subject is not. It will not tell the court, the probation officer, or the police where the subject is," said Sheppard.

"To do so, requires the use of an equally available technology known as continuous offender tracking. Various methods of continuous offender tracking are available and in use. Probably, the best known to the general public is a global positioning system often used on high-end luxury motor vehicles, often used by hikers and campers, certainly used by mariners for navigational purposes. This is a fully mature and fully operational technology which can track a person to within a few meters. This is a technology that would continuously monitor any individual subject to it. It is not dependant on that subject having a permanent address, it is not dependant on that subject having a telephone line and it would, of course, deal with the monitoring of the other conditions of probation which are not subject of this variation application."

Sheppard said his decision was a difficult one, with the court having to "balance public safety with the individual's rights and his rehabilitation."

"The court accepts and finds that both these systems intrude on an individual's life. It becomes important at this point to remind ourselves that the notice initiating this application states that Mr. Whitmore 'presents a large risk to public safety and, as a result, we need to know where he is at all times.' Continuous home monitoring only tells us where he is not. After we learn where he is not, it would require good old traditional police work to find out where he is. Precisely the type of police work that resulted in Mr. Whitmore being detected as committing the offence to which he pled guilty before this court," said Sheppard.

But continuous offender tracking would tell us with reasonable certainty where Mr. Whitmore is. And it would clearly aid in determining that the probation is being followed. However, that is not the system that the government is seeking."

Sheppard was denying the application. But he wasn't finished. He next took aim at the corrections system, questioning the early release of an untreated Whitmore back into the community.

"Mr. Whitmore is a pedophile. Statutory remission has resulted in his release when he was only half-way through the Ontario Correctional Institute's program for pedophiles. He would have needed to be at the Institute for a further four to five months to complete the program. In part, this is because of bureaucratic slowness and resource constraints and lack of cooperation from other correctional authorities. It is not, as suggested by the Crown Attorney in his submissions, entirely the fault of Mr. Whitmore. But whose fault it is is not the important factor. The important factor is that the program has not been done and has not been completed," said Sheppard.

Sheppard said he was stunned by one particular revelation about Whitmore's treatment. Prison officials had started him on a drug therapy program for sex drive reduction – known more commonly as "chemical castration" – just one day before his release from custody.

Whitmore had given his consent to the treatment months earlier – as is required in Canada – yet no action was taken. And now Sheppard worried it may have been too late.

"Given that such a medication regime can have a therapeutic effect within one month, so the court was advised, it is likely that Mr. Whitmore was a greater threat on his release date, November 10th, than he needed to be," he said.

Whitmore had continued to take the medication since his release and was seeing a doctor regularly, court was told.

"Seven weeks have passed, there is some reason to believe that he may be a lesser threat now than he was on November 10th, assuming at all times that he is compliant with that therapeutic program," said Sheppard.

Sheppard cited other potential problems with the electronic monitoring bid; including the fact Whitmore was having trouble keeping a fixed address. He had already bounced between four different residences since his release, largely because of ongoing public backlash, a lack of community supports and no financial resources.

Although Whitmore wouldn't be fitted with the ankle bracelet, Sheppard did agree with the Crown's request to impose a nightly curfew against Whitmore. Sheppard told Whitmore he had to be off the streets between the hours of 6 p.m. to 6 a.m., a move that would hopefully help keep his behaviour in check. The curfew would last until April 2, 2002, and any breaches would land Whitmore back behind bars facing new criminal charges.

Outside court, Brodsky was declaring victory for his client – but said the entire sad, sordid affair should have all Canadians concerned.

"There have been a lot of screw-ups in this case," Brodsky said.

And there were more to come.

# CHAPTER SIXTEEN

## TORONTO, ONTARIO
FEBRUARY 15, 2002

Peter Whitmore was gone – yet again.

Toronto police officers had come to his cheap downtown motel in the early evening hours, making yet another in a long list of curfew checks. To date, Whitmore had seemingly been following the rules and given police no reason to pull him back into custody. Until now.

Police were greeted with an empty suite on this latest visit, an alarming sign that triggered the immediate obtaining of a Canada-wide warrant. Officers began asking other guests and tenants in the motel about Whitmore, hoping to put a more detailed timeline together about his recent movements.

They got more than they expected. One of his neighbours, a single mother of three young children, was stunned to learn that the friendly man living just down the hall was one of Canada's most notorious sex offenders.

Whitmore certainly hadn't offered that detail about himself when they'd first met a few weeks earlier, shortly after he moved in. In fact, he hadn't even given his real name. Whitmore had introduced himself as "Rob Edwards."

Now the woman was an emotional wreck, recalling every single encounter she'd had with Whitmore during that time. He had taken an immediate liking to her boys, aged five, two and seven months. Whitmore had spent the most time with the oldest child, even going so far as to play-wrestle and tickle him on a number of occasions.

And while the mother had always been in the room during the visits, she was sickened by the thought that Whitmore had put his hands on her children – with her consent.

Police now had grounds to lay additional charges. Whitmore, of course, was under a lifetime ban from being alone with children unless he'd obtained written consent.

Although there were no new sexual assault allegations, police believed Whitmore's contact with children and his sudden vanishing act was a sign that he was once again preparing to self-destruct. They had to find him. And fast.

● ● ● ● ●

## CHILLIWACK, BRITISH COLUMBIA
## FEBRUARY 25, 2002

He had come west, apparently wanting to spend time with his closest living relative. But now, a bearded, scruffy looking Peter Whitmore was back in custody, after police received a tip that he was in same community as his aunt, Lynn Hopkins.

Police made a disturbing discovery shortly after re-arresting Whitmore. Pictures of children. Binoculars. Latex gloves. Lubricant. Zip ties. Duct tape. An application for a Canadian passport. And child porn website addresses. It was an all-inclusive tool box for an experienced pedophile, a sure sign that Whitmore was preparing to strike again.

His lawyer, Dan Brodsky, disagreed. He immediately went on the offensive, saying this wasn't an example of his client trying to run away and hide so he could continue to victimize children. Instead, he said Whitmore was just frustrated with the endless media coverage and lack of substantial treatment he was receiving in Ontario. Brodsky also disputed claims of a so-called "rape kit", saying Whitmore may have just been gathering hunting supplies.

Police and prosecutors weren't buying it. They believed Whitmore was the author of his own fate, a manipulative conman who seemed to always want to play the "poor me" card whenever he got caught in the act.

Brodsky immediately began negotiations with the Crown, attempting to strike a speedy deal that would see Whitmore immediately admit to his latest breaches. In exchange, Whitmore wanted a guarantee that he could remain in B.C. to serve whatever jail sentence he received.

The Crown briefly considered the offer but decided against it, not wanting to make any deals with a man who'd burned them – and the public – so many times before. He would be brought back to Ontario.

· · · · ·

News of Whitmore's latest arrest quickly spread across Canada. Many people began questioning how closely he really was being monitored in the community. Others were furious about the judge's decision to not make him wear an electronic monitoring bracelet.

Rob Sampson, Ontario Corrections Minister, said plans were quickly underway to bring in satellite tracking systems that could better manage the Peter Whitmores of the province.

He noted the ankle bracelet would only have told justice officials Whitmore had fled his apartment – but given no actual clues as to where he'd gone.

A global positioning system would change that, using 24 satellites and cellular technology to track a person's every movement around the clock. Although Canada had yet to introduce GPS technology, at least 27 American states had already been using it for years to track an estimated 1,200 high-risk offenders. Sampson promised that Ontario would be the first to get on board – a move directly related to the outcry over Whitmore's case.

Some justice critics also began questioning what it would take to brand Whitmore a dangerous offender, which would give him an indefinite jail sentence. According to Corrections Canada, using 2000 figures, 297 Canadians had been declared dangerous offenders.

They also claimed the following:
- 99 per cent of temporary absences are successful.
- 94 per cent of those released on day parole did not commit a new crime.
- 87 per cent of those released on full parole did not commit a new crime.
- 85 per cent of those released on statutory release did not commit a new crime.

As well, Corrections Canada said previous offenders were responsible for:
- 1.3 of every 1,000 violent offences.
- 0.7 of every 1,000 sexual offences.
- 1.2 of every 1,000 drug offences.
- 1.1 of every 1,000 property or other federal statute offences.

By law, the breach charges alone against Whitmore likely wouldn't be enough to satisfy the onerous dangerous offender requirements. There would likely have to be a more substantial offence – such as an actual attack on a child – to make the case.

CTV's Canada AM, which had been following the Whitmore case over the years, devoted a lengthy segment to the latest developments.

Steve Sullivan, president of the Canadian Resource Centre for Victims of Crime, and Karen McArthur, an Ontario defence lawyer who had represented numerous pedophiles, weighed in with their thoughts on Whitmore's latest arrest and the fact he'd been given early release from his prior jail sentence.

"I think parole works for a lot of offenders who can be released into the community and need a little bit of assistance. The problem is when you have someone like Peter Whitmore and pedophiles who have a very high recidivism rate it doesn't matter if you put them on parole. It doesn't matter. Unless you have a parole officer with them 24 hours a day these people have a very high recidivism rate, particularly pedophiles like Peter Whitmore. And if you give them a chance they will reoffend," Sullivan told a national television audience.

Host Lisa Laflamme asked both panellists about whether they supported electronic monitoring.

"If they're properly supervised, yes. But I think the difficulty Judge Sheppard faced last fall was that the attorney general and the solicitor general didn't have the proper resources in place for the tracking system. The Crown wanted it but it just wasn't properly available. It wouldn't have worked," said McArthur.

"Well, I think the judge made a good point. It's not a question of whether he should've been on a tracking device;

it's whether this particular tracking device would have really made a difference. And I think it probably wouldn't have. And the solicitor general, or the minister of corrections, in Ontario is looking at an improved tracking device which seems to offer some better protection for society. But at the end of the day, as long as we have a system that will release people like Peter Whitmore either early or at the end of their sentence, untreated, who are still at risk to society, society is going to be at risk and there are going to be children who are victimized," said Sullivan.

Laflamme asked how society can be protected.

"Well, in 1993 the Liberal government, before they became government, made a promise in their Red Book that they would send sex offenders who were still at risk to reoffend at the end of their sentence to mental institutions for further treatment. They have never done that. And until there is some mechanism in our system to say, "Look, you have reached the end of your sentence but you are still at risk, we're not going to let you go," until we do that we are always going to be at risk from people like Peter Whitmore," said Sullivan

Talk shifted to existing dangerous offender legislation and why it isn't being used in cases like Whitmore.

"I think it should be used judiciously because if you use it too frequently people will just be ending up serving life sentences for offences that don't warrant it," said McArthur.

Sullivan said a recent inquest examining a sex offender who spent his life in a mental institution – then killed a man shortly after his release – shows how difficult it is to "treat" pedophiles.

"The mental health system is not currently set up to deal with people like Peter Whitmore," he said.

"I agree with Steve that there are gaps in the system. But I think the way to deal with it is to deal with it cooperatively, collaborate. I have done that in one case, worked successfully with the police and integrated quite a notorious pedophile back into the community successfully without any breaches. But it takes working together as opposed to always approaching it from the adversarial system. It takes a new and different, integrated approach," said McArthur.

"We worked with mental health professionals, we worked with the policing system, and we worked with just medical professionals. And the person's family. And we set up a realistic plan that has worked for almost a decade."

Sullivan said it's clear Whitmore's release plan wasn't a good one.

"As long as we're going to release them I think the community has to take some responsibility for protecting themselves. And there are circles of support where community members will assist the sex offenders who are being released and who are a high risk, but they have served their entire sentences. So I applaud Karen, I applaud the police across the country who are trying to do those imaginative things. As long as we're going to release these people we need to take steps in our communities to protect society," he said.

"But I still think we need a mechanism in our system that says if you are still a high risk to reoffend at the end of your sentence we're not going to let you go. There are Charter issues but I think they can be overcome."

• • • • •

Angry members of the public were flooding Canadian talk radio shows and sending off Letters to the Editor expressing their views on Whitmore's case.

Naomi Gold, a resident of Thornhill, Ontario, fired off the following to the *Toronto Star* in early March 2002.

*"Lawyer Dan Brodsky quoted as saying it's up to Corrections Minister Rob Sampson to prepare a treatment and release program for Peter Whitmore because 'he's going to be released sooner or later.' If Brodsky is so concerned with Whitmore's treatment, maybe he should invite Whitmore to live with him in his own home. If Brodsky is not willing to subject his own children to the vile menace that Whitmore possesses to children, perhaps he should work to see that he is locked up for a long time. The Canadian 'justice' system being what it is, however, I suspect that Whitmore's 'rights' will be protected, and more children will be placed in harm's way before he is declared a dangerous offender and locked up for good."*

# CHAPTER SEVENTEEN

## TORONTO, ONTARIO
JUNE 18, 2002

"Children are a precious resource."

Ontario Court Justice Ivan Fernandes delivered the message – along with one of the country's longest-ever sentences for breaching court orders – just moments after Peter Whitmore pleaded guilty. Whitmore was sentenced to three years in prison – one less than the maximum allowed by law – following a joint-recommendation between Crown and defence lawyers.

Justice officials backed down from seeking a four-year term once Whitmore agreed to plead guilty and spare the resources which would have been needed for a preliminary hearing and trial. The move also meant the traumatized young mother of three who was befriended and duped by Whitmore wouldn't have to take the witness stand.

Crown attorney Jennifer Crawford told court that police and the mother are satisfied her children were never sexually assaulted by Whitmore. But she said he remains a "serious threat" to the public.

Whitmore showed little emotion and said nothing during the sentencing hearing, which included extensive details of his previous criminal history from being read out.

"Your record is an appalling record," said Fernandes.

The Crown said Whitmore appeared to be preparing to find his next victims by putting together the "rape kit" found by investigators in B.C.

Crawford said his use of a fictional name to get closer to the woman and three young boys fits a disturbing pattern.

"History has shown he seeks them out," Crawford said. "He grooms them."

Brodsky said the disturbing items found on Whitmore could also have been used for things like camping and suggested his client may have just been trying to escape into the woods rather than attack another child. But he admitted Whitmore had clearly messed up again.

"He suffers from an illness," said Brodsky.

The judge recommended that Whitmore serve his sentence at Kingston Penitentiary, where once again he could be offered multiple treatment options.

Brodsky said his client planned to complete programming this time and seek parole after doing just one-third of his sentence.

He also repeated Whitmore's request to be transferred to B.C. to do his time and be closer to his maternal aunt. Brodsky said it would also allow Whitmore to escape the "public hounding" he'd endured the past few years.

Lynn Hopkins filed an affidavit, saying she continued to stand behind Whitmore despite his criminal history.

"I am very aware of the background and charges of my nephew. I would sincerely appreciate the opportunity to have

Peter serve his sentence in B.C., close enough for me to visit him regularly," Hopkins wrote.

"I have a good relationship with Peter. It is my intention to provide daily support and supervision upon Peter's next release in B.C."

Fernandes recommended that Whitmore be allowed to serve some of his time out west, provided he shows legitimate progress while behind bars.

• • • • •

News of Whitmore's potential return to B.C. wasn't sitting well with many local residents.

"Pedophile not welcome" was the headline of one letter-to-the-editor, published days after Whitmore's sentencing in the *Chilliwack Times*.

*"If the people of Chilliwack take the time to protest something so dumb as the opening of our courthouse and protest to save some tree in the middle of nowhere, I hope those same people and many more will be out with their signs to make sure that pedophile Peter Whitmore does not move to Chilliwack,"* resident Nicole Brinson wrote.

*"A repeat offender is exactly that – a repeat offender. Maybe we should invite him to work at one of our workplaces and then we find out what a nice guy he is, then maybe we should get him to be our softball leader or better yet we will hire him to be our babysitter. A certain offender has only done it three times, right? Wrong. That's how many times the offender has been caught. That's why they keep doing it. They know that a child won't tell. Ask me because I am one of them. He is ruining children's lives and affecting how his victims love their own children.*

*Let's vote to save our children. Not to find this pedophile a job. We don't want you in Chilliwack."*

However, a June 21 editorial in the same paper – titled "Better The Devil You Know" – offered a different take.

*"Peter Whitmore has been harassed and hounded out of any community he has tried to live in since he was first convicted of sexual offences involving children.*

*And no wonder. Who would want an untreated, unrestrained pedophile living in their community?*

*Whitmore needs treatment. That said, there is no proven, effective treatment for someone with his urges. Perhaps his best course would be to volunteer for castration. As his track record shows, his hormones just keep leading him back to prison. Castration could allow this troubled man to live in peace in the community.*

*And Whitmore will have to live somewhere. He's fortunate that his aunt, who lives here, has offered to look after him. Whitmore's lawyer said she deserves a medal and we agree. It can't be an easy thing to take on someone like him.*

*Chilliwack has one to three years to prepare for Whitmore. We'll have to accommodate him, if not actually make him welcome because he has to live somewhere. We can't just say not in this backyard and send him underground.*

*It's better that we know who he is and what he does. It's better that we help to ensure that he stays away from children. It's better for him and for us if he has a job and something to do with his days, than if he has free time on his hands.*

*It's a scary thing to have someone like Whitmore in the community, but Whitmore's lawyer made a chilling comment, when he told us that there are lots of people like Whitmore.*

*There are lots of people who might hurt our children and we don't know who they are. Safeguards have been put into place to check up on people who come into contact with children. We do our best to tell our kids not to talk to strangers, not to agree to go anywhere with anyone and to kick and scream if someone tries to take them away. And still, children are hurt and kidnapped every day and we don't always know by whom.*

*At least with Whitmore, we'll know what he looks like and where he lives. And unlike Etobicoke, where he was run out of town, we'll have to learn to live with him."*

●　●　●　●　●

Lynn Hopkins deserved a medal. At least that was the opinion of her nephew's lawyer, Dan Brodsky, who said the retired school teacher deserved credit for standing by Whitmore in his time of need.

"Nobody wants Peter Whitmore living in their community – nobody," Brodsky told *Chilliwack Times* reporter Lisa Morry for a story published on the front page.

Hopkins agreed to an interview with the local paper, explaining why she continues to support Whitmore.

"I'll do it and I won't give up until I've done it," she told the *Times*.

Hopkins, who cared for her ailing husband and worked in a local convenience store, said she has a long history of helping her community. From an elementary school teacher to three years spent as an Ontario alderman in an Ontario, Hopkins said she is always looking for a "cause".

"When I go about things, I know what needs to be done," she said.

She likely ruffled some feathers with her own assessment of Whitmore, saying "he's never done anything violent or mean."

"He's done some stupid things. The early things were teen experimentation... He knows now, but he didn't know then, what right and wrong were. He has said to me 'I could never hurt another child'," said Hopkins.

Despite his countless breaches, Hopkins believed her nephew was a low-risk to the community. And she suggested Whitmore was just "being made an example of" by a vindictive public and justice system.

"The things he did, he did when he was young. He's served his time, he deserves a chance to prove that he's not going to reoffend," she said. "I have children. I have grandchildren. I had many classes of children and I care a great deal about children. I wouldn't let any child be harmed and I will do my very best. I feel there's a 95 per cent chance he won't reoffend."

• • • • •

With nothing but time on his hands, Whitmore began hammering out what he titled his "Autobiography." It came following several jailhouse sessions with a psychologist who thought writing might be therapeutic. It was a dark, sordid look into his disturbed mind, a world filled with conflict, confusion and chaos.

His 7,000 word opus contained rationalization for his many crimes, detailed explanations of so-called evidence never presented in court, wild personal claims that had not and could not be verified and seemingly candid admissions of the impact he'd had on his many victims.

*I was going to say some things but I thought better about it and decided that I would take the responsibility to describe my first 10 years to the best of my ability. However I will be leaving out names, countries and towns that would give any details that would leave to a criminal investigation against certain family members. Also during my later years, I will also leave out the names, places, and countries of any and all things that could lead to criminal charges. There are two incidents that are known to police but no details about the actual crime, as this information is not known to police.*

*As I do not know the names of all my victims I will call them the following, boy, child, and victim. This will also help me not to give out any names that belong to any undisclosed victims*

*I will also not give my company names, locations, or countries that they are in. But I will give the types of companies there are I would ask the psychologists not to mention the whereabouts or the names of my companies as I do not believe that their disclosure would benefit either myself as the group also I do not want anyone to use the information for wrong I did either criminally or morally, I will also not discuss any financial assets either liquid or property.*

*Now I want to clear up something now, not one of us has lied to officials or friends to hide their criminal activities or their past.*

*I used to do it all the time so I was called a compulsive liar. I really did not care about this label as long as my*

*past stayed there but over the past several years I have
devised a plan where I could talk about my past as long as
I disclosed no names, crimes or countries so this is what I
have been doing since.*

*Now I'll begin. The first 10 years of my life has been
told to me through family members - some of them who
went through the same as me. Also I have obtained several
hospital reports, police reports, and school records from
foreign countries. Interpol is a great source of information
for someone.*

*I am changing the beginning of my autobiography
after a phone call with a family member who corrected me
on some of my details.*

*I was taken from my parents at 2 weeks old. The actual
reasons why are still unclear. All I know was that I had
some sort of brain injury.*

*My brothers and sister were removed as well. Three of
my family actually took us from the home. We were placed
in separate homes. I with a family member, my brothers
and sister with another family. For approximately one
year I stayed with this family member. Then I was moved
in with my brothers and sister. It was here that we were
shipped to different places and countries for sex. At
about 2-3 years old while being back in the country I was
hospitalized. It was here that the first reports of sexual
abuse were noticed. I had anal scarring.*

*We were removed from the home and placed on a farm.
The problem was that these were friends with the other
home. So we continued being sent abroad on weekends
and holidays. There were times that I even missed school
for quite some time. It was these families that sold me and
my brothers and sister into the sex trade. But I was the*

*money maker as I was blond, blue eyes, and extremely young.*

*In two countries the police sent me back to Canada when I was caught. I was part of an international child porn ring. So were my brothers and sister. To this day there are 1000's of children in the same circumstances.*

*As for feelings about this part of my life, I really do not have any. For two reasons:*

*# 1    I do not know if I am being told the entire truth about my childhood*

*#2    I do not know what exactly happened to me.*

*I can only imagine what happened plus official reports. But all these reports and thinking what may have happened does not bring any sort of feelings out. You can not feel what you do not remember.*

*At around 9 years old I stayed with a good family. For about one year. However during this time I was destructive, troublesome, and sexually interested in the female body of their daughter who was the same age as I was.*

*We were caught exploring each other's body and I was beaten/hospitalized and then moved to my real parents.*

*There I met my brothers and sister again. I was 10 years old. I was there only two weeks when my oldest brother raped me both orally and anally. No charges as I was not believed by my parents. He was the good boy of the family and could do no wrong. However this was the only time he did this. But I remember every detail even to this day. I beat him up several times over the years but when I shot his car up while he was in it I missed but he left the country and has not been seen since. I tried to kill him.*

For the first several months I was at my parents, my other brother tried to kill me several times. Finally a teacher noticed a severe rope burn around my neck and he brought me to the hospital where charges were laid, but later I withdrew them. However because of this incident I was put in a psych ward. During my time there I was examined by several psychologists and psychiatrists. I was diagnosed with acute emotionally disturbed socially maladjusted childhood psychosis anxiety disorder

Also, during my stay there we tried to have family counselling, but after two sessions we never had any more.

I was released shortly thereafter. I was placed back into my parents' home, 'till I was 12. During this time I was physically abused, to the point that I hid from everyone and would sneak out for food after midnight when I knew everyone was asleep. I stayed away from home for as long as I could. I began stealing from stores and my school. But I never got caught.

I then stole some vehicles from the Ministry of Transportation.

I got caught but the police returned me home. I got a really vicious beating that night. The next day my parents felt so bad, that they did anything I wanted for the next several days. It was great.

I was also used as a pawn between my parents. They would fight over me; literally at times each would grab an arm and try to pull me apart.

Then one night one of my brothers found out that my dad was having sex with my sister. He pulled a gun and was going to kill him. The gun was taken away from him but given to me. I hid the gun in my room. I played with it for a while decided on whether or not to kill everyone.

I decided against it at the time but know I think I should have.

I was an angry child, confused, and constantly worried about my safety, and the safety of others. I was also scared that I was going to get beat again. The days that I did not get beat was the worst. As I would at least know after a beating that I was safe till the next day, but on the days I wasn't the anticipation and worry were real tortures. I used to act out on these days just to get a beating and get it over with.

At 12 I was moved by my relatives to another town and placed in C.A.S. I went to an intake farm where I was raped on a daily basis by the man and the four older boys. I stayed there approximately two months. I finally told my relatives and was removed from C.A.S care. My relative then paid for a private firm to look after me but before I was allowed to move into a group home I needed to be accessed first.

I was placed in a special home sort of like a jail. It was here that I had my first consensual oral sex with a boy what was a year younger than me. This only happened once.

I did not do well there. I was again very anti-social and I did not get along with anyone. I continually fought authority and went into my dream life all the time – the same thing I do now. I read books and become the character or watched movies and become that person, which is why I watch a lot of family movies.

I was also checked out and assessed at a psych ward for 30 days again similar diagnoses.

# DEVIL AMONG US

*I was approved for a special group home for abused kids with emotional difficulties. At this time I was always regressing to a boy of 9 or 10 years old, and still do this to this day. It is a security feature for me while in this state. I don't care what you do to me.*

*During my time in this group home I had two sexual encounters with two boys. One boy lasted two weeks till he told. I was 13 and he was 10. The other boy for one night in a tent was oral sex only.*

*The police were involved with the one boy but it was decided that no charges be laid. I was however removed to a room of my own there was no counselling offered to me at this time.*

*Then when I was 15 I lost control and became very violent towards the staff. I do not remember what set me off, nor do I remember what I did but when I came back to myself there was a lot of people sitting on me. I was told after that one of the staff touched me sexually and I became a different person. The staff was removed.*

*I ran away shortly after that, because I was afraid of what I was capable of doing. I was caught, returned and then underwent a court battle to go back to live with my parents. As soon as I moved back with them, nothing had changed so I ran away*

*During my travel I realised that people gave me money if they could suck my dick. Truckers especially.*

*I finally ended up in Hollywood, California where I became a prostitute. I met my wife there. She was working at a church of scientology place as a security guard. After a few weeks of having fun we decided to get married for the hell of it. She knew my preference was for young boys and the gay life but she did not care.*

So we took her dad's car to Las Vegas and got married. We drove to Mexico and lived there. However I always drove back to San Diego and Hollywood to continue my prostitution for money.

It was at this time that I called a family relative, and asked for money. I was told that I had a trust fund and that I would be given a monthly allowance and a credit card.

We built a house somewhere in Mexico and had 3 children. All boys, I had to leave them when my oldest turned three years old. I just could not handle the pressure of parenthood, changing diapers and being responsible for another human being. It also cramped my life style. I enjoyed traveling alone.

So we divorced and now got everything including money every month to raise the boys, I still visited them several times a year and they also visited me where I was. My ex-wife and I are still on very good terms. I spent six weeks with them in 2000.

I travelled to Canada several times of course I always got into trouble and spent 60 days in a juvenile detention centre open and closed, and also spent several small 30 days or less for property crimes same as the states.

In 1992 I few to Canada for my sisters second marriage, while here I met a young boy that I found out was offering very young boys and girls for people. We started a very reasonable friendship. Through him I met other people who did the same thing.

When I wanted a boy all I had to do was pick up the phone and call someone and a boy would be ready to pick up or he would be dropped off. This lasted all summer in 1992. I moved to a small town and fell into a sexual relationship with boy. I also had several other *relationships during this time. All but two victims were 11-13.*

*My friend and I went to a public pool and met an 11 year old boy who was one of my friend's working boys.*

*There was only one boy that all I wanted from him was to have oral sex performed upon him. This was the boy that was at a pool and on occasion had done work for my friend.*

*I spent the night with him. He suggested that I try other things with him as I was paying him. I let him perform oral sex on me for about two minutes but could not get aroused or even an erection. Then we decided on anal intercourse but again I could not get aroused or even excited about the process. All I could think about was that this would hurt him and it did not interest me.*

*As stated in court, I could not get an erection during the process of my crime; therefore what was I really after?*

*All I was after was that I needed to feel wanted. I know the boy thought there was something wrong with him when I could not get aroused and he told me so. I told him that he was a very beautiful boy but I am only interested in giving pleasure of oral sex to boys, nothing else and that it was not his fault. The next day I took him shopping and bought clothes and other stuff for him and his family. This is how I was caught, because I used my own checks and credit cards to pay for the purchases and left the receipts in the stores own special bags.*

*I was also charged with four other boys, these were my friend's boys who I paid for sex. Some charges were withdrawn due to a lack of evidence so I ended up with only three boy victims.*

*Here is what I wanted from them...*
*CRIMES AND IMPACT*
*In regards to all my victims*

*My like of boys is not entirely a sexual idea. I find boys to be non-judgemental, very good listeners, not aggressive, kind, caring, compassionate, and with no ulterior motives in what they do. I also find boys more willing to show affection, hugging and willing to keep you company.*

*At first I would feel bored with myself then lonely. When I became lonely I needed companionship. I have always felt very comfortable around young boys. If I was going to do something wrong or did something wrong, I would not listen to an adult. However if a child explained things to me or if I was angry and upset 90% or the time I would listen to the boy, and do as he says. It has been said over the years that I have never matured emotionally so my emotional level is that of a child. However that being said I can cope in the adult world exceptionally well in terms of business practices and have been known to have intellectually stimulating conversations with people.*

*I am always aware of any and all international politics and world economies. I am also a strategist. I will formulate a plan and do everything to accomplish it. The downfall being, there are times when I plan for unreasonable acquisitions or plans.*

*Anyways, getting back to my offences. I would call a friend and ask him to provide me with a boy for the day or weekend. The boy could come over or I would meet him somewhere. The prearranged price would be paid at the time however there are some friends I keep a current balance with and money is deducted this way.*

After meeting with the intended boy we would always go to a restaurant and talk and eat for a while. The kid's discussions would normally include what I wanted from him while he was with me. My requests are always the same so I'll say them now

- I would ask for companionship for him to at least pretend to be my friend and that he act like he really like me and cared about me.
- That he listen to everything I wanted to talk about. Even if it did not interest him
- That he makes me the centre of his world while we are together
- That he shows affection towards me - not sexual but rather like an older brother.

And then I would tell him that in return for this I would do the following.

- I would take him to fancy restaurants, movies of his choice, shopping for anything he wanted all at my expense
- We would spend the day together like true friends and then at night when we got to my place and he was either getting prepared to go home or stay the weekend I would perform oral sex for him, to show that I really appreciated his company and that I liked him as a friend

WHAT THEY PROBABLY THINK OR ACT NOW
I believe now that my victims felt like the following:

- Ashamed of what they were doing
- Feeling that they have to do this to please others, that this may be the only way to be loved by a man

- *Suicidal, feeling that they are in a no win situation and may not be able to stay no to others who only want to use them for sex*
- *Alone, thinking that they are the only ones doing this*
- *They may take constant showers because they keep feeling the man on them or may even feel that the man left something in them and they want it off, but no matter how many showers and scrubbing they do they still feel dirty and unclean*
- *Confused, belief that this is the only way to show love*
- *Anger. They bottle their anger up about what's happening to them or what they're being forced to do, until they explode*
- *They feel that they may have done something to deserve this stuff that's happening to them.*
- *They feel they must do this to please their friends who may be threatening them or their family*
- *Scared that if they don't comply with certain sexual demands that something will happen to them or their family*

*But I think their biggest fear is what if this guy is a whacko and intends to kill them?*

*I received 15 months for my victims and a 16 month sentence for abduction. I was charged with abduction because I did not have his parents' consent to have him.*

*Once released my Canadian Company – called C.P.S – had been open for only about a year.*

# DEVIL AMONG US

*I met a man in jail who told me about the problems he was having obtaining his infant son. I told him I could help him. He did not know what I was in jail for.*

*I worked with the courts and police to get his son back. I succeeded in this task and we got a court order granting him sole custody so we used the police to apprehend the child from his mother who was psychologically unbalanced.*

*We got to the house with the police, went into the apartment and while the police dealt with her – she was holding a knife – I was told to search the house for the boy.*

*I found him and removed him from the house into a waiting car with the father in it. He immediately left. They left the eight year old girl in my car. The police finally came out and I followed the police back to the station where the father was waiting there. The police would not let us leave until we had a baby seat so a hospital was called and I and the girl went to pick it up. This was about 12 am*

*When we got back to the station the crazed mother was there waving a knife at me in the car. I locked the door and honked my horn till the police came out. We were walked into the police station into the back room. We stayed there till about 3 am when the police saw the woman had left. We got into our car. The girl is mine.*

*Just down the road I played the distracter when the mother then showed up. I used my car as a physical barrier between us and the baby. The police were following and when the van turned into a gas station to get ahead of me, I pulled around and she tried to ram my car. The police pulled her over.*

*The other car with the infant was gone on ahead; it took us about 1.5 hours to get to her place. We got inside the apartment, when the mother showed up with a knife and tried to gain access to the apartment. I used my body weight against the door while he called the police. She was sent away from the property. I stayed out in my car to provide protection for the apartment.*

*In the morning, I drove back to my common laws apartment. This was just a business arrangement - she needed money and I needed a family to look good for my investors before going public.*

*That night about 1 a.m. the father called me and asked me to pick up his daughter for one week till things cooled down. So my common-law and I drove 1.5 hours to pick her up and another 1.5 hours back while she was at the apartment.*

*I took her shopping. I locked my keys in the car so I went to the police station in the mall and left the girl in their care while we decided on how to get my keys out. About two hours later a tow truck came and got my keys out.*

*I picked up the girl who was having a blast with the police. The next day I took her to Canada's Wonderland. When we got back the father had called. I called him back and he told me he knew I was in jail for and was coming to get his daughter and that he would deal with me.*

*I panicked and took the girl with me. I did not know what to do so I bought a tent and we spent the night camping. During the night I asked her to perform oral sex upon me. She refused so I went to sleep. In the morning I took her to a mall and sent her back home. I gave the taxi driver my business card with my name address and telephone number.*

*I left for Nova Scotia. I was arrested in Nova Scotia and charged with numerous sexual offences against the girl. During trial the medical examiner proved the girl was still a virgin both anally and vaginally so all charges but the invitation was left. I was found guilty and sentenced to 5 years.*

*At the same time I was accused of having oral sex with an 8 year old boy. I pleaded guilty to this however it was not him I was doing but rather another boy and he caught us together. But I cannot go into this in order to protect myself from criminal charges. The 8 year old boy blackmailed us. In his statement to police the last line he said was 'When do I get my $5000?'*

*All my crimes except the sexual ones were done for thrills. I enjoyed getting everything I could for free or I just enjoyed stealing cars and driving them everywhere.*

*Once I was released I was arrested and transported to Toronto to sign an 810.1 peace bond. I signed it knowing full well that in a few hours I would be on my way to Mexico.*

*I was arrested in Mexico for not making a phone call to the police and not having an address in Canada. I was given one year for not making a phone call.*

*I was released once again and my passport was seized so that I could not leave the country.*

*While staying in Toronto I met several street people. I bought them meals, clothing and rented them motel rooms to stay in. I met two boys who said they were 16 and showed me Identification to verify it. I showed them my peace bond and explained who I was. The street people had already told them. I bought the two boys food and clothes. I rented them a hotel room for two days. The first* night I stayed with the street people and the two boys in the hotel room. Everyone took showers. When the boy was taking a shower they left to go get a coffee across the street. I was watching TV so I stayed. They called the police and when the police arrived the boy was getting dressed. I was fully dressed. I was arrested, while they went through the boys ID. They said that if everything checked out I would be released right away. It turned out the boy was 13, one week from turning 14. There was no sex between us, but I was hoping that there might be later on.

I was convicted of being with a minor under 14 and sentenced to one year.

I spent the first four months fighting the system not willing to change. Finally after an incident in which pictures were found in my bunk I settled down and concentrated on the program. I did very well, which was a real surprise to me. But I still had some rough spots.

I left the program at my warrant expiry date.

With media attention at its highest I moved into a motel in Scarborough. There I met a lady with three boys aged 6 months, 3 years and 5 years. The mother comes over to my place to play cards a lot. I told her not to bring her kids, she did not.

Every morning I would go over for coffee and spend about 15 minutes. I played with the children. I was then asked to take her friend and her 5 year old to the flea market to pick up some things. I did this and I told my probation officer and he said that there was no problem. He lied.

He called the cops and pulled my probation. I found out through some sources and fled to B.C. I was caught there - however I hated the cops and was wondering what I could do to piss them off and to do more work so I had an idea. I would make a rape kit.

I bought duck tape, straps, KY jelly, and gloves and put them in a small backpack. When I was caught they found the stuff. They did freak at first till they realized that everything was still in its original packaging. So that did not work the way I thought it would.

I was convicted of not being with an approved adult when I was around children and fleeing to B.C. I was given three years.

Since then I went to the Royal Ottawa Hospital to undergo testing for my sexual preferences. After eight hours of testing I was told that I like older women and children only a little. I did not like the results. I had my probation officer get me tested again. However the only test we did was pictures of children only. No adults and not children under five and no older than 13 years old. The test results came back boys 5-13. It was a set up

I know I prefer boys 11-13 years. I also like older men 16-25 and I like the company of men 50-70

Now my psychologist says I should just touch on my companies. I own several companies. This along with my allowance allows me to live my life the way I want. I enjoy travelling and do so at every chance I get. But I will never come back to Canada

I am in this program to learn how to control my sexual impulses towards children and understand more about myself and why I do what I did.

I have been told that some of my abuse in my early years has caused me several problems in my life as a teenager and adult. It has caused me to act as a 10 year old child to an adult. As you all know I bounce in and out of this stage every day. I also have an inability to form close friendships or relationships with men or women. It has caused me to bottle my feelings and all my anger and that by growing up in several countries with different morals and attitudes towards sex; it has warped my thinking towards children.

I have no social ties or friends in Canada. However in other countries I have a lot of acquaintances and family.

Fantasy life did not revolve around sexuality; instead it formed around characters on TV or in books that look like they were enjoying their family life

I wanted to be them so in my fantasies I became them.

Only since coming to jail/prison has my fantasy life began to include young boys. Porn of young boys also became a major part of my personal life.

As for authority figures such as psychologists, doctors, police, or anyone in charge of children I have a very strong dislike for them. I also do not like people in authority over me.

I know most of my problems, and now I learn how to deal with them.

It took me a long time to really look hard at myself to figure out my problems, to identify them and to realize that they were really a problem. Not just because someone says it's a problem. I needed to find out these things for myself.

While here I hope to learn social skills, economics, how to live without depending on everyone else to do things for me, schooling, anger management and to try and deal with my life. Upgrade my schooling and to raise my self-esteem.

# CHAPTER EIGHTEEN

Peter Whitmore was full of shit. At least that was the conclusion reached by his oldest brother following review of Whitmore's so-called biography.

"Most of the things he mentions are not true, although he may have gone over them so much that he's actually started to believe that they were true," said the man – who now lives in the United States, has distanced himself from his family and doesn't want to be named.

He wanted to set the record straight. Most concerning was Peter's claim that he had raped him when they were younger.

"If this had happened it would have been brought to someone's attention. I didn't really associate with the others since I had my own friends and hung out with them. If he was orally assaulted by me then there would be something he remembers about the description of my private parts, since I am not normal down there," the brother said.

Peter was the youngest of four children. Their father was a clerk in the Air Force who frequently moved the family around. He separated from their mother in about 1970 – prior to Peter even being born. He quickly faded from the picture and played little role in any of his children's lives.

"Our mother was a little different. I didn't really notice much until I grew up and saw some of the childish behaviour," the brother said.

"I was the one that took care of the house and did the dishes and cooked the meals and did the laundry so that everyone else would eat and have clothes to wear. My mother didn't change at all over the years and was still a child in a woman's body."

He disputes many of Peter's claims, including the allegation he was taken from his parents at two weeks old.

"He was almost a year old when we were taken and he wouldn't remember how it all went down," said the brother. "It was my aunt and the police that took us from our mother as at the time she was unfit to care for us."

The man said he and his sister – the second oldest child – were being abused by their mother's boyfriend.

"Peter and the rest of us were all placed in one home for roughly two years. Then our mother kidnapped us and so the saga continued. Peter again was too young to remember this. We were then retrieved again by our aunt and the police and put into another home, a friend of hers took us in," said the brother.

He eventually moved to Germany with an uncle, while Peter and his other two siblings were kept together in another Canadian placement. All of the children continued to have limited supervised visits with their mother, he said.

The brother scoffs at Whitmore's claim he suffered a childhood brain injury. "As far as I know there never was one," he said.

He also was stunned by Peter's claim that he was "sent abroad" on weekends and holidays to be used in the sex trade.

In his biography, Peter claimed he got caught "exploring" the body of a young girl whose parents had taken him the Whitmore children in. Peter claims they were both nine years old at the time and he was beaten and hospitalized because of what he did.

"This family did not have a daughter," said the brother. "And he was never beaten by this family. Since I was the oldest I was taught to take care of them at any cost."

Peter also claimed to have beaten his older brother up on several occasions.

"I was his protector and as far as him beating me up that would be impossible since I was twice the size of him back then and after everything that happened to me I was actually considered a hard-ass," he said.

The brother also denied Peter's claim that their other male sibling "tried to kill me several times", including an incident where he tried to strangle him with a rope.

"Peter was at home, and it was roughly eight or nine at night when this happened. He called the police and made an accusation that my other brother had tied him up with a rope. This was a lie. Peter had been sleeping on a quilt and the marks from the quilt had left marks on him. The marks went away very vividly since I had just returned home with my girlfriend and saw the police taking my brother away in handcuffs. I was beating the hell out of the cop car when they took him away," said the brother.

Peter claimed he later "withdrew" criminal charges against his brother.

"He never did. They were dropped once the police did their investigation. My brother then moved out of the house and swore not to return. His life became a living hell after that with numerous run-ins with the law," he said.

The brother said Peter's claim that he was used "as a pawn between my parents" is also laughable.

"Now this would have been funny since our father had nothing or wanted nothing to do with any of us," he said.

The brother denied they ever learned that their mother's boyfriend had molested their sister, as Peter claimed.

"If this would have happened I would have killed him with my bare hands," he said.

Peter also claimed his brother got a gun and was going to kill the man, but changed his mind and gave him the gun instead.

"Who in their right mind would give Peter a gun," he asked. "Although, our mother's ex did have a rifle under his bed locked up with a trigger guard and case."

The brother said Peter seemed to be living in a "fantasy world" as a child and believed "everyone was out to hurt him."

"Peter was, I believe, 17 when he finally left home. Not by running away but by moving out. Our mother had taken up with another guy with whom she is still with to this day. I had my outs with him as well when it came to Peter getting punished by him. Nobody was going to lay a hand on Peter when I was around. (The boyfriend) was roughly 200 pounds and a large man but I didn't back down and he respected that," he said.

The brother also wanted to clear the air about Peter's bizarre relationship with Terry, who had lived with him in the early 1990s.

"She lived in Canada and he met her through a prison letter exchange program, like a pen pal. She was in a wheelchair and was roughly twice his age. I met her once and that was enough for me," he said.

The brother also takes issue with Peter's claim that he's fathered three children.

"As far as the family knows, he has no children," he said.

He doesn't doubt Peter was prostituting himself, considering he used to visit their sister by showing up in a limousine. Peter would also talk big, including plans to buy an apartment building and "striking it rich."

"There are so many stories he's told over the years that have come back to bite him. His life was not as traumatic as he likes people to think," said the brother, who hasn't spoken to Peter in many years.

· · · · ·

After what seemed like a non-stop barrage of media coverage spanning several years, Peter Whitmore finally had the peace of mind he claimed to have wanted for so long. Now serving his three-year prison term, Whitmore gradually faded into obscurity as the country's attention turned to other more pressing matters.

However, debate was still raging over the way high-risk offenders were being handled. Statistics Canada released an eye-opening report in 2003 that offered some light at the end of what many saw as a very dark tunnel.

Despite all the outrage over paroled criminals, Statistics Canada found that the number of inmates being forced to serve their entire sentence was actually climbing. In 2002, 257 federal offenders were not given any reduction of their sentence. They served every last minute – just like Whitmore had done with his five-year sentence years earlier.

The number was up substantially from the 215 inmates who were "gated" – the term used to describe those who aren't given statutory release after doing two-thirds of their sentence – in 2001. In 2000, 209 inmates were held for their full sentences.

Could it be that public outrage was making a difference?

The federal government had passed legislation in 1986 that allowed for inmates to be kept behind bars for their entire sentence, provided prison officials could show the prisoner posed as substantial risk of violent re-offending.

The new law was introduced during an emergency summer session of Parliament, in response to a wave of murders and violent attacks that had been committed that year by paroled offenders. The federal government estimated at the time that about 50 inmates a year would be affected. In fact, the number quickly swelled.

The all-time high was in 1996, when 484 inmates were denied any form of parole. But it began a steady decline the following year before beginning what now appeared to be a slow climb. There was no doubt that keeping a dangerous prisoner behind bars for their entire sentence was an effective way of ensuring that person can't re-offend for a longer period of time.

But the jury was still out as to whether the move had any significant longer-term impact on crime reduction. Many experts said it did not.

John Vandoremalen, a spokesman for the parole board, told the *Toronto Star* "it doesn't serve the interests of public safety, in the long run, for them to go all the way to the end of their sentence and be released cold turkey onto the street."

He noted a 1996 internal study which found the re-offending rates between those kept behind bars for their entire sentence was 12 per cent. By comparison, the rate only increased to 14 per cent for those who got early release.

Allan Manson, a Queen's University law professor and expert on prison and parole issues, told the *Star* he believes public opinion is playing a role in parole decisions.

"I don't doubt there are some instances when the parole board is very concerned about how they are perceived in public, and that becomes an important influence on decision-making," he said.

Dan Brodsky, Whitmore's long-term lawyer, quickly waded into the discussion. He noted that forcing Whitmore to serve every day of his previous five-year term did nothing to stop him from re-offending. And he predicted justice officials were going to make the same mistake again by keeping his client behind bars for the duration of his current three-year term.

Brodsky said that would simply leave Whitmore back in the same old position of being back on the streets, without any type of structure of support. He said the key issue is treatment, something Whitmore was still having trouble obtaining despite the high-profile nature of his case.

"This is a guy who really needs to be released on parole," Brodsky told the *Toronto Sun*. "It would be in everybody's best interest for him to live under supervision and be gradually released rather than just kicked back onto the streets because we know it doesn't work."

Chuck Cadman, a Conservative Alliance MP from British Columbia who was serving as vice-chairman of the parliamentary justice committee, admitted keeping prisoners locked up longer carried a steep financial cost. Federal figures show it costs about $70,000 a year to keep an inmate in jail, versus about $15,000 a year to supervise them in the community.

"When someone re-offends the community just goes wacko, and rightfully so, saying 'We don't want these guys'," Cadman told the *Star*. "What price are we going to put on a victim's life?"

• • • • •

Peter Whitmore had finally completed his first intensive treatment program – but he wasn't exactly getting glowing remarks from those in charge of treatment.

Yes, he'd gone through the high-intensive sex offender group program at the Regional Psychiatric Centre, finishing up his requirements in March 2003. But many wondered whether he'd actually learned anything.

Just weeks earlier, a routine search of his jail cell had uncovered a familiar yet disturbing sight. Whitmore was keeping a notebook and had a long list of websites listed that contained child pornography. He swore to prison officials the notes were from years ago and not an indication of any pending or future plans.

Jim Blackner, the executive director of the treatment centre, wrote a detailed report on Whitmore later that year. Among the many highlights:

Blackner said: "The circumstances of these offences (previous criminal convictions) are of paramount concern. Not only do they demonstrate his continued lack of respect for the rule of law but they also have direct implications regarding his offence cycle, which continues to result in sexual offences against innocent children. It is clearly evident in the file material that Mr. Whitmore's criminal history has a well-established pattern of sexual offences against children."

Regarding his most recent conviction, Blackner said: "The context of his current offence of failing to comply with a recognizance becomes much more relevant and troubling. Mr. Whitmore has already demonstrated a pattern of sexual violence against children. However, despite any controls the court has imposed, he has simply disregarded them, instead placing his own sexual gratification and impulses at the forefront. His own admission regarding his sexual preferences, and the age of his current and prospective victims speak volumes regarding the level of risk in this case. It is very apparent that Mr. Whitmore has very limited insight into his sexual behaviour. He continues to see these acts as consensual and that the victims were 'willing participants'. In addition, he has no appreciation for the psychological damage imposed upon his victims. In essence, his act of befriending, studying, fantasizing and engaging young children into sexual contact appears to override any sense of what is moral or legal."

On attempts to reduce Whitmore's risk through programming, Blackner wrote: "Clearly any attempt to control Mr. Whitmore's sexual deviance through incarceration, court orders or probation has failed miserably. He continues to demonstrate a poor attitude and a total disregard towards any mechanisms that may assist in controlling the risk of prevent the initiation of an offence cycle that has led to violent sexual offences. Mr. Whitmore has been participating in the high intensity sex offender program at RTC, however a verbal account of his performance provided by his psychologist indicates that 'Mr. Whitmore has made minimal gains as a result of the program'. In fact, during treatment Mr. Whitmore refused to partake in arousal reconditioning simply because he did not wish to stop his fantasies regarding children."

Finally, Blackner summarized the bleak outlooks as follows: "Essentially, Mr. Whitmore is an untreated homosexual pedophile who has established a clear pattern of sexual offending against children. Any previous attempts at managing this behaviour through treatment or imposed conditions has only led to further convictions involving more innocent victims or behaviour that characterizes the onset of his offence cycle. Mr. Whitmore's risk for re-offending in a sexual manner in particular, is high, and his own admission regarding these sexual preferences and desires only exacerbates the risk should he be released prior to warrant expiry."

• • • • •

Whitmore's treating psychologist, Carey Sturgeon, filed his own report in late 2003. His main focus was Whitmore's "dangerous thought patterns."

"Mr. Whitmore exhibited several cognitive distortions related to perceiving himself as a victim based on his personal history of sexual abuse. He also denied and minimized victim harm using distortions regarding prostitutes (e.g. "the prostitutes enjoy the sex that they are paid for", "I am helping prostitutes by getting them off the street and having them work for only me instead of hundreds of other people each year", "They are already dysfunctional, so it doesn't matter if I use them") and his sexually assaulting behaviours (e.g. "I am not hurting children by performing oral sex on them," "I am not hurting them because I don't beat them," "I am not hurting them because they consent to it and they like it," "I am not hurting them because I do nice things for them and treat them better than most people do"). He further exhibited distortions related to entitlement (e.g. "I am entitled to sex if I pay for it," "Everything I want I can take"), the sexualisation of children (e.g. "Children can act seductively," "Children understand sex," "Children enjoy sex"), and the fulfillment of his adult emotional needs in relationships with children (e.g. "Children aged 11 and older can give me love, attention and support that I want," "Children will not reject or criticize my feelings or sexual desires"). Moreover, he exhibited nonsexual antisocial cognitive distortions (e.g. "It's only to blackmail people to get what I want," "Everyone is corruptible," "Everyone is for sale at a price," "I must take revenge"). Overall, Mr. Whitmore was proficient at challenging intellectually his distortions related to sexual offending; however, he did not integrate these challenges at an emotional level, as he reported that he did not believe that the challenges applied to him. That is, he was reluctant to accept that his sexual deviancy was problematic apart from it being against the law."

Sturgeon also raised serious questions about Whitmore's intention to change his behaviour.

"Mr. Whitmore failed to identify specific release plans or long-term goals. Moreover, Mr. Whitmore had not yet integrated his understanding of relapse prevention into his behaviour, as evident by his ongoing use of deviant sexual fantasies and refusal to participate in arousal reconditioning. Further, it is unclear whether Mr. Whitmore will be motivated to implement his relapse prevention plan upon release given his entrenched belief that his sexually deviant behaviour is acceptable. In addition, although he indicated that his primary deterrent for re-offending was the potential for his designation as a dangerous offender and indeterminate incarceration, he also reported that he preferred incarceration to living in the community. He later clarified his position that he would rather be released for a few months every few years than be incarcerated indefinitely as a dangerous offender."

Sturgeon offered a detailed glimpse into therapy, portraying Whitmore as anything but a model student.

"He was antagonistic in group sessions (due apparently to the presence of the male facilitator given his distrust of adult males), reluctant to address treatment issues in individual sessions, and did not complete his homework during the early stages of treatment. However, when he was confronted regarding his lack of progress, his performance improved... Mr. Whitmore demonstrated a significant intellectual understanding of most treatment-related concepts. Moreover, he integrated his treatment gains concerning anger management and problem-solving into his behaviour, as evident by a reduction in reports in his conflict with some staff. However, he failed to integrate his understanding of his offence cycle and relapse prevention into his behaviour, as evidence by his ongoing endorsements of cognitive distortions related to sexual offending, use of deviant sexual fantasies, refusal to participate in arousal reconditioning and reluctance to address issues related to his meeting his intimacy needs with children. Obstacles to Mr. Whitmore's progress in treatment included his lack of motivation to address issues related to his sexual deviancy, his pathological lying and his emotional immaturity."

As a result, Sturgeon suggested that further treatment would simply be a waste of valuable time and resources.

"Mr. Whitmore would be unlikely to benefit from further treatment to address his sexual offending at this time. However, if he were to become motivated to address issues related to his sexual offending in a forthright manner in the future, it would be necessary to reassess his suitability for treatment," he concluded.

The ball was back in Whitmore's court. And the dangerous game was about to continue.

• • • • •

As the country prepared to celebrate Christmas, Peter Whitmore was apparently feeling homesick. Still stuck behind bars in Ontario, Whitmore wrote a letter to prison officials asking once again to be transferred to B.C. to serve the rest of his sentence. He also appeared confident that he would be granted early parole.

Whitmore's letter, dated Dec. 23, 2003, was also copied to his lawyer, his aunt and Toronto police.

*"This letter will confirm a request that I have made several times before. It is my request to be transferred to British Columbia, Canada, where I intent to reside upon my release.*

*I wish to ask the Correctional Services of Canada and the institution which I will be released from in British Columbia to assist in my reintegration of that province.*

*For the record, if I cannot be transferred to British Columbia, prior to my release from custody, I thought it would be appropriate for you to have in writing from me, my intentions.*

*Upon release, it is my intention to travel to British Columbia and take up residence in that province. Accordingly, would you please ensure that whoever needs to know this information be informed as soon as possible? Also, that all necessary files be transferred to British Columbia.*

*The time for my release is growing rapidly near. In the past it has taken quite a bit of effort to find a place to live. I would suggest that we begin working on that issue A.S.A.P."*

• • • • •

## MARCH 5, 2004

Evidently, Peter Whitmore's release wasn't as "rapidly near" as he thought it was. Early parole was being denied.

"The board is satisfied that, if released, you are likely to commit a sexual offence involving a child before the expiration of the sentence you are now serving according to law," they said in written reasons.

Whitmore had actually contributed to the decision, admitting he didn't have any kind of release plan in place. He actually requested an adjournment for his hearing, saying he needed more time "to canvass potential release plans."

The parole board refused, saying they were governed by law to make a decision at least 90 days before a prisoner's statutory release date. Since Whitmore was fast approaching that deadline, the hearing had to proceed.

The parole board had been given a mountain of evidence regarding Whitmore's continued risk, much of which was recapped in their decision.

They noted Whitmore's longstanding request to be moved out west to do his time and said a transfer was likely going to be granted within the next few weeks.

"The board agrees that this would be a prudent move in your case given that you clearly have positive family support in another region," they wrote.

The parole board also expressed concern about the February 2003 search of Whitmore's cell that uncovered the notebook filled with child porn addresses.

"You claim that these addresses were written long ago and they had been in your notebook for some time. The board cannot conclude that there is reliable and persuasive information to indicate that you are planning to commit another sexual offence involving a child, however, the board notes that there is certainly ample information to suggest that you are still consumed by deviant sexual fantasies and cognitive distortions," they wrote.

"In conclusion, your risk continues to be rated as high, even after having completed a high intensity sex offender program. Your criminal history demonstrates that you are either unwilling or unable to abide by your conditions of release and you have not proposed any viable release plans at this juncture. You are hopeful that you will be able to develop release plans in another region where you have community support. The board agrees that this would be the most prudent course in your case."

• • • • •

## AGASSIZ, BRITISH COLUMBIA

Peter Whitmore had gotten his wish. Federal prison officials had green-lighted his request to go west, moving him to Mountain Institution. The medium-security federal penitentiary is about an hour's drive east of Vancouver and specializes in housing inmates who require protective custody.

Sex offenders are always at the top of that list, given their place in the prison pecking order as the low men on the totem pole. Mountain had recently undergone major renovations, expanding their prisoner capacity to 480 and replacing their old, dormitory style living quarters with several new, modernized buildings.

Whitmore's transition to Mountain had been smooth and seemingly non-eventful, and he was acutely aware of the dwindling time left on his sentence. He was getting visits from his aunt, Lynn Hopkins, and appeared pleased to have "come home" following several tumultuous years out East.

Perhaps the change of scenery really was going to make a difference.

# CHAPTER NINTEEN

## SEPTEMBER 3, 2004

It's often been said the best way to survive in prison is to simply shut your mouth and know your role. Not everyone adopts that motto, of course, which is why the potential for violence is always high.

Guards are usually privy to the latest gossip and rumours making the rounds and try to put out as many small fires as possible before they can ever develop into infernos.

Rival gang members are kept apart. Sex offenders – also known as "skinners" – are given protection. Those who are known to have co-operated with police and justice officials – usually called "rats" – are also kept apart from those who might be looking to improve their peer status by dishing out some jailhouse justice.

In a perfect world, inmates and prison officials would work together to create a peaceful, harmonious existence. Prisoners would come forward without fear of reprisal to discuss their current environment, pointing out any problem areas which could then be quickly acted upon by those in power.

But prison is anything but perfect. And most inmates would rather take a bullet than be seen co-operating with their keepers. And on those rare times where an inmate does purport to have vital information, it always has to be taken with a grain of salt.

What are their motives for coming forward? Do they have some kind of personal axe to grind or is it strictly a matter of doing what seems right? What is their relationship, if any, with the person they're informing on?

Peter Whitmore, serving the final months of his latest prison sentence, had clearly rubbed a lot of fellow inmates the wrong way while behind bars. The obvious reason for this was his crimes, which would have made him a moving target in most of the institutions he'd been in. That's why so much of his time had been spent in protective custody and segregation.

Whitmore's personality could be abrasive as well, which had led to several personality clashes in the past. Over the years, guards had witnessed some of these hostile encounters and heard stories about others after the fact, including some from fellow inmates.

Given his track record, guards were prepared to hear – and believe – just about anything about Whitmore, including the following report, which Corrections Officer Joe Clay recorded and submitted to his superiors for follow-up.

On this day, an inmate identified only as "Willoughby" came forward regarding a direct conversation he claimed to have had with Whitmore. He said it had happened while both men were in treatment together.

"Peter commented that he'd like to take a boy child and fuck them," Willoughby told Clay. "I was so shocked it worried me all the next night. Then he showed me another book with children, males aged 3 and up."

• • • • •

NOVEMBER 22, 2004

They had been watching him. And now, finally, they had the smoking gun. A search of Peter Whitmore's cell revealed yet another disturbing stash which only reinforced the tip that had come in from his fellow inmate two months earlier.

Parole officer Lois Gerstman summarized the findings in her report.

"Photographs of young boys, one being of children of another inmate in Mountain Institution taken during a family visiting event, were seized during a search of Mr. Whitmore's cell. Also seized were some cut-out pictures from magazines of young children. Mr. Whitmore indicates that the only photographs he had were of family members and his aunt verifies that she did, in fact, send him pictures of family members i.e., his sons and various nephews. However, until his aunt can identify these pictures they have not been given back to him," wrote Gerstman.

She said there was also information from police that Whitmore may have been trying to find a way to get child pornography brought to him in prison. Whitmore denied the allegation.

"Mr. Whitmore indicates the only thing he has solicited from the community is a subscription to 'People' magazine, which has not actually arrived to him as yet. The corrections management team continues to investigate this new information. It is also of note that cut-out pictures of clothed children pasted into a People's magazine and a Reader's Digest magazine were found in another inmate's possession and reportedly belonged to Mr. Whitmore and also had Whitmore's name on the envelope that contained the magazines. Mr. Whitmore suspects that another inmate is setting him up and denies ownership of the magazines found in possession of the other inmate."

Gerstman included her report in a document titled "Assessment for Decision", which would be forwarded to the parole board in advance of Whitmore's next shot at early parole.

Other reports would soon follow, including a summary of Whitmore's recent meeting with senior psychologist Douglas Boer.

Whitmore was asked how he planned to deal with high-risk situations once he's back on the streets. His answer did little to ease concerns about his future.

"There are no guarantees and I recognize the possibility of re-offending. I can only say that I have made interventions that are necessary to cope with my cycle of deviant thinking and will hopefully signal a better response on my part not to re-offend," said Whitmore.

"I first of all believe that I do not want to re-offend, and to strengthen that I have surrounded myself with a strong support team. I have personally taken steps to correct my life so that I may be able to enter the community safely."

• • • • •

Now less than six months from his mandatory release date – and still with a shot at earlier release – the evidence was piling up that Whitmore was certainly not the changed man he claimed to be.

His psychologist weighed in on the likelihood of obtaining yet another section 810 peace bond against Whitmore once he was out.

"Mr. Whitmore has failed to comply with prior 810 orders and appears not to appreciate the severity of his prior sexual offences. His statement, in prior interviews, that he has not committed any further sexual assaults minimizes his need to appreciate that he can no longer have any contact with minors," wrote Douglas Boer.

"He is also aware that, at least in Ontario, any further sexual offending may have led to the consideration of a dangerous offender application. In light of this, Mr. Whitmore has persisted in having pictures of children in his cell during this incarceration, and his sexual deviancy appears to have remained egosyntonic, in that, he has not been distressed about his sexual crimes apart from their legal consequences," Boer continued.

"Sexual deviance is among the strongest predictors of sexual recidivism. Actuarial and predictive measures place Mr. Whitmore's risk to sexually reoffend as high and his risk for general and violent recidivism as moderate to high. Treatment attempts have been incomplete and treatment reports have not been positive and therefore he remains an 'untreated' sexual offender. This must be prefaced by his understanding of the various components of the sexual offender programs but his failure to adequately internalize what he has learned. It is evidence from file information that Mr. Whitmore has the ability, to some extent, to respond appropriately to questions regarding his history, offences, risk factors, and relapse prevention strategies. However, Mr. Whitmore would benefit from more sexual offender programming provided that he was sufficiently motivated to address his sexual deviancy. At this point, there have been few changes from Mr. Whitmore's prior detention decision date, and release into the community is not supported."

• • • • •

## FEBRUARY 7, 2005

With Whitmore's next parole hearing just days away, parole officer Lois Gerstman summarized her concerns in a final report.

"Although Mr. Whitmore could identify his typical pattern of offending, he generally lacked insight regarding the origins of his offence chain. Although Mr. Whitmore successfully completed the high intensity sex offender program, he was unable to integrate his understanding of relapse prevention into his behaviour, as evidenced by his ongoing use of deviant sexual fantasies and refusal to participate in arousal reconditioning," said Gerstman.

"Further, it is unclear whether Mr. Whitmore will be motivated to implement his relapse prevention plan upon released given his entrenched belief that his sexually deviant behaviour is acceptable...It is the belief of many of the present corrections management team that, while although Mr. Whitmore can repeat what he is taught, he is really not making the connections relating the concepts to his behaviour. Mr. Whitmore stresses that he doesn't want to hurt children in any way and can't understand how fantasizing to fully clothed children is in any way hurting them."

• • • • •

## FEBRUARY 16, 2005

There would be no early release this time – Peter Whitmore was going to do every last second of his sentence. With absolutely no evidence of any significant progress, the National Parole Board quickly ruled they had no other choice but to keep him behind bars as long as possible.

They recapped the previous parole denial from last year and noted Whitmore had done little to address the concerns raised back then. He still had no solid release plan. He was still rationalizing and minimizing his crimes. And he still viewed treatment as more of an inconvenience than a necessity.

Many of the same terms that had been used to describe Whitmore in the past were once again being used.

"You are an untreated sex offender at risk to re-offend."

"You have demonstrated a blatant disregard for your previous release orders."

"You have identified your victims as willing participants."

"You are likely to commit a sexual offence involving a child."

If Whitmore was indeed going to strike again, the parole clearly didn't want it to happen on their watch.

• • • • •

**FEBRUARY 22, 2005**

Was this Peter Whitmore's version of "Fantasy Island?" Another routine search of his prison cell had unearthed the most disturbing discovery to date.

A new stash of pictures, mostly young boys, had been found hidden inside several CD cases. Like previous seizures, some of the pictures were of National Geographic variety and contained nude or partially nude kids. Other images were taken from a calendar which showed nude cherubs.

Guards were especially shocked by a detailed diagram they found inside Whitmore's cell which showed some kind of Secret Island he had apparently dreamed up and drawn out. The crude map included a living quarters surrounded by a dog-run and two large Rottweilers.

Whitmore had written out a sadistic shopping list, including KY lubricant, baby wipes, baby powder and duct tape. There was also a list of preferred food items.

Guards also found another set of papers which spoke of Whitmore's plans to obtain a boat that was equipped with thick soundproof walls and included living quarters isolated below the deck.

Whitmore had some hand-outs he'd been given at a previous treatment session. But they certainly weren't being used for the intended purpose. Instead, Whitmore had hidden a picture of a nude boy in between the pages.

Finally, guards found another list of Whitmore's favourite websites including a special CNN page that had been set up featuring stories about child survivors of a massive tsunami. He had also ripped several pages out of a book – apparently obtained through the prison library – that featured a story about a serial child molester named "Tree Fog". Whitmore had highlighted several areas on the pages that referred to sexual activity with children.

Psychologist Kamie McConnell was asked by prison officials to weigh in on the seizure, which seemed to mirror the one made back in 2002 following Whitmore's last arrest in B.C.

"There is grave concern that Whitmore's fantasies and deviancy is increasing rapidly," said McConnell. "With the detail that he is able to describe his plans, whether fantasy or reality, is concerning."

He was eventually confronted and interviewed regarding the items found inside his cell. Whitmore downplayed the discovery, claiming it was no big deal.

"He stated they had nothing to do with planning to re-offend. He said that he would just use the pictures as a source of income by selling them to other inmates," McConnell wrote in her report.

"He said he just liked to make lists. He said that the island diagram was a place to keep people out, not keep someone in."

• • • • •

Whitmore was transferred in March 2005 to a new sex offender program on the west coast. Called the "low functioning" program, it was the last shot at treatment before Whitmore would be a free man.

It wasn't long before his commitment was being called into question. Whitmore again refused to participate in so-called arousal reconditioning and continued his pattern of making disturbing statements.

As part of the program, inmates were shown a video depicting a woman being raped and then asked for their response. Whitmore quickly jumped in, saying "He had the power when he raped her but she had the power when he went out in cuffs."

McConnell said his answer "is an indication of...his lack of victim empathy in that he saw being taken away in cuffs on the same level as rape."

• • • • •

**JUNE 17, 2005**

The day had arrived. And the message being delivered to all Canadians was sadly familiar.

*"RCMP are warning about a well-known sex offender. Peter Whitmore, 34, was released by Corrections Canada Thursday after serving his entire three-year sentence for breaching a probation order, which was implemented following past sexual offences against children. Whitmore is Caucasian with brown hair and blue eyes. He's 183 cm tall and weighs 110 kg. He's not allowed to be within 300 metres of any park, playground, school ground, swimming area, daycare, recreation/community centre, library or other place where children under the age of 18 are usually found..."*

# CHAPTER TWENTY

## CHILLIWACK, BRITISH COLUMBIA

With the latest section 810 peace bond in place – and the accompanying community warnings from police – Peter Whitmore made a relatively uneventful transition from prison to community living.

His aunt, Lynn Hopkins, had been of great assistance and immediately put Whitmore up in one of the apartment properties she was managing. Whitmore was saying and doing all the right things, complying with his probation and adamant about finally making a fresh start.

He made one noteworthy change shortly after his release, telling police and probation officials he no longer wanted to go by the name of Peter. Instead, Whitmore asked to be called Robert.

This most recent release hadn't generated the same national media buzz as his others. Perhaps it was because he was out of the intense spotlight of Ontario. Or perhaps it was the Karla Homolka factor. Whitmore could thank Canada's most notorious female killer from taking some of the heat off him.

Homolka had just been released from prison after serving her entire 12-year sentence for her role in the sadistic sex-slayings of two Ontario girls. Justice officials had quickly obtained a section 810 peace bond against her, and radio talk shows and newspaper editorial boards across the land were being flooded with callers and writers seething over the justice system.

Whitmore's didn't escape the glare entirely as name was brought up in some of the Homolka coverage, with critics pointing to Canada's inability to control him in the past. Many wondered how Homolka's case would be any different.

With Homolka dominating the headlines, Whitmore quietly began meeting weekly with a local psychologist. The doctor had no expertise in the field of sex offenders and was dealing primarily with issues of social phobia and anxiety.

Whitmore developed a trusting case relationship with Chilliwack RCMP Const. Laural Mathew, who was one of the officers tasked with keeping a close watch on him. Whitmore also enrolled in the Circle of Support and Accountability Program. Any success, however, was short-lived.

Maureen Donegan, coordinator of the program, wrote a report on Whitmore's status in the fall of 2005.

"Robert has displayed a consistent and adamant refusal to discuss any issues related to his offence cycle. He has consistently claimed to the Circle that he has had no deviant sexual fantasies; that he has done nothing to act out such deviancy; that he is adequately accountable to several professionals including police and probation, and therefore does not wish to address accountability issues with his Circle," Donegan wrote.

Whitmore was being kicked out of the program.

Cindy Field, Whitmore's primary case manager with probation, weighed in on Whitmore's situation later in the year.

"Client is currently living alone at City Centre Manor. His aunt, Lynn Hopkins, manages this building. He receives Level 2 disability. Peter has now chosen to go by Robert since the public notification. Peter will continue involvement with two of the women from the Circle of Support and Accountability group; however, there is no tie between the COSA and his support from these women," Field wrote.

"My concern is that Peter is highly manipulative. There was concern that he was manipulating these women and as a result two men were added to his COSA group. This is where the problems began for Peter, as he did not like this. Peter has power and control issues (which he will fully admit) and when he was no longer able to control the group, he wanted it shut down. He still managed to have things his way, by maintaining contact with these two women. Peter was unwilling to admit to the extent of his breaches, his risk, possible fantasies, etc. He wanted to spend his support group time talking about his own agenda and having them provide the assistance he wanted," she said.

"At the present time Peter is upset with me that I will no longer consider these women a formal support group for him and has requested a joint meeting between the four of us. Peter was served with documents to comply with the National Sex Offender Registry. He is fighting his obligation to comply, however has complied pending the court process."

Field said there was concern about the amount of time Whitmore has been spending working on computers.

"He appears to have put together a fairly decent computer system. He admits to talking to persons from around the world. He picks up odd jobs rebuilding and fixing computers. He admits to 'scrubbing' his computer daily. My concern will remain that he may be dealing with child pornography over the Internet and of talking to young persons over the Internet. He adamantly denies this," said Field. "Peter remains a high risk sex offender and will be treated as such."

· · · · ·

In early 2006, Whitmore was asked to begin seeing a forensic psychologist who specializes in pedophiles. He travelled to Vancouver for one meeting, and then declined to see the man for any future sessions.

Whitmore came up with several excuses, claiming a lack of money and transportation. His case manager, Cindy Field, proposed a series of ideas including financial reimbursement and arranged travel. Whitmore wanted nothing to do with it.

He eventually claimed to be suffering from a "phobia" about going to Vancouver. Field noted Whitmore didn't seem to have any problem heading to the big city after he bought a vehicle in the spring of 2006.

Whitmore lost his legal challenge and became part of the sex offender registry, which had been unveiled in 2004 by the federal Liberals.

The idea behind the registry was to form a national database that tracks the movements of convicted pedophiles and rapists and potentially assists in helping police identify suspects in cases.

Whitmore had also been attending bi-weekly group counselling sessions but was deemed a "disruptive" force.

"He attempted to take on a facilitator role and his approach to other group members was at times authoritarian. He attempted to be the main focus of attention in every meeting and would interrupt others while they were talking. These interruptions would have nothing to do with the conversation of topic being discussed and appeared to be an attempt to place the focus of the group back on him," Field wrote.

•  •  •  •  •

## MORINVILLE, ALBERTA
## JUNE 2, 2006

After nearly a full year on the west coast, Peter Whitmore was apparently looking for a change of scenery. He got the blessing of his B.C. case manager to make a short weekend road trip to Morinville, a town of 6,500 located about 35 kilometres north of Edmonton.

Whitmore had been in touch with his brother, David, and arranged for a visit. Police had been notified he was coming.

Brent Miller, a corporal with the Morinville RCMP, greeted him upon arrival. He then sat down with both Peter and David Whitmore to discuss the prospective move.

David explained that he owned his own company, DW Finishing, and did work in new home construction in the Edmonton area. He said he was well aware of Peter's criminal past but was willing to look to the future and give his brother another chance.

As well as a job, David said he wanted Peter to come and work for him as a labourer. He would also open his doors and let his brother live with him.

Miller was tasked with compiling a geographical "risk assessment" of the area and noted 16 "high risk" locations that fell within short walking distance of the trailer park the men would live in. These included parks, playgrounds, swimming pools and elementary schools. Miller also noted there were several young families with children living in the same trailer park.

David Whitmore said he had planned to have his 16-year-old niece and 13-year-old nephew stay with him for the summer – but Miller made it clear that Peter Whitmore would not be allowed to stay under those circumstances.

David told Miller he believed his brother had been "rehabilitated to a point" but agreed that, if unsupervised, he may re-offend. Miller asked Peter Whitmore a series of questions regarding his current feelings toward children. Whitmore was quite candid with his responses, which were noted in a police report.

"The offender openly admits that he is attracted to young males, 12-14 years old. Whitmore stated that he commits sexual offences when he is under stress and that under these circumstances he resorts to offending against street people," police wrote.

"He claimed that he currently copes with stress by playing games on the computer or by watching TV. Furthermore, he advised that he will always have sexual urges towards 12-14 year old boys but that he manages his behaviour by masturbating to his mental fantasies. Whitmore stated that he expected to go to jail for life if he committed any new sexual offences, and that he does not want this to happen."

Police decide the community should be warned that Whitmore has come to town.

• • • • •

JUNE 3, 2006

"Police are warning families in St. Albert and Morinville to keep a close eye on their kids this weekend, when a convicted sex offender visits the area for the next three days," reporter Peter Boer wrote in the pages of the *St. Albert Gazette*.

"This individual represents a significant risk to offend against young male or female victims and poses a considerable risk to the community."

•  •  •  •  •

CHILLIWACK, B.C.
JUNE 12, 2006

His mind was made up. Whitmore was ready to move. The only thing that could stop him was his section 810 peace bond – but that was about to change. The one-year order expired today.

Police had been planning for a renewed application that would see him controlled for at least another 12 months. Whitmore initially agreed to the new order but changed his mind.

A court date was set for June 15 to argue the matter. But with no court order in place, Whitmore was truly a free man for the first time in ages. So he hopped in his car and hit the road. He was off to see his brother.

•  •  •  •  •

JUNE 15, 2006

The Crown's application for a new peace bond had just hit a major snag. Justice officials had recently discovered a 13-year-old criminal charge against Whitmore languishing in their system. He had been charged way back in 1993 with writing a bogus $1,000 cheque to a Black's photography store in Edmonton.

The case somehow got overlooked as Whitmore was sentenced for his first set of sexual offences. Now, the plan was to have it transferred to B.C. so Whitmore could finally deal with it.

The plan was to do the false pretences sentencing at the same time as the peace bond renewal. However, the required paperwork hadn't been brought to court.

Whitmore's hearing – both on the bad cheque charge and the peace bond – was adjourned until July 13. The scene was now going to have to shift to Alberta, where Whitmore had now moved.

Police were quickly notified about the developments and began making their own plans to obtain an 810 order. Time was of the essence.

A "Risk of Significant Harm" report was prepared by Morinville RCMP in advance of the peace bond application which included a detailed history of Whitmore and notes about the recent police interview with him and his brother.

A hearing had been set for June 29 – 17 days after the last order expired. Whitmore was aware of what was happening and promised to be there.

●  ●  ●  ●  ●

MORINVILLE, ALBERTA
JUNE 29, 2006

The courtroom was empty. Whitmore was gone.

# DEVIL AMONG US

• • • • •

## TOPSAIL, NEWFOUNDLAND

Something just wasn't right about the new guy on the block. He had introduced himself to the friendly residents of this community on June 28 as "Robert", a grieving father of two young boys whose wife had recently died of cancer.

He moved into a small apartment on Annie's Drive, a cul-de-sac brimming with young families and kids, and paid his rent through August. Two children lived upstairs from him.

Robert said he was looking for a "fresh start" and was hoping to land a job and permanent residence on the East Coast. He immediately began contributing to the neighbourhood.

A young boy, about seven years old, was upset that his dirt bike wasn't working. Robert jumped at the chance to help out, walking the boy a few blocks down the street to a nearby repair shop.

He bought several neighbourhood kids candy from the corner store, bringing smiles to their faces and handing it out to them in front of their parents.

Robert helped neighbour Brad Durnford, a married father of two young children who works with the Coast Guard, build a small fishing pond for the local Canada Day block party.

He claimed to have a $1.6-million property back home in B.C. But Robert left their community almost as quickly as he entered, disappearing on July 5 after only eight days. He claimed one of his boys was sick back home in British Columbia and needed him.

He promised to be back – bringing his two kids with him.

# CHAPTER TWENTY-ONE

## BROADVIEW, SASKATCHEWAN
JULY 31, 2006

Bernard Tremblay quickly opened his eyes, which immediately darted towards the clock. Worry turned to relief when he saw the time. He had only slept for 20 minutes.

Although his body was begging for more, Tremblay knew it was all he could afford right now. The veteran corporal with the RCMP major crimes unit in Regina was facing the most important challenge of his career.

Youngsters Kyle Mason and Adam Munroe were still missing, their fate in the hands of a dangerous pedophile who likely realized he had nothing left to lose.

Tremblay put his car into gear and backed out of the parking spot he'd found behind the Broadview Hospital to catch a quick nap. He was already feeling guilty about taking a pause – his first since the manhunt began a day earlier.

Tremblay – who found himself thinking a lot about his four young children – began working the phones, calling several fellow officers for an update.

The Amber Alert had been issued following an emergency overnight meeting involving several officers. It had been an easy decision, with all the required criteria being met in this case. Now it was a matter of hoping and praying for a quick and peaceful resolution.

Police detachments across Canada had been sent a bulletin about Peter Whitmore and two missing boys. Tremblay and several officers had personally called nearly every RCMP detachment big and small in Saskatchewan overnight – in some cases waking members up from their sleep and telling them to hit the road immediately and watch for Whitmore's vehicle.

Senior members of the RCMP had given the green light to any overtime that was required. There would be no shortcuts taken.

Tremblay reminded all officers to check every hotel, gas station, campground, parking lot and restaurant they could find. Look at the main roads, the side roads, the back roads – anywhere and everywhere.

Calls were made to the Canada Border Services, to airports and bus depots, and to the Ontario Provincial Police just in case Whitmore had gone east.

Police also contacted a well known criminal profiler who had done extensive work with sex offenders. They wanted to ensure nothing was missing, no stone left unturned.

There was constant communication with the Winnipeg Police missing persons unit, beginning early in the morning when Tremblay had first noticed the bulletin about missing Kyle Mason.

Police had quickly grabbed a photo of Kyle and showed it to the Munroe family – who confirmed he was the same boy that had been in their home and taken their son out for the bike ride that had ended with his kidnapping. Tremblay saw the pain in the Munroes eyes and desperately wanted to bring them a happy ending.

Police set up a public tip line and the calls started pouring in early Monday morning. Tremblay was being briefed about them all.

Most were vague and based largely – if not entirely – on hunches rather than specific, detailed information. But RCMP vowed that no tip would be ignored, and began fanning them out to members across the province – or beyond – as soon as they were received.

One caller, near Minnedosa, Manitoba, was certain he had seen a white man matching Whitmore's description camping there in recent days with a young native boy. The story was true – a white man was camping with a native boy. But it wasn't Whitmore.

One particular phone call did stand out. It was a trucker, out on the western edge of Saskatchewan near the Alberta border, who had spotted something bizarre while making a pit-stop at a gas station washroom. He had even taken a photograph of it to support his claim.

Scrawled on the wall of a bathroom stall was the following: "KYLE...911. HELP."

It seemed straight out of a Hollywood thriller – but it was likely just the product of someone's cruel imagination.

"It's got to be a hoax," Tremblay told fellow officers, who nevertheless followed the requisite steps to follow it up as best as they could. And a hoax is exactly what it proved to be. The prankster, unfortunately, would be difficult to hunt down and identify.

Police couldn't believe someone would take advantage of such a tragic situation and turn it into their own personal punch line. Not that police needed it, but it was yet another reminder of the type of sick people that inhabit the world.

• • • • •

"It's him, it's him. It's Robert on the news. He's kidnapped some kids."

The search for Peter Whitmore had quickly spread across Canada, providing a sudden jolt to residents in Topsail who had welcomed the mysterious stranger to their Atlantic community only weeks earlier.

Brad Durnford saw the television report and immediately felt like he'd been hit in the gut. It had only been a few weeks ago that he was working side-by-side with the man he knew as Robert Summer during the community's annual Canada Day party.

He had grown suspicious since Summer had left suddenly, vowing to return soon with his two children. Durnford had even gone online – mostly at his wife's urging – to try and find out whether the man might be a sex offender. No results had turned up for the name of Robert Summer. Now Durnford knew why.

The good people of Topsail had been conned. Just like the residents of Whitewood. Only Topsail hadn't lost a child. However, it apparently wasn't for lack of trying.

Shortly after news of Whitmore's deception hit the newswire, a family had come forward to police in Newfoundland with a disturbing story.

Whitmore – known to them as Summer at the time – had tried to molest their young son. He paid him $40 for a chance to touch the boy's penis over his clothing. The boy fled.

Durnford and many of his neighbours were now asking themselves one very important question. Were the two "sons" Whitmore spoke of bringing back to Newfoundland the boys he was now accused of kidnapping?

· · · · ·

"We want to do more."

Malcolm Green, the mayor of Whitewood, was on the phone with police. He wanted them to know the community was ready to get involved. He also pointed out the obvious – local citizens were outraged.

That wasn't a surprise to police, who had already received several calls and emails on their tip line with a variation of the same theme.

"Kill Whitmore."

It seemed like everyone wanted a peaceful end to the manhunt – but only for the two boys. They wanted to see Whitmore come out in a body bag, not handcuffs.

Police were feeling the same frustration but couldn't waste valuable time on it. Every second that passed was another opportunity for Whitmore to be harming his two prisoners.

Tremblay had also done a quick read of Whitmore's history and saw the pattern of escalating behaviour. Whitmore seemed to know that he'd likely face a dangerous offender designation if caught – which likely only made him more desperate not to.

Could he actually resort to murder? The possibility was playing repeatedly in Tremblay's head.

· · · · ·

"I know where Adam Munroe is," the woman on the line told police.

She had identified herself as a psychic. Police immediately knew to take anything she said with an enormous truckload of salt. "He's with Amber Redman. And Tamra Keepness."

Redman and Keepness were two Saskatchewan girls who were currently missing and believed to be dead in separate, unrelated cases. Police thanked the woman for her call and hung up.

•  •  •  •  •

## WHITEWOOD, SASKATCHEWAN
## AUGUST 1, 2006

It was the question seemingly everyone in this community was asking. Why had Kyle Mason stayed silent?

There had been several opportunities for him to speak up and say something about his plight. Instead, Mason had seemingly played right along with Whitmore. And that was generating a lot of discussion – and anger.

"It's very easy to brainwash a child," Roz Prober, the co-founder of child advocacy organization Beyond Borders, told the *Winnipeg Free Press* in an interview as the desperate manhunt continued.

She said people who believe victims like Kyle can simply run away or scream for help don't understand how pedophiles like Whitmore operate.

Prober said there have been several high-profile examples of similar situations, including the 2003 abduction of 14-year-old Elizabeth Smart from her home in Utah. Smart was found alive nine months later, living with a polygamist drifter and his wife.

After being reunited with her family, Smart later went on the talk show circuit to explain what happened. She told Oprah Winfrey that Mitchell made her keep a daily diary and write things such as "I like it here. They are nice to me" in reference to him and his wife.

However, Smart wrote several entries in French that stated how much she hated what she was going through.

Sex offenders like Whitmore are experts at "grooming" child victims – and even their parents – into a position of trust and compassion that makes them easy prey, said Prober.

"They can sniff out vulnerability for sure," she said.

Pedophiles pass themselves off as "lots of fun" to kids and convince them life is better in their company. And too often, children like Kyle Mason get blamed if they don't put up a struggle, she said.

Prober said the Kyle's background would likely have been music to the ears of Whitmore – a troubled, somewhat hardened young kid from the big city with a prior history of running away from his family.

"Parents would be putty in the hands of a skilled con artist like Whitmore. He's used to having his needs met by children. He's developed very sophisticated skills to disarm those who might question him," she said.

There were several others riding to the defence of Kyle Mason and his family, including Winnipeg police.

"This individual (Whitmore), he duped the family. He became their friend," Const. Jacqueline Chaput told the media.

Lianna McDonald, executive director of Child Find in Manitoba, had met with the Mason family following Kyle's disappearance and said she was shocked at how Whitmore had manipulated them.

"They are completely torn apart over how this whole thing unfolded," she said. "It's beyond concerning."

She reminded parents to be careful about any men who show an over-interest in their children and suggest activities that could get a child away from parents – such as camping.

• • • • •

Vic Toews, the federal justice minister, was closely monitoring the Whitmore situation and getting swamped with media requests for interviews.

Toews was careful in his comments, given the ongoing situation, but promised changes would be coming. He said it was obvious the justice system had failed to stop Whitmore from re-offending and tougher measures were needed to control the likes of him.

"We should never be releasing dangerous offenders cold into society," Toews told the *Winnipeg Free Press*.

He suggested a more Americanized-version of parole might be needed in which an offender who had served their full sentence could be hit with a slew of tough conditions upon release.

Of course, section 810 of the Criminal Code – the peace bond provisions which Whitmore had twice been under – was supposed to address that very issue.

Toews did turn some heads across the country when he brought the up the issue of dangerous offender legislation. He questioned why Whitmore had managed to dodge the label – and the mandatory indefinite prison sentence that comes with it – despite his long criminal history.

He suggested prosecutors might have dropped the ball in that regard.

"There could have been a dangerous offender application by one of the provincial attorney generals," he told the *Free Press*.

The federal Conservatives had already promised new legislation was coming that would see anyone convicted of a third violent and/or sexual offence – and hit with a federal prison sentence of at least two years – facing the onus of proving why they shouldn't be declared a dangerous offender.

Toews said perhaps the "three-strikes-and-you're-out" law might need to be expanded to include people who get provincial sentences of less than two years, as Whitmore had done in some of his priors.

Toews said the easiest way to use the dangerous offender provision to protect society was to get the country's justice ministers to agree to a standard protocol which would ensure the rarely-used Criminal Code section is more frequently used regardless of the province.

Failing that, Toews said he could look into legislation which would require judges to consider the provision if certain requirements were met.

"Does it need to be protocol; does it need to be actual legislation? That is something my department is examining in conjunction with provincial departments at this time," he said.

• • • • •

Al Scott, a veteran Winnipeg police commander, had his own ideas on how to stop high-risk sex offenders. He called on Ottawa to fix the national sex offender registry – something he called good in theory but poor in execution.

Scott felt compelled to speak out after some members of the public and media started questioning how Whitmore was able to slink across Canada so easily without being detected.

Scott said it was time the public realized what police were forced to deal with.

"We just can't access the registry on any missing person's case. Law enforcement in Canada has long sought for improvements in the registry because we find it very restrictive," he told the *Free Press*.

Case in point – Whitmore's name was one of 13,550 known offenders currently entered in the national database. However, police had no authority to begin poking around once the initial missing persons report on Kyle Mason came into their office. That's because access is only allowed in the case of a reported sex crime. According to federal stats, the two-year old registry had been used a total of 44 times across Canada.

RCMP Cpl. Al Fraser echoed Scott's concerns while trying to explain how police lost track of Whitmore after the peace bond lapsed.

"Once he's free and clear he has rights and freedoms as any other Canadian," he told the *Free Press*. "It's not that hard for someone to disappear. It's a big country."

• • • • •

## NEAR KIPLING, SASKATCHEWAN

Pat Beaujot couldn't stop thinking about those two boys. The Saskatchewan farmer had been following the Peter Whitmore story closely and was sickened by what was happening.

He had given his nine-year-old son a few extra hugs these past two days and told his wife, Judy, to make sure she watched the boy closely while he was at work. They even went so far as to show their son a picture of Whitmore and telling him he wasn't to leave their yard until further notice.

It was a major downer for a curious young boy living on the Prairies in summer, but Beaujot would rather be safe than sorry.

Beaujot had read and heard about the Amber Alert and closely studied the description of Whitmore and his vehicle. Like everyone in the area, he was keeping his eyes open for anything unusual.

It was early afternoon on this day when Beaujot was heading home for lunch from the local seed equipment business he owns.

Beaujot decided he'd drive a little slower, take as many back roads, and watch a little more closely about what he saw along the way. He was trying to pay special attention to any outlying buildings – such as sheds and huts – and properties he knew to be abandoned. One of those happened to be just down the road from his place, about a quarter-mile away.

It was owned by Don Toth, the provincial MLA for the Moosomin region. The dilapidated, two-storey farmhouse had sat empty about 18 years and had become a bit of a local nuisance. It was a popular spot for local teens to gather and drink alcohol after dark, as evidenced by the shards of broken glass which littered the property.

Toth knew it had to go but had hung onto it for sentimental releases. It originally belonged to members of the Varjassy family, who were well-known in the Kipling-area.

Geraldine Varjassy still lived nearby, just one property to the north, and cherished the place where her late husband had been born and raised. She held many fond memories of family gatherings inside and was saddened by what it had become.

With his search winding down and lunch on his mind, Beaujot decided to take a quick peek at the old Varjassy homestead. Beaujot drove by slowly, at first spotting nothing except a thick cover of trees and bushes. But his eyes were soon drawn to an unusual sight. Tire tracks.

The metre-long Prairie grass had been pushed down; the direction indicating someone had recently entered the property. Beaujot went a little closer, now in sight of the driveway. He followed the path of the tracks, his hands gripped tightly on the wheel and his eyes focused straight ahead.

Beaujot was now close enough to the main property to glance inside. The back door appeared to be slightly opened. But he saw no movement inside, nor any evidence of anyone being around. The tire marks continued to lead towards a run-down garage.

Beaujot pulled up close, first spotting a KFC chicken box and some discarded bones lying on the ground. He looked up. His heart nearly stopped.

Parked inside was a blue Dodge Caravan with wood panelling on the sides and Alberta licence plates. Beaujot recognized it immediately.

It was Peter Whitmore's.

# CHAPTER TWENTY-TWO

## REGINA, SASKATCHEWAN

The timing couldn't have been worse.

Bernard Tremblay had been looking forward to a long overdue visit with his out-of-town parents – until the biggest case of his career wiped away the prospects of spending some quality family time together.

Still, with the plane tickets already paid for, Tremblay and his folks decided they should come to Saskatchewan regardless. Any other plans beyond that remained up in the air and subject to change.

Tremblay felt bad, but knew his parents would understand. His work was important to him – and this was no ordinary case.

Tremblay at least wanted to greet them on arrival, so he arranged to be available by cell phone and pager while he made the quick trip to the Regina Airport.

The stress of the past two days was taking its toll on Tremblay and his co-workers. Seeing his parents, even if just for a few minutes, would be a welcome relief.

Tremblay got the airport just in time. His mother and father were on the ground, having already collected their luggage. He gave them both a big hug.

*Ring. Ring. Ring.*

It was Tremblay's cell phone. He pulled out of the embrace and immediately answered the call. It was the news he'd been waiting for.

They'd found the missing boys.

•••••

## NEAR KIPLING, SASKATCHEWAN

Pat Beaujot was waiting on the highway, at the end of the overgrown driveway, when the swarm of police cars began to arrive.

It had only been a few minutes earlier that Beaujot had raced to his nearby phone and yelled for his wife, Judy, to call for help.

"I found Whitmore's van," he said.

Beaujot didn't want to place the call himself for fear of giving Whitmore – who he suspected was holed up inside the abandoned farmhouse with the two boys – a chance to escape. He sped back to the scene, parked on the highway and waited.

A million thoughts and questions ran through Beaujot's mind. What was going on inside the house? Could Whitmore see him? And what was he going to do if the fugitive tried to escape?

He had convinced himself Whitmore probably heard his truck running, or maybe the sound of the garage door opening and closing. Would that only leave him more desperate, more dangerous?

Beaujot had called for some backup in the form of Vernon Varjassy, a good friend and neighbour who lived right next door. The two men then positioned themselves at the end of the driveway, prepared to do whatever it took to ensure Whitmore didn't get away and the two boys were saved.

• • • • •

Const. Tim Schwartz and members of the RCMP Emergency Response Team were prepared for anything. They knew they were dealing with a very dangerous man. There's no telling what he had done to the two boys.

And the possibility that one or both of them were dead had entered their minds on more than one occasion. They had all driven as fast as possible, coming from all directions in rural Saskatchewan, to converge on the farmhouse. More than a dozen in total,

There were no sirens – for fear of alerting Whitmore they had found him. Upon arrival, police began setting up a command post on the highway. There was a definite sense of urgency. But there was also a need to be careful, to avoid inflaming an already volatile situation.

The first step was trying to confirm that Whitmore and the boys were in fact inside the home. The next step was trying to establish contact, find out their conditions and hopefully coax Whitmore to come out.

Three trained, experienced crisis negotiators were on the way and would be given the enormous responsibility, where lives literally hung in the balance and any mistakes could have deadly results.

Beaujot and Varjassy were told to leave the area. The men, thankful for police arrival, were happy to oblige.

Schwartz, among the first to get to the scene, stepped out of his vehicle to get a closer look. He couldn't believe his eyes.

There, in the distance, was the image of a little blond-haired boy running towards him. Schwartz knew right away what was happening.

Adam Munroe was making a run for freedom – straight into Schwartz's open arms.

• • • • •

It was a remarkable scene, the stoic police officer and the frightened little boy locked in a dramatic embrace. Schwartz quickly retreated back to his vehicle, taking Adam with him. The boy looked to be in relatively good health but was clearly terrified.

Several officers soon came to Adam's side, telling him repeatedly that he was safe, in good hands, that his parents had been so worried and would be very happy to see him. He was given water and re-assured that his nightmare was over. Adam managed a smile.

There were questions, so many questions. At the top of the list was the whereabouts of both Kyle Mason and Peter Whitmore. Adam explained what had happened.

Whitmore had seen the police pull up to the property. He knew he was caught. He ordered both boys to grab whatever they could from inside the main farm property – candles, flashlights, some food – and then directed the to a small barn on the back of the sprawling yard.

The others were still inside the barn. But why had Adam been able to break free but not Kyle? Why didn't Whitmore stop him?

"He told me to go," said Adam.

• • • • •

Police were shocked that Whitmore would simply allow one of his kidnapping victims to leave. Perhaps that was a sign the matter would end quickly, as Whitmore had given up what could have been a major bargaining chip in any kind of stand-off situation.

Still, he had Kyle. And police knew they still had work to do.

They had much more to ask Adam but knew this wasn't the time or place. But just before they whisked him from the scene to the police station – and a happy reunion with his family – police wanted to know a little more about what they were up against.

Did he have any weapons?

"Yes," said Adam. "He has a gun."

It wasn't the answer police were hoping to hear. What's more, Adam explained how Whitmore had pointed the weapon at both him and Kyle during their ordeal.

"He said it can shoot through body armour," said Adam.

• • • • •

## WINNIPEG, MANITOBA

"Jennifer, they found him!"

Janet Stewart, the supper-hour news anchor of CTV Winnipeg, had called her neighbour the moment the development had come across the newswire. And while

Jennifer Mason's son, Kyle, remained inside the farmhouse with Peter Whitmore, there was reason to be optimistic.

Kyle was still very much alive. And police were now working on his release.

"It's almost over, sweetheart," said Stewart, a compassionate woman who had been hit hard by her personal connection to this story.

Mason was quickly in contact with the Winnipeg police missing persons unit. Det.–Sgt. Randy Antonio came over to the Mason home to debrief the family. He also warned them a deluge of media was likely to follow. They drew their blinds and took their phone off the hook.

Antonio assured Mason police would do everything possible to ensure Kyle remained safe. They were working to establish communication with Whitmore to find out what it would take to bring the case to a swift, safe conclusion.

Mason wanted to believe that would happen, that it wouldn't be long before she could hold Kyle in her arms the way the Munroes were likely embracing Adam this very moment.

But she couldn't escape the feelings of utter helplessness and dread as she waited anxiously by the phone, Kyle's fate still hanging in the balance.

• • • • •

## NEAR KIPLING, SASKATCHEWAN

Tension was high inside the police command post. Officers had called in every available resource – including the canine unit and a police robot – and had officers on the ground and in the air.

An ambulance sat in the distance, ready to respond if needed. Police hoped that wouldn't be necessary – at least not for Mason.

Police had managed to deliver a walkie-talkie to Whitmore to finally open the lines of communication. But what they heard was grounds for concern.

"Maybe I should just come out shooting," he said.

Negotiators told Whitmore that wasn't necessary, that this could all be resolved peacefully by talking it through. They asked for assurances that Kyle was okay.

Whitmore insisted he was, then held the walkie-talkie out and was heard saying "Tell them you're okay." A boy's voice was heard in the background, confirming as much.

Police turned the discussion to Adam Munroe, how the boy was back safe with his family and how Kyle's family wanted a similar resolution. Whitmore briefly explained why he had elected to let Adam go.

"He was too young," he said. "He was suffering."

Police told Whitmore he'd done the right thing. Now he just needed to do it again and let Kyle go. Whitmore said he couldn't do that. He knew he had messed up and would be going to jail for a long time. Whitmore said he'd run out of chances, that this would finally be the crime that would land him behind bars forever.

Police tried to downplay any criminal consequences, telling Whitmore he didn't have to worry about that right now and everything would work out. Just let Kyle go.

No, said Whitmore. He knew police would come after him, probably shooting, the moment he was alone. He couldn't let that happen. Whitmore said he was ready to go back to prison but that he needed some glimmer of hope.

"I don't want to be a dangerous offender," he said.

Police told him nothing was concrete, that there was room for discussion. Whitmore seemed interested. He wanted to know more.

Police said they would get back to him.

• • • • •

## INSIDE THE FARMHOUSE

"You're my only friend, the only one who understands me."

Peter Whitmore was a master at the art of mind control. And he had managed to get inside the head of the 14-year-old pawn that remained in his possession.

Kyle Mason desperately wanted to be back with his family. The past few days had been a nightmare filled with fear and worry and confusion.

But he also felt the need to stay. Whitmore had told him so many stories, threatening to go back to Winnipeg and kill his mother and sisters.

And then there was the claim that Kyle's family had paid Whitmore to take him from them.

"Your mom and step-dad gave me $6,000 to take you. They didn't want you. They said you were nothing but trouble," said Whitmore.

It sounded ridiculous. But Kyle knew he had given his parents fits in the past and was hardly the perfect son. He was so confused.

"If you leave me, I'll kill myself," Whitmore told him now as they hid out in the barn.

The sun was beginning to fade. Night would soon be taking over. Kyle had seen the gun, watched Whitmore point it at Adam and stared down the barrel himself. And he had listened to Whitmore offer to give it to him, practically begging Kyle to shoot him.

"I want you to kill me," he said.

Kyle couldn't do it. He refused to take the weapon.

Whitmore appeared to be growing more agitated by the hour, clearly affected by the knowledge that his time was nearly up. In a momentary fit of rage, he grabbed whatever he could find – a pack of tobacco and a can of WD-40 – and mixed the items in a glass of water. He then poured the concoction down his throat in what Kyle thought was a suicide attempt.

Only nothing happened. Whitmore remained alert and Kyle was still his prisoner.

Just when the situation started to look hopeless, police were back on the walkie-talkie with an interesting proposal.

They wanted to make a deal.

• • • • •

"We believe Kyle is in good health. But all of our information on him has come from Mr. Whitmore."

RCMP Sgt. Tammy Patterson had come out to address the media, which was gathered just behind the police roadblock set up on the highway.

She was not authorized to provide any specific details but confirmed that negotiations were ongoing and police remained hopeful the situation would end soon.

But she said police weren't going to rush into anything and would take as much time as needed.

• • • • •

The offer seemed too good to be true. But Peter Whitmore had been assured by police they were serious.

A senior Saskatchewan Crown attorney, Jeff Kalmakoff, had spoken with police and agreed on a document that promised justice officials would consider NOT seeking a dangerous offender designation or life sentence against Whitmore in exchange for his guilty plea.

Police had the paper in their hand and told Whitmore they weren't trying to trick him. As well, Kalmakoff said they would recommend he be placed in a private, segregated cell to ensure other inmates couldn't get at him.

Whitmore was aware his latest crimes were generating plenty of news coverage and would make him an easy mark behind bars.

The letter read as follows:

*"To Whom It May Concern. Re: Peter Whitmore. I will recommend to Saskatchewan Justice that the Crown prosecutor will not seek a dangerous offender designation for Mr. Whitmore. Nor a life sentence. Mr. Whitmore has agreed to plead guilty to any offences he has committed in the last 24-48 hours. Mr. Whitmore has requested to be housed in a single cell under complete segregation and I do not oppose that request. I have discussed this with Mr. Jeff Kalmakoff, Crown Prosecutor, Saskatchewan Justice, Regina."*

Whitmore was pleased with the proposal and felt a sense of pride that police had listened to him and taken his demands seriously. He knew his back was against a wall and there was no way to escape. But at least he'd just guaranteed himself a good shot at getting out one day.

It was just after 11 p.m. the deal was finally consummated. Kyle came out first, slowly and cautiously, and was immediately whisked away by heavily-armed officers who had surrounded the barn.

Whitmore followed, his hands in the air. He was ordered at gunpoint to the ground, laid down and immediately swarmed.

It was over.

# CHAPTER TWENTY-THREE

## WINNIPEG, MANITOBA
AUGUST 2, 2006

"We have your son here. Do you want to talk to him?"

Jennifer Mason couldn't believe what she was hearing. Her prayers had been answered.

"Of course, put him on!" she screamed excitedly at the officer who was calling from Saskatchewan.

Kyle took the phone. He was crying.

"Why did you leave me with this guy?"

Mason felt sick. She had no good answer for him. Kyle continued to weep, telling his mother how scared he was.

"He kept telling me he was going to hurt you guys," he said.

Mason assured him they were just fine. Perfect, actually, now that he was safe. Their conversation lasted several minutes and ended with Mason vowing to come to Saskatchewan right away to see him.

Police said they would be waiting at the detachment in Broadview. Jennifer quickly grabbed a few essentials, hopped in the car and started driving through the night.

· · · · ·

## BROADVIEW, SASKATCHEWAN

It had been a joyous reunion, a family back together after the most horrendous 48 hours of their lives.

And now the parents of Adam Munroe wanted to make a brief public statement to thank everyone – the police, the community, the Amber Alert system and all their friends, family and neighbours.

"We cannot express our deep felt gratitude...for helping Adam to find his way home," Larry Munroe said, his voice trembling and cracking as he stood outside the RCMP station reading a prepared written statement. "The system really worked."

Munroe asked the media to respect his family's privacy at this difficult time, saying they now wanted to focus on making sure their son gets all the support he needs.

"Adam is doing as well as can be expected. My son did everything I knew he would to get away. He's a very strong little boy. And he will get better," he said. "We've been humbled by all the love and support."

Paula Munroe couldn't bear to face the cameras herself and had stayed inside the police station. Her husband quickly re-joined her, unable to continue talking. They were so happy to have Adam back home.

But they knew, in many ways, the hardest battle was still to come.

· · · · ·

It was every tool a child predator would need.

And a search of the farmhouse – along with two other nearby properties where Kyle Mason said he and Whitmore had "squatted" during their week in rural Saskatchewan – uncovered a disturbing cache of tools.

Police fanned out to search every inch of the properties, wanting to collect as much evidence as possible. Investigators quickly located the gun that Adam Munroe had told them about – the one Whitmore had held to the boys' heads and claimed could pierce through police armour. It turned out to be a pellet gun, albeit a very realistic looking one.

Police also recovered a knife that had been used to threaten the boys, several packages of lubricant and a long chain that was attached to a bed in the farmhouse. They would later learn the horrific relevance of that device.

Police also recovered some pubic hairs which would be sent for analysis and later found to belong to Kyle Mason.

Finally, there was the stash of computer disks that Whitmore had been carrying around. Police opened up the files and found 49 pictures of children – mostly young boys in swimsuits.

More disturbing were 31 video files which showed boys engaged in sexual activity with adults. None featured Whitmore and they hadn't been locally produced, but it was clear Whitmore had been using them for his own pleasure and likely to help entice his victims.

• • • • •

Kyle Mason's embrace was strong and firm, the young boy not wanting to let go of his crying mother as they reunited inside the Broadview police station.

"Mommy, I never thought I'd see you again," said Kyle.

Al Baxter stood quietly at the side. He had joined his common-law wife for the drive but knew seeing Kyle again was going to be tough. He was still blaming himself for what happened and knew Kyle likely harboured all kinds of anger.

"I'm so proud of you," he said.

Police explained that they would need to speak with Kyle about what happened. The same process would be done with Adam. Family members were encouraged to sit in on the interviews for support.

Police warned both victims it could be difficult, as they would have to take the boys through every step of their ordeal. They wanted to ensure Whitmore was punished for everything he did, so full disclosure was a necessary evil.

* * * * *

*Winnipeg Free Press* EDITORIAL – "How Did It Happen?"

*How does this happen? How does a career pedophile such as Peter Whitmore once again become the object of a police search and a national effort to rescue a 10-year-old boy who was abducted from Whitewood, Sask., and to locate a 14-year-old boy from Winnipeg, when his record of the sexual molestation of children extends back 13 years and has been relentless in its consistency?*

*Police believe that Mr. Whitmore first abducted Winnipeg teenager Kyle Mason, who was last seen on June 22 in Brandon. They believe that he then abducted 10-year-old Adam Munroe in Saskatchewan. But how could a serial pedophile have been roaming freely through the small towns and cities of Canada, trolling for young boys?*

*Mr. Whitmore has not been convicted of anything in this case, but his record as a pedophile is appalling. In 1993, he was convicted of abduction and five sexual crimes committed on four young boys in Toronto. He served 16 months, an indication of how seriously that court, at least, regarded such crimes.*

*Only nine days after his release, he abducted an eight-year-old girl, for which he was sentenced to more than four years in jail. Released from prison in November of 2000, he was arrested in a Toronto motel room with a 13-year-old boy. For that he was sentenced to one year in jail.*

*And finally, in 2002, he was sentenced to three years in jail after being caught with a five-year-old-boy and a "rape kit" in his backpack.*

*Mr. Whitmore served the entire three years of that sentence before being released. He is now accused of abducting two more children.*

*What went wrong here? Apparently, just about everything. In the last 13 years, Mr. Whitmore has been sentenced to a total of nine years and 10 months in prison for sexually assaulting and/or abducting seven young children. No one in the judicial system seems to have noticed that he might be a habitual pedophile, a dangerous offender who should be jailed indefinitely. He did his time – short bursts, all of it – and went on to offend again.*

*Federal Justice Minister Vic Toews said yesterday that he will look at ways to apply the dangerous offender provision more widely, but that does not explain why it was never used against Mr. Whitmore.*

*Curiously, Mr. Whitmore himself understood the situation better than did his prosecutors and his judges. In 1993, when he was first convicted of sexual offences, he told the court that his compelling sexual desire for young children would inevitably lead to "more serious harm" if he was not stopped. As his subsequent convictions prove, he was exactly right. Why did no one in a position to do something about this pay any attention to what he said?*

*This case caught the attention of the nation and focused it on the judicial system. Mr. Toews promises changes, but it is not really change that is needed so much as a determination to use laws that are already on the books.*

• • • • •

Rural Saskatchewan was still buzzing about the sudden resolution of the case – and many were now openly questioning Kyle's role in all this. Some locals speculated that perhaps the teen would end up facing charges as well. After all, hadn't he helped Whitmore kidnap Adam?

Some of Mason's extended family members back in Winnipeg were also beginning to worry. They felt the news coverage of the case had been tilted largely towards painting just Adam Munroe as a victim. Kyle, it seemed to them, was being given the short shrift.

Police quickly put an end to the suspicion when they announced later in the day that Whitmore was going to face a slew of charges pertaining to both young boys.

Kyle, like Adam, had done nothing wrong. Both were victims.

And the heartbreaking police interviews with both had revealed the extent of the damage the sadistic Whitmore had done to them.

• • • • •

Dan Brodsky hadn't been surprised by the phone call. His old client, Peter Whitmore, wanted to talk. Police had arranged for the chat while holding Whitmore in custody shortly after his arrest.

From his Toronto office, Brodsky had briefly touched base with Whitmore and been given an overview of what had gone down the previous night. He knew the police had made some promises. And he intended to ensure they were kept.

Brodsky was hoping he might be able to act for Whitmore but knew there would likely be some challenges. The Saskatchewan government likely wouldn't be very happy about the prospect of paying taxpayer dollars to an Ontario lawyer to represent the most notorious criminal to come their way in some time.

But Brodsky was prepared for a fight – and he believed he had plenty of ammunition at his disposal.

• • • • •

REGINA, SASKATCHEWAN
AUGUST 3, 2006

Wearing a scowl on his face and a grey sweatshirt with the word "Canada" written across it, a tired Peter Whitmore shuffled into the packed provincial courtroom shortly after 9 a.m. under heavy security.

His hands were cuffed behind his back and Whitmore briefly scanned the scene but didn't stop to make eye contact with anyone during his two minute court appearance.

A Legal Aid lawyer spoke on Whitmore's behalf, asking for the matter to be adjourned for a week. He said Whitmore wanted to be represented by Dan Brodsky but there were funding issues that would have to be resolved.

The Munroe family didn't travel from their Whitewood area home for the appearance, while the Masons had already driven home to Winnipeg. However, the court appearance wasn't lacking in drama.

The public got its first glimpse at the charges Whitmore was facing – and they hinted at the kind of horror the two boys had been put through.

The celebratory mood of finding the two boys alive was certainly dampened a bit as the public learned of the 15 charges in total, which read as follows:

- Forcible confinement of Kyle Mason between July 23 and August 1.
- Numerous sexual assaults causing bodily harm against Kyle Mason between July 23 and August 1.
- An additional count of sexual assault causing bodily harm against Kyle Mason between July 23 to August 1.
- Abduction of Adam Munroe on July 30.
- Forcible confinement of Adam Munroe on July 30.
- Numerous sexual assaults causing bodily harm of Adam Munroe between July 30 and August 1.
- Uttering threats to kill Kyle Mason between July 23 and August 1.
- Uttering threats to kill Kyle Mason's family between July 23 and August 1.

- Uttering threats to kill Adam Munroe between July 30 and August 1.
- Assaulting Adam Munroe between July 30 and August 1.
- Possessing a weapon – to wit a pellet gun – between July 30 and August 1.
- Possessing a weapon – to wit a knife – between July 30 and August 1.
- Possessing child pornography between July 23 and August 1.
- Making child pornography available to Kyle Mason between July 23 and August 1.
- Making child pornography available to Adam Munroe between July 30 and August 1.

The sexual assault charges meant publication bans would be placed immediately on the names of both boys.

"There's a fucking rapist in court," one angry member of the public said outside the courtroom. The woman's comments likely reflected what much of the community, and country, were thinking.

• • • • •

Tammy Patterson, the RCMP spokesperson, held court with reporters following Whitmore's court appearance. She wanted to set the record straight in regards to questions that were being asked about Kyle Mason.

The teen never was considered anything other than a victim, she said. The questioning of him – in the presence of his family – was routine and part of the normal course of investigation.

She noted the charges which had been laid, which police hoped would clear up any perception that Kyle had done something wrong.

Meanwhile, Patterson said the police officers involved in the case were battling a range of emotions.

"There's a great sense of relief and they are happy it's been resolved," she said. But privately, many officers were stunned and horrified at what Whitmore had done to the boys and wondering if they could have done anything else to find them sooner.

• • • • •

Jennifer Mason was too upset to speak publicly at this time. But the Winnipeg woman wanted everyone to know how much she appreciated their support. She recorded the following message on her voice mail upon returning home to the city, her son at her side.

"I'd like to thank everybody for their concerns and support during this difficult time. I'd also like to thank those who were directly for the safe return of Kyle. May the Creator be with you and all your families. From our family to yours, we thank you with all the love in our hearts."

• • • • •

Peter Whitmore's arrest and the new charges were making headlines everywhere and prompting people to speak out. Public pressure was clearly mounting for some kind of explanation as to why Whitmore was free to roam about the country and attack two more innocents – despite all the previous warnings about his high risk that were now being repeated to the entire country.

Canadian Prime Minister Stephen Harper promised his government would take action in the wake of the case.

"We're protecting our children from sexual predators by raising the age of consent from 14 to 16. And we will be toughening dangerous offender legislation, as well," he told reporters during a stop in Cornwall, Ontario.

Police in Newfoundland were also confirming an active investigation following a complaint from a young boy and his parents about their contact with Whitmore during his brief, mysterious stay out east.

Insp. June Layden of the Royal Newfoundland Constabulary admitted police had no idea Whitmore was in their community until they heard from residents.

"He sure hit the jackpot when he moved in here. There are so many kids that in his eyes he must have been delighted. There are always a dozen, maybe 15 kids playing out there in the cul-de-sac at any given time," local resident Brad Durnford told the *Winnipeg Free Press*.

"We are angry. This is just awful. It's a sign that our laws in Canada need changing. What happened out there in Saskatchewan could have easily happened to us here."

Residents of Topsail were now wondering what Whitmore's plans were for their community. The fact Whitmore left behind a car and rented apartment suite – and claimed he would be returning with his two boys – has led to speculation he might have been planning to bring the two kidnapping victims to Newfoundland.

And why did he leave so abruptly?

"Maybe with the sexual assault incident that's come up here, he got freaked out, tried something that didn't work out and had to leave," said Durnford. "But I believe he planned to come back."

• • • • •

Dan Brodsky knew how to get the public's attention. And that was exactly what the veteran lawyer was trying to accomplish when he gave an exclusive interview to the *Winnipeg Free Press* and revealed how the Peter Whitmore case could quickly be wrapped up.

"This whole fiasco could be resolved in two weeks," said Brodsky.

The solution was simple. Whitmore would immediately plead guilty to kidnapping and sexually assaulting his two victims – sparing them from testifying – if justice officials honour the signed deal that led Whitmore to surrender.

However, Brodsky warned there would be problems if justice officials tried to renege on the deal. He said a long, drawn-out legal process was in store "for years" if the Crown didn't agree to spare Whitmore a dangerous offender designation that could mean he would remain in prison forever.

"But this is about much more than Peter Whitmore. It's about the integrity of the police. Police can't do their jobs if the message that comes out of Mr. Whitmore's case is that when you speak to a police officer, all you're speaking to are liars and cheats," Brodsky insisted.

He said Whitmore only agreed to come out and end the stand-off after being assured by police they wouldn't seek the maximum penalty against him.

Brodsky had now received a copy of the RCMP letter, which was written and signed by both Insp. Len Del Pino and Saskatchewan prosecutor Jeff Kalmakoff during the course of negotiations. Brodsky said because the prosecutor's signature was on the document, the agreement should be binding on justice officials.

Saskatchewan Justice Minister Frank Quennell responded to Brodsky's proposal, saying he wasn't part of any deal to get Whitmore to surrender and noted that police can't bind justice officials about how they will handle a prosecution.

Quennell told reporters he supported any "appropriate and legitimate" methods used by police to capture Whitmore and that his office would deal with the case "in a way that protects the public."

Brodsky said the best resolution for everyone involved would be to honour what was in the letter and bring a speedy conclusion to a case that gripped the country.

He said the Crown wouldn't be prevented from asking for a long prison term and obtaining a long-term offender designation, which would add 10 additional years of intense supervision upon Whitmore's release. The decade of parole-like conditions would be suspended each and every time Whitmore was caught in violation and sent back to prison, Brodsky said.

"It's almost a matter of certainty he would get (a long-term designation). He could sit in the penitentiary for decades if he's not willing to comply," he said. "I don't believe the Crown is giving up very much here."

Roz Prober, an international child-rights advocate based in Winnipeg, told the *Free Press* she backed the deal the police used to get Whitmore to surrender.

"They made a deal and they have to stick with it. You have to look at the situation that police found themselves in. They had a 14-year-old highly vulnerable victim and an individual who was desperate and desperate people do desperate things. They had to get the kid out," Prober said.

The deal also put Whitmore behind bars for longer than he had ever been locked up before on a single case.

"The issue people can look at here is, they did throw Whitmore a bone, but it's a very bare bone indeed," said Prober.

Brodsky said he thought justice officials would have difficulty getting a dangerous offender label against Whitmore because one of the requirements is that an offender has shown no ability to be monitored and supervised in the community.

"The exact opposite is true with Mr. Whitmore. When he had a roof over his head and was being supervised (under a court-ordered peace bond that expired earlier this summer), he was being managed and stayed out of trouble," Brodsky said.

"It's when he had no supervision and conditions (the peace bond was never renewed by police) that he reoffended. So how are they going to convince a judge to give him dangerous offender status?"

# CHAPTER TWENTY-FOUR

## AUGUST 5, 2006

*Winnipeg Free Press* EDITORIAL – "Doubtful Dealing"

*The first priority of police surrounding an abandoned farm house in Saskatchewan where career pedophile Peter Whitmore allegedly was holding a 14-year-old boy captive was to get the boy out safely. They accomplished that on Wednesday when the boy, who is from Winnipeg, was freed. Another 10-year-old boy from Saskatchewan had fled the farmhouse the previous day. Mr. Whitmore gave himself up.*

*The second priority of police seeking to arrest Mr. Whitmore should have been to protect every other child in Canada, now and in the future, from his notorious and well-documented tendencies. He has a record of the sexual abuse and abduction of children going back to 1993. Since then, Mr. Whitmore has been sentenced to a total of almost 10 years in prison for the abuse or abduction of seven children. He is now accused or suspected of the sexual abuse of children in three provinces. Even before these latest charges, it was known that he is an unreconstructed pedophile who has admitted that he needs the judicial system to stop him and to protect children. On this count, the RCMP bumbled badly.*

*After Mr. Whitmore's arrest and his arraignment on charges of multiple sexual abuse against the two boys, it was reported that the RCMP had cut a deal with Mr. Whitmore. He would not be charged as a dangerous offender, the Crown would not seek a life sentence, and he would receive a private cell in a segregated area of the prison. In return he would plead guilty and avoid the cost of a lengthy trial and the ordeal that would present for his alleged victims when they had to testify.*

*The RCMP reportedly put this offer in writing. If that were all it was, that would not be binding on the prosecutors except in the sense that if the police cannot deliver on what they promise, they lose their credibility in negotiations with criminals.*

*Mr. Whitmore's lawyer, Daniel Brodsky, however, says that Crown prosecutor Jeff Kalmakoff also signed the document, which leaves less wiggle room for the Crown. The question now is should Saskatchewan authorities try to wiggle out of it.*

*The question involves principle, practicality and politics, with the principle and the politics for once pretty well meshing. The principle is that the laws should be enforced as they were meant to be, convicted criminals getting the punishment they deserve – it is difficult to believe that Mr. Whitmore was not long ago declared a dangerous offender since he offended at every opportunity he had. The politics is that we have a federal government that claims it wants to get tough on crime and a population appalled by what has happened in this case.*

*The practical part is the tough part. If the deal is honoured, Mr. Whitmore avoids facing a life sentence or dangerous offender status. Many Canadians will be outraged, but the conviction is certain and the children are spared a trial of a different kind. He can still receive a lengthy sentence, and as much as 10 years of close supervision after the inevitable parole. There is a certain sense to that, except for this ultimate irony – by the time he is out of jail, his victims may have children of their own, vulnerable themselves to career pedophiles who are too readily released back into society.*

• • • • •

**AUGUST 8, 2006**

Dan Brodsky was ready to pour some more fuel on the fire. With Saskatchewan justice officials still tight-lipped on what many had started calling the "Deal With The Devil," Brodsky tried to press the issue by suggesting perhaps Whitmore shouldn't go to prison at all.

"We know that pedophilia is a sickness. Well, you're not supposed to put sick people in jail, or criminalize the mentally ill," Brodsky said from his Toronto office.

He said his client was prepared to fight to be proven not guilty by reason of mental disorder – a move which would send Whitmore to a psychiatric hospital for an undetermined period of time.

"If you accept as a premise that this guy is sick in the head, why shouldn't he have a better quality of life than a criminal in prison?" asked Brodsky.

Most Canadians could likely have suggested a few reasons. But Brodsky said those who just want Whitmore to suffer severe punishment are missing the point. He said it was highly probable Whitmore would remain in a mental-health facility for the rest of his life and never be released, considering there is no actual "cure" for pedophilia.

"Why should the public care if he's got prison bars on his windows or is in a hospital if they know their child is protected from harm?" asked Brodsky.

As a federal prisoner, Whitmore would face possible violent backlash from other inmates, and most prisons don't have resources to treat the sexual deviancy that has continually landed his client in legal difficult, said Brodsky.

"A guy like Peter Whitmore isn't very high on the totem pole. Most of the other inmates have families and don't like people who have harmed other people and their families (in a sexual way)," said Brodsky.

Not surprisingly, Brodsky's suggested insanity defence wasn't well received by the families of his most recent victims.

"Holy shit. You've got to be kidding me," Al Baxter said upon hearing the news.

He was likely speaking for much of the country.

• • • • •

## AUGUST 9, 2006

David Matas, a Winnipeg lawyer who works with the Beyond Borders child advocacy group, had heard and seen enough. Angered by Whitmore's latest crimes and frustrated with the Canadian justice system, the well-respected Matas sat down and explained his four-point plan to protect other children from dangerous predators, submitted it for publication to the *Winnipeg Free Press*.

*Canada is not doing enough to protect children from sexual abuse. That much seems clear from the Peter Whitmore saga. Whitmore, a chronic, convicted sex offender is accused of kidnapping two boys, a 14 year old from Winnipeg and a 10-year-old from rural Saskatchewan. The police negotiated his surrender in Kipling, Sask., last week.*

*There are at least four ways protection could be improved. One is raising the age of consent for sex with adults. Right now it is 14. It is chilling to realize, but Whitmore cannot be convicted with sexual abuse of the 14-year-old from Winnipeg unless it can be established either that Whitmore sexually exploited the child or that the child did not consent to sex.*

*The government of Canada has introduced legislation into Parliament to raise the age of consent from 14 to 16 with a close-in-age exemption for a partner who is less than five years older. That legislation needs to be enacted as soon as possible.*

*Second, the threshold for dangerous offender designation needs to be lowered. Dangerous offender designation means that an offender can be sentenced to life in prison not for what he has done, but for the danger he poses, what he will do.*

*Whitmore was never designated a dangerous offender because, although he had been convicted many times for sexual abuse of children and was an obvious danger, he had never met the threshold for that designation.*

The designation can be imposed only if a person has committed a serious personal injury offence.

None of the offences for which Peter Whitmore was convicted fit that description. When it comes to chronic sex offenders, the potential future danger combined with convictions of any sort relevant to the danger should be enough.

Third, dangerous child sex offenders should not be given passports. Whitmore had violated a supervision order in 2000, going to Mexico, where, according to media reports, he "cultivated relationships" with children. He was found with a notepad containing the names and ages of 13 children.

The Canadian Passport Order authorizes the government of Canada to refuse a passport for only one offence, the fraudulent use of a certificate of citizenship. The list needs to be expanded to include repeated sexual offences against children.

That same order allows revocation of a passport if the passport is used in committing a serious offence abroad. But a passport cannot be revoked simply because a person has committed child sexual abuse offences in Canada and is likely to do so abroad. Yet, that should be possible.

Fourth, Canada needs a publicly accessible sex offender registry. The B.C. police allowed Whitmore to visit Alberta for four days and even issued a press release he was going there. Whitmore stayed in Alberta beyond the authorized time. His court ordered supervision expired, in mid-June, while he was still there. A court date was set for the end of June to extend the supervision order. But Whitmore did not show up.

*If the public in Alberta had known, through a publicly accessible sex offender registry, who Whitmore was, the public could have been after the police to get a court ruling to extend the supervision order before it expired. The police oversight would have been a good deal less likely to have happened.*

*Right now, there is a national sex offender registry maintained by the RCMP. But the information on the registry is available to police only and not to the public. Moreover, even for police, the registry is available only to investigate unsolved crimes of a sexual nature. The police in Alberta knew about Whitmore. But it was no thanks to the sex offender registry, which even they could not access, because at the time Whitmore was not a suspect in an unsolved sexual crime.*

*A sex offender registry can be too accessible, as the case of Stephen Marshall showed. Marshall, a Canadian from Cape Breton, looked up on the Internet the names and address of two sex offenders, Joseph Gray and William Elliott, on the Maine sex offender registry, went down to Maine and shot and killed them. When confronted by police on a bus in Boston in April this year, he shot and killed himself.*

*There are legitimate issues, once public sex offender registries are established, about who should be on the registry, how access is obtained and how much information should be available to the public about the offender. Only those who are truly a danger to the public should be on a publicly accessible registry, not every person who has committed a sexual offence. Public access should require some form of police screening for those who seek information about offenders, to prevent vigilantism. Information about the offender on the registry should be specific enough to prevent cases of mistaken identity.*

*It is easy to think of what, for a sex offender registry, might be too much. But what we have now nationally, a registry accessible only to police and only even for them for the purpose of investigating unsolved sex crimes, is far too little.*

*The Whitmore incident has made it as plain as day that Canada is not doing enough to protect children. We should learn from the drama to improve our protection.*

• • • • •

A place that held so many happy family memories had been forever tarnished. And now the owner of the ramshackle farmhouse that served as a hideout for Peter Whitmore said the only option was to bring out the wrecking ball.

Don Toth, MLA for the Moosomin area, said it was time to level the dilapidated, two-storey home near Kipling – and not just because it was a house of horrors for a pair of kidnapped youths. He said the farmhouse had become an eyesore in recent years and a popular spot for local teens to gather and drink after dark.

"The only reason the house is still there is for sentimental reasons. But I'm thinking recently that maybe it's time to push the thing down," he said.

Geraldine Varjassy, who lives just one property over to the north, said demolishing her late husband's childhood home is probably for the best.

"It gives us a different feeling when we drive by," she said. "It's hard to balance thinking about all the good times with the bad things that happened there."

# DEVIL AMONG US

• • • • •

It was the answer everyone was waiting for. And Saskatchewan justice officials decided they wouldn't drag out the suspense any longer.

Just moments after Whitmore's second court appearance, the lead Crown attorney stopped outside the downtown courthouse to address the public.

There would be no deal. Whitmore would be taken to trial. He would be found guilty. And he would feel the full weight of the law come crashing down on him.

Prosecutor Anthony Gerein said that meant, for the first time, seeking a dangerous offender designation against Whitmore and hopefully having him put away for the rest of his life.

But what about the document given to Whitmore to coax him into surrendering?

"The Crown has never made a deal, and there is no deal with Mr. Whitmore," a defiant Gerein told a throng of reporters.

Gerein said the RCMP "have honoured the terms of that letter" by making the recommendation to avoid a dangerous offender designation and life sentence.

"The Crown sees no basis to accept that recommendation. We believe there is a reasonable likelihood of conviction and upon conviction a reasonable likelihood he would be designated a dangerous offender," said Gerein.

Gerein said police "should be commended" for the way they brought a peaceful resolution to the high-profile case.

Whitmore's court appearance had been otherwise non-eventful. He was brought-in looking slightly dishevelled, his hair messy, his eyes baggy and a scowl on his face. He was wearing the same "Canada" sweatshirt he had on during his first court appearance a week earlier.

• • • • •

## WHITEWOOD, SASKATCHEWAN
## AUGUST 11, 2006

It was the family's first – and only – interview, and it came during an emotional afternoon and evening filled with laughs and tears around a campfire. Larry and Paula Munroe, along with their three children, agreed to sit down with the *Winnipeg Free Press* to discuss what they'd been through.

Until the previous week, the only invaders these self-described 'simple farm folks' had to worry about were the coyotes and foxes trying to get at their barnyard animals. But then along came Whitmore, with a 14-year-old Winnipeg teen in tow, and a story that preyed on their trust and cost them their son and his innocence.

The freckle-faced Adam takes a reporter by the hand to proudly show him the greeting card he'd personally picked out for the Regina RCMP officer who helped rescue him.

"I made a wish. And you came true," the 10-year-old recites with a sweet smile.

Paula, a strong and deeply protective woman, is once again near tears as he reads it aloud.

"It's the card that makes Mommy cry," she tells her son.

Larry – a gentle, kind-hearted soul – also admits to getting a lump in his throat.

Adam says he plans to send the simple but very powerful message to Const. Tim Schwartz, whose open arms were there to meet him as he sprinted to safety, finally free from Whitmore's clutches.

After reading the card, Adam quickly returns to acting his age – playing with his toy robot and teasing his two sisters, aged nine and 12, how his "invention" – a coffee machine made out of a cardboard box, tape, foil and Styrofoam cups – is better than theirs.

They share a good-natured laugh and life, it would appear, is back to normal. But it is difficult to escape the reality of the family's current situation for too long.

The family is reluctant to discuss specific details of the allegations against Whitmore but offer a few disturbing revelations.

Adam says he was given dog food, water and crackers to eat during the 48 hours he was held captive. He also says they were holed up inside the abandoned farmhouse the entire time, and he always believed he would escape.

"I told police that very first night he would try to run, that he wouldn't fall prey to that scum," Larry tells the reporter.

Fortunately, Pat Beaujot came along and stumbled across the hiding place.

"He's a hero, and we are very, very grateful for Mr. Beaujot," says Larry. The family has spoken with Beaujot by telephone and plan to have dinner with him soon to offer personal thanks.

"Now we have him," Larry says, hugging Adam tightly. "You're the centre of attention – but you're our little world."

Try as they might, there are daily disturbing reminders of what has happened. Adam begins to protest when Paula reminds him he has to take his medicine, which a doctor has prescribed as a precaution given the sexual assault charges against Whitmore.

"I don't want to take my medicine," he says softly. "How much longer?"

"Well, you have to take it 28 days. And this is nine. So how many more is that?" she asks.

"Uh, 19," he replies, briefly putting his concerns aside to take praise for his quick math skills. "I was top three in my class last year," Adam boasts, adding he's looking forward to starting Grade 5 in a couple weeks. "I want to be a scientist," he says.

"Devastating," is how the boy later sums up his ordeal, which the Munroes say they now want to use as a springboard for political change. And they want other outraged Canadians to join them.

"My God, I don't want anyone else to have to go through what we're going through," Larry says.

Earlier in the day he met face-to-face meeting with his local MP and has plans to meet with federal Justice Minister Vic Toews in the coming weeks.

Larry says the family will eventually give up their right to anonymity and fight for better monitoring and stiffer punishment of sex offenders in full public view.

"We want justice. Not just for us but for everyone out there. Our medical issues with (Adam) are our number 1 issue right now. But we plan on getting a grassroots movement going. We'll take this anywhere we have to go," he says.

The family was relieved the Crown prosecutor assigned to Whitmore's case phoned them earlier in the week and asked for their input before announcing they would not cut a deal with Whitmore.

The family urged the Crown prosecutor to go to trial and seek the maximum penalty, even if it meant a long, drawn-out legal battle. And they simply scoff at Dan Brodsky's suggestion Whitmore may try to be sent to a hospital instead of prison on the grounds he is mentally ill.

"We want to fight this. It doesn't matter if (our son) has to testify. He's already faced the worse he's going to. He has to live this every day of his life," Larry says.

"We're not scared of Mr. Whitmore. If he thinks we're going to back down he's wrong. We'll meet him in the courtroom. My boy is very strong. Much stronger than we are. (Whitmore) has no idea who he's dealing with."

The family realized they were dealing with a very complex issue that had rocked their world. "It's peaceful out here," Larry said while serving up hotdogs to his family and guest. "We live a quiet life."

"We used to," Paula says immediately.

They recall how Whitmore showed up on their sprawling, 360-acre property with a blown tire on his van, claiming the Winnipeg teen was his nephew and telling the family his wife had recently died and he was looking for work and property in the area.

"We think now he deliberately damaged that tire. It was a setup," says Larry.

He shook his head as he discussed taking Whitmore to a local repair shop that evening while Kyle Mason stayed behind at the farm to play Adam – a move that would culminate in the fateful bike ride the following day.

The entire family is now undergoing counselling and working closely with victims' services personnel in Yorkton, whom they describe as "wonderful." They also praise the police for all their work and thank local residents – and the entire country – for the outpouring of support.

Cards and letters have been coming in from strangers across Canada, while others have chipped in with financial donations at the local bank – something the family wasn't even aware was being done.

"You've got a lot of people who are thankful you're home," Larry tells his son, who looks up from playing with his two pet rats to give a smile.

"No rats at the dinner table," Paula says firmly before everyone breaks into a laugh. She admits to being a little more on edge since her son returned home safely. "I'm like a mother bear now," she says. "I don't want this to change the way we are. But we haven't been sleeping well. If I get my chores done, it's a good day."

For now, the focus is on feeling better. And fireworks.

A relative brought over more than $300 worth of fireworks, which the family set off in a spectacular celebration in honour of Adam's first night home.

"It sounded like a shotgun going off," Adam says with wide-eyed glee.

The family has saved one last item, a $40 sky-dancer which the Adam says he may set off on his 11th birthday next month.

"We're saving it for a special day. I think I have a day in mind," Larry says with a sheepish grin and acknowledgment of the long road still ahead.

"But I don't know if we want to wait that long."

# CHAPTER TWENTY-FIVE

Letter to the Editor:

*"There is no sentence a judge can impose that would fully assuage the feelings of the victims, their families and the community at large in the case of my client, Peter Whitmore.*

*Every pedophile leaves, in his or her wake, varying amounts of sorrow, grief, anger, fear and frustration. In all cases, young lives are shattered or ruined and families are devastated and torn apart.*

*I suppose it's a normal sentiment to wish the perpetrator is locked up forever, tortured, and even killed. The imposition of sentence, however, is governed by statute and fixed principle, not by emotional reaction. It does not measure the value of the victims either in absolute or in relative terms and it is not revenge.*

*The judge must impose a fit sentence, no more and no less. In this case the court will be asked to determine if pedophiles detained indefinitely should be managed by the Federal Correctional Services of Canada or the Provincial Ministry of Health in Saskatchewan.*

*I will remind the court of the fate of Joseph Fredricks when he was sent to prison rather than a hospital and argue that the dangerous offender designation is nothing more than a backdoor method of achieving capital punishment. (Fredricks, a convicted pedophile, was on parole from prison when he killed 11-year-old Christopher Stephenson in 1998).*

*In the United States, pedophiles are diverted to the mental health regimes. They are not criminalized. The American Sexually Violent Predator laws in the United States are civil, not criminal, mental health enactments. It's a myth that other countries imprison their pedophiles in penitentiaries and criminalize the mentally ill.*

*Perhaps it's time to do the same."*

*–Dan Brodsky*

• • • • •

He may have had an outside shot in a court of law. But Dan Brodsky's campaign to convince Canadians his client was mentally ill was being rejected by the court of public opinion.

His letter-to-the-editor was published in several papers across the country.

"I don't think this approach is going to work," said Roz Prober, the co-founder of advocacy group Beyond Borders, which runs campaigns to end child-sex exploitation in 70 countries.

She said the very nature of Whitmore's crimes proved he wasn't too sick to be found criminally responsible.

"In the courts, the test is whether you knew right from wrong and no lawyer can prove that he is mentally ill – because the level of deception he went through to do it," said Prober. "He knew what he was doing."

• • • • •

AUGUST 18, 2006

*Winnipeg Free Press* OPINION PIECE –
"Containing Sexual Predators"
By J.F. Conway, political sociologist, University of Regina.

*The case of pedophile and sexual predator Peter Whitmore, who is accused of abducting and sexually assaulting two boys aged 10 and 14, has resulted in the usual public outcry for harsher measures to enhance public safety. Typically, such measures focus on the criminal justice system and involve demands for longer prison sentences and easier access to dangerous offender designations for convicted predators.*

*A case can be made that the criminal justice system cannot effectively deal with those suffering from dangerous sexual psychopathologies, either in changing the offender's behaviour or in protecting future victims. I came to this conclusion in the mid-1960s when working as a psychologist intern at the Saskatchewan Penitentiary in Prince Albert.*

*One case, seared forever in my memory, led me to this conclusion, a conclusion that was confirmed for me by an examination of all the files of those convicted of violent sexual offences.*

During my first summer, the penitentiary psychologist invited me to observe the "out-routine" for a violent rapist at the end of his sentence. The "out-routine" involved moving the inmate from his maximum security cell to a dormitory for the period leading up to his release. The inmate was assessed by the psychiatrist, the psychologist, and a classification officer. Interviews to assist with post-release planning were arranged with professionals from the John Howard Society, the Salvation Army, and Canada Manpower.

The inmate fit one of the classic profiles of the violent rapist, in his 30s at the time with a long record of sexual crimes from adolescence onward, each assault more serious and more violent than the last. In appearance he did not fit the stereotype of a violent rapist. He was slight in stature, extremely good-looking, and diffident and shy in manner. As a result, he found it easy to persuade women to trust him as he stalked them in preparation for his attack. When attacking his victims, he became increasingly violent in each case. After the last attack he was convicted of rape with violence. He repeatedly raped a woman while holding a knife at her throat. He was sentenced to eight years.

He was a very well-behaved inmate, working as a gardener in the warden's yard (partly for his own protection from other inmates and partly because he was assessed as a non-flight risk). Repeated assessments by the psychiatrist, the psychologist and classification officers concluded he would reoffend upon release and fears were expressed the violence of his attacks would escalate. He refused all treatment. During the last few years of his sentence, many efforts were made by classification officers, the psychologist, and representatives of the National Parole Board to convince the inmate to take early, supervised release. Their reasoning was that since he continued to be at high risk to reoffend, early release under mandatory supervision would provide at least some measure of oversight. The inmate refused all offers for early release, preferring to serve out his full time so that, upon release, he was unencumbered by mandatory supervision.

The psychologist's final assessment, written after a number of clinical interviews and a battery of psychological tests, was scary. The inmate was suffering from an untreated deeply rooted sexual psychopathology that led to a pattern of sexual gratification realized only through the violent rape of women. The inmate would inevitably rape again and his future assaults, given the pattern of escalating violence, could result in the death of his victim. Both the psychiatrist and the classification officer reached substantially the same conclusion in their reports. I protested that surely we shouldn't release him under the circumstances because we could be sentencing some woman to death. Yes, we shouldn't, the psychologist sadly noted, but under the law, we had no choice.

The inmate was released. Within days he was the most wanted man in Canada. He travelled to Edmonton where he gained entry to the apartment of two nurses (or student nurses, I can't recall). He raped the two women repeatedly and then cut their throats. He was quickly identified because one of the cuts wasn't deep enough, the blood coagulated, and one woman survived to identify him from his mug shot. Last I heard, he was serving life with no chance of parole in Millhaven.

What had this sexual predator learned as a result of his harsh, eight-year sentence? He learned that henceforth he would kill his victim in order to avoid incarceration. And this was too often the pattern of the criminal justice system at the time because of its nature. Dangerous sexual predators could only be incarcerated for life after they had murdered a victim. Later, the Criminal Code of Canada was amended to allow the Crown to seek a dangerous offender designation, resulting effectively in a life sentence, but such designations are difficult to obtain. Section 810 was also added to the Criminal Code requiring that those sexual predators deemed a threat could have conditions imposed upon them even though they had served their full sentence. This has proven ineffective, as the Whitmore case demonstrates (Whitmore was under Sec. 810). In the absence of complete surveillance, a determined sexual predator under Sec. 810 can easily reoffend, and perhaps even get away with it, at least for a time.

The criminal justice system operates on a number of premises. First, the system takes Bentham's utilitarian view that humans are importantly motivated by rationally seeking pleasure and avoiding pain. Hence, the theory of deterrence, i.e., if a behaviour, no matter how temporarily gratifying, results in enough pain, and then it will not be repeated. Thus, a jail term will convince an offender not to reoffend. Further, others will be deterred from the forbidden behaviour by witnessing the pain inflicted on those who cross the line. Second, the criminal justice system assumes individuals take action after making a rational calculation, given their circumstances, that the behaviour will pay off. Thus, a poor person might rationally calculate that it is worth the risk to steal rather *than suffer destitution. A jail sentence, or the threat of a jail sentence, might convince him/her to change that calculation of benefits and risk.*

*Such an approach is hopeless when dealing with those suffering from dangerous sexual psychopathology. Such people are not rational. They are mentally disturbed, at least psycho-sexually. They do not fit the technical requirements under the law for an insanity defence, since they know what they are doing is wrong and unlawful, and they often carefully calculate their actions in order to avoid detection. But they are not sane. The motivating forces behind their behaviour are rooted in madness and delusion, and the behaviour itself is not that of a sane person.*

*Those suffering from dangerous sexual psycho-pathologies, after a trial confirming their guilt, should be committed by court order to a highly secure psychiatric institution for treatment. Such individuals should only be released when a panel of experts on sexual psychopathologies declares they are no longer a danger to the public. And such release should require continuing monitoring and the powers to recommit upon threatened relapse. This approach would both secure the safety of the public and ensure appropriate psychiatric treatment for those suffering from the malady.*

*Since Whitmore's first conviction in 1993, involving assaults on four boys, there have been five subsequent victims of this predator that we know of – an eight-year-old girl in Guelph, Ont., a 13-year-old boy in Toronto, a five-year-old boy in B.C. He has been accused of assaulting the 10- and 14-year-old boys in Saskatchewan. There may be more charges, stemming from his time in Newfoundland.*

*All these subsequent alleged victims would have been spared the experience had Whitmore been committed in 1993 to a secure psychiatric institution. That is where he belongs until he is cured of his dangerous sexual psychopathology.*

• • • • •

## REGINA, SASKATCHEWAN
## SEPTEMBER 8, 2006

It's been said that a person who represents themselves in court has a fool for a client. Either Peter Whitmore hadn't heard that expression. Or he didn't care.

Now more than a month after his arrest, Whitmore had apparently grown tired of watching long-time lawyer Dan Brodsky fail in his bid to secure Legal Aid funding.

"I'll be acting on my own behalf," Whitmore told provincial court Judge Linton Smith, reading from a written statement that Brodsky had helped him craft during phone conversations.

"You understand that's unwise?" Smith asked.

"Yes," Whitmore replied.

Whitmore then asked to set dates for a bail hearing and a preliminary hearing. Whitmore had been granted the services of two Saskatchewan legal-aid lawyers but was refusing to co-operate with them. He wanted Brodsky – or nobody.

Brodsky had been working for free up until now but said he needs a funding arrangement with the province before he agrees to travel to Saskatchewan and take on the case full-time.

He said he was willing to be paid the same fee as a legal-aid lawyer. But that offer was refused by legal aid.

Brodsky suggested his would-be client's rights had been violated by the Crown's refusal to turn over all of their evidence against Whitmore. He accused Saskatchewan justice officials of trying to gain a "tactical" advantage and suggested extreme measures were just around the corner.

"If this situation persists I will bring an application on Peter Whitmore's behalf to stay the proceedings," said Brodsky.

Outside court, Gerein told reporters there is case law in Saskatchewan that allows for certain restrictions to be put on how defendants receive disclosure of evidence while acting on their own behalf.

"Of course, anyone in Canada has the right to represent themselves if they so choose," Gerein said. "But when it's disclosure in a sensitive case, it's open to the court to put certain controls on how that disclosure will be used and won't be used, where it will be held and so on."

A compromise was reached days later when justice officials agreed they would provide a copy of the evidence against Whitmore to Brodsky in Toronto, who would then advise his former client on an "unofficial" basis while he continued to be self-represented.

• • • • •

## WHITEWOOD, SASKATCHEWAN
## SEPTEMBER 16, 2006

They were mad as hell – and they weren't going to suffer in silence.

Led by their vocal mayor, the nearly 1,000 residents of this tight-knit community announced they were banding together to call on the Canadian government to create stiffer penalties for pedophiles like the one who terrorized them.

The town of Whitewood had started a petition asking Ottawa for changes to legislation that would include mandatory electronic or other form of monitoring for pedophiles released from custody.

"I think it's time that we can make it safe for our young people to be able to live normal lives," Mayor Malcolm Green told reporters. "We're asking to put stiffer penalties and better protection and more information in people's hands than is available today."

Green said the petition was launched because people in the town felt it was time for action.

"I think people get to the point where something just sparks and (they) say enough is enough and I think this incident has done that," said the mayor.

• • • • •

## SEPTEMBER 21, 2006

It was being dubbed as Canada's three-strikes-and-you're-out law. And after promising major changes were on the way following the Whitmore debacle, the federal government was ready to deal with specifics.

Justice Minister Vic Toews promised a new bill – dubbed C-2 – would be introduced to make it easier to designate three-time criminals as dangerous offenders and jail them indefinitely after a third serious conviction.

Opposition parties and other critics quickly decried the coming legislation as an affront to Canadian values of fair punishment and a violation of the Charter of Rights and Freedoms.

"It flies right in the face of Canadian criminal justice," Louise Botham, president of the Criminal Lawyers Association, told the *Winnipeg Free Press*. "I don't think it would withstand constitutional scrutiny."

Unlike California's famous three-strikes-you're-out law, the proposed federal bill will not trigger an automatic life sentence for repeat offenders. What it would do is reverse the burden of proof in dangerous-offender hearings for people already found guilty of three violent crimes.

Malcolm Green said the legislation was music to the ears of his community and likely would have made a big difference in the case of Peter Whitmore.

"It's probably a step in the right direction as far as we're concerned," he said.

Under the present system, someone convicted of a violent offence can be declared a dangerous offender after a court hearing initiated by Crown prosecutors.

The new legislation would make it much easier for judges to slap three-time offenders with the designation which brings an unlimited prison sentence, although offenders could still begin applying for parole after seven years.

"At present there is an onus on the prosecutors at all levels to demonstrate dangerous offender," Toews said. "We feel that once a person has been convicted three times, a presumption should apply that the individual is dangerous because a court has found that individual to be so."

Toews conceded the Whitmore case played a part in the drafting of a new bill.

"I can't comment on specific cases, but I can say we took a look at a number of cases to see whether or not this legislation would catch those kinds of situations," Toews said.

· · · · ·

After weeks of delays and public posturing, there was finally a sign of progress.

Dan Brodsky had lost his bid for public funding, and Whitmore was now reluctantly accepting the help of a pair of in-house Legal Aid lawyers.

A judge ruled there was no reason to drag the matter out any further.

The Crown had its case ready to go – and they would take the first major step in proving Whitmore's guilty at a preliminary hearing set for early January.

· · · · ·

## JANUARY 6, 2007

It had been a dream vacation to Disneyland – but now the Munroe family had returned home to face a nightmarish situation.

After getting Adam prepared to face his attacker – including a guided tour of the courtroom in Regina – Larry and Paula had just learned the preliminary hearing was being adjourned.

It seems Whitmore's desire to have Dan Brodsky act as his own lawyer had taken its toll on the two Legal Aid lawyers who had been thrown into the case. The men announced, on the eve of the important court hearing, that they were withdrawing their services based on a "fundamental loss of confidence" between them and their client.

Whitmore was now back to square one, once again representing himself.

Larry Munroe figured enough was enough – he was urging justice officials to order a direct indictment against Whitmore. Such a move would avoid the need for a preliminary hearing and move the case directly to trial. It would also mean the young victims only testify once.

The Crown has the authority to direct-indict without consent from the accused. They had been reluctant to take that step because they wanted to cover all the bases and make no mistakes in their prosecution.

Meanwhile, the Mason family was also stinging by the news. Kyle had been having a difficult time lately, including plenty of anger issues and wild mood swings.

He hadn't been looking forward to testifying – but his mother thought she had finally convinced him things would be okay. Now she had to tell him, through tears, that it wasn't going to happen. At least not yet. The waiting would continue.

"This is not a good thing that it's going to drag on," she said. "We just have to stay strong as a family and keep going."

Brodsky was coy about the development but admitted Whitmore was frustrated by the legal situation. He suggested Whitmore might end up acting as his own lawyer after all.

Judge Linton Smith told Whitmore it would be "very foolish" to continue without counsel. And he warned these types of delays wouldn't be allowed to continue.

● ● ● ● ●

**REGINA, SASKATCHEWAN**
**JANUARY 12, 2007**

Saskatchewan justice officials didn't wait long to pull the trigger. Crown attorney Anthony Gerein consulted with senior management and got authorization for a direct indictment. They weren't going to allow Whitmore to dictate the pace of the prosecution.

Whitmore was clearly upset at the development.

"How can I appeal the decision," he asked in court.

Judge Carol Snell said he couldn't.

"I'm not allowed to look at my disclosure, I'm not allowed to have a bail hearing, I'm not allowed to have a preliminary hearing," Whitmore fumed while leaving the courtroom in the company of sheriff's officers. "I have no rights in Saskatchewan."

• • • • •

## REGINA CORRECTIONAL CENTRE

Peter Whitmore's frustration was beginning to manifest itself in bizarre, even dangerous, ways.

Guards inside the city's holding cell had their hands full dealing with a pair of institutional incidents that left some wondering whether Whitmore actually might be mentally ill.

The first involved a series of cuts he made to his own stomach. Whitmore then defecated inside his cell and rubbed the feces into his wound. He was taken to the prison medical facility for treatment, bandaged up and then placed on suicide watch for several days.

Upon his return to the general jail population, Whitmore wasted little time before he launched a second attack on himself. This time he jabbed his scrotum with a ballpoint pen, breaking it off and leaving several small pieces embedded inside. He was rushed to hospital for surgery and put back on suicide watch.

The *Regina Leader-Post* learned of the incident, which was reported to be an attempted self-castration. As expected, the news generated plenty of buzz across Canada.

Inside the jail, some speculated Whitmore was just trying to create attention for himself and get out of segregation for a few days in exchange for a hospital trip.

Whitmore had once again been appointed a lawyer by the court and remained angry at the fact he couldn't have Brodsky. While Merv Shaw declined to comment publicly on his new client's well-being, Brodsky said it proved Whitmore wasn't well and needed serious medical help.

But if Shaw was planning to use an insanity defence at trial, he wasn't tipping his hand.

# CHAPTER TWENTY-SIX

## WHITEWOOD, SASKATCHEWAN
JULY 18, 2007

Saskatchewan justice officials stunned the public – and sparked a tidal wave of anger – when they revealed that a mutual agreement had been struck with Peter Whitmore. The pedophile had agreed to plead guilty to all his crimes, in exchange for a life sentence that could see him apply for parole in seven years.

And what of the dangerous offender application that the Crown had vowed to pursue? It was off the table.

"That can't happen. If we don't put an end to this right now, he's going to get out one day and do it all over again," an angry diner at the local highway truck in Whitewood told several customers.

"Anybody who does that to a child should be shot. Or worse," added a waitress, who paused from dishing out midnight platters of bacon and eggs to give her two cents.

A provincial election was expected this fall in Saskatchewan, and the deal with Whitmore would likely become a political issue, local residents predicted. The long-reigning NDP government would have a hard time explaining the sudden flip-flop, especially since Crown attorney Anthony Gerein was on the record promising that Whitmore would not be offered a plea bargain.

While the public's collective blood pressure rapidly began to rise, two families were surprisingly at ease with the decision. The Munroes and the Masons had actually signed off on the Crown's intentions. They had been quietly working behind the scenes with Gerein and Whitmore's lawyer, Merv Shaw, in the preceding weeks.

And they had all agreed that putting the boys on the witness stand to relive their ordeal wasn't worth it. Whitmore would still be eligible to apply for parole after seven years even if declared a dangerous offender.

And while it's true the stigma of such a designation makes it very difficult to get released, so, too, does having a life sentence with the kind of background Whitmore already has.

Larry Munroe knew the news wouldn't go over well in his home community.

"You won't want to be in this town when this goes down. You'll get crushed by the stampede (of angry people) down to the courthouse," he predicted.

But Larry and Paula weren't prepared to put their son through a torturous cross-examination just to appease the public.

"Our concern is what's best for (the boy). Today, tomorrow and in the future. I know what they do to Whitmore makes a lot of difference to me, (Paula), the community. But it doesn't much matter to (Adam). We can't go back and change what's happened," he said.

"I guess this is our fault. But there's no way we're putting a 10-year-old boy on the stand to be cross-examined by Whitmore and his lawyer. He's been through enough."

He predicted Whitmore wouldn't be getting out of prison anytime soon, regardless of any deal that is made.

"Right now, Whitmore is where he belongs. And it's our goal to keep him there. As far as I'm concerned he's never getting out," he said.

Director of public prosecutions Murray Brown was forced to defend the move, saying his department had the best interests of the alleged victims in mind by sparing them a lengthy, emotional trial. He said a life sentence was "functionally the same" as a dangerous-offender designation.

"Both are indefinite sentences, both allow for parole at seven years and both provide him with the same access to resources and treatment programs in the federal correctional system," Brown said.

"Frankly, if somebody that we were thinking about doing a dangerous offender on agreed to a life sentence, I would be hard-pressed to explain to the public why I would spend the resources to pursue a dangerous-offender proceeding."

Brown admitted the deal has some benefits for Whitmore, including what he can tell the parole board when his time for review comes – "I didn't put the kids through it."

Brown's explanation fell on deaf ears with the opposition and many callers who flooded open-line talk radio.

Saskatchewan party Leader Brad Wall said he was shocked the Crown agreed to bargain with Whitmore – noting that after Whitmore's arrest last August, provincial Justice Minister Frank Quennell boasted about the province's track record in getting dangerous-offender designations

"If Peter Whitmore is not a dangerous offender, no one is," said Wall.

Regina MP Adam Scheer brought the issue into the federal forum, calling on opposition MPs to quickly pass Bill C-2 when the House of Commons resumed in September. The federal government introduced C-2 in the wake of the Whitmore case. The bill calls for repeat sexual offenders to automatically be considered dangerous offenders unless they can prove otherwise.

"When Whitmore is released and reoffends, who will take responsibility for his subsequent crimes?" Scheer said in a statement.

The National Parole Board also spoke out, saying it puts dangerous offenders under the same microscope as those serving a life sentence when it comes time to consider their release.

Bernard Pitre, Prairies regional director with the parole board, told the Canadian Press the procedure under which a dangerous offender or a lifer seeks parole is the same.

"Basically, for all intents and purposes, the review is based on the same principles," Pitre said. "The same factors are being looked at with the ultimate goal of assessing that, if released, the offender would present a risk to the community."

According to figures supplied by the parole board, as of July 2006, there were 3,721 first- or second-degree murderers serving life sentences in the system. Of those 1,361 or nearly 37 per cent were out on either day or full parole. As of April 2007, there were 370 dangerous offenders in the system. Of those, only 18 or five per cent were on some form of conditional release.

But the parole board argued that the statistics were misleading because they applied generalities to highly specific cases.

The Munroes and Masons weren't concerned about politics right now. They just wanted what was best for their children. And that meant getting the matter over as quickly as possible.

# MIKE MCINTYRE

•••••

JULY 20, 2007

*Winnipeg Free Press* EDITORIAL – "Cause For Outrage"

*Justice is not usually well-served when the administration of it creates public outrage, as has resulted from the deal that Crown prosecutors in Saskatchewan have cut with notorious pedophile Peter Whitmore. A plea bargain will let him escape a dangerous-offender designation when he pleads in court next Monday. Dangerous offender had been the sentence that the Crown had originally promised to pursue and would have allowed authorities to keep Mr. Whitmore, a career pedophile who is considered to be incapable of being rehabilitated, in jail for the rest of his life. Instead he will be allowed to plead guilty to charges of kidnapping and sexual assault in exchange for a life sentence that makes him eligible for parole in seven years.*

*The outrage in this case, however, may be misdirected. Saskatchewan's director of public prosecutions, Murray Brown, defended the decision on the grounds that it spares Whitmore's victims the ordeal of testifying at trial and results in basically the same circumstances. Dangerous offenders can be imprisoned for life but their sentences are eligible for review after seven years.*

*If Whitmore in fact pleads guilty on Monday under the terms of the reported plea bargain, the situation has hardly changed – he can still be imprisoned for life. The fact that he will be eligible for parole after the same seven-year period does not necessarily mean that he will get it.*

*Mr. Brown told a press conference "if somebody that we were thinking of a doing a dangerous offender on agreed to a life sentence, I would be hard-pressed to explain to the public why I would spend the resources to pursue a dangerous-offender proceeding." And that makes a certain sense.*

*There are grounds here for outrage, but not particularly in this plea bargain. What the public should be outraged by is the fact that Whitmore, a serial pedophile who has been in and out of jail for sexual assaults on children of both sexes over a period of 14 years, and who has admitted that he will offend again, was not jailed for a longer time a long time ago. Several children would have been spared.*

*The deal struck allows for him to be kept in jail for life. The parole system, however, is legitimately regarded even more dubiously than the justice system by the public – how do unrepentant pedophiles get paroled? In this case, Canadians should perhaps save their outrage for another seven years, until they see the results of Whitmore's first appearance before the parole board.*

• • • • •

**REGINA, SASKATCHEWAN**
**JULY 23, 2007**

Larry and Paula Munroe sat near the front of the packed courtroom, surrounded by other family members who'd come in from Alberta for moral support. Their children remained in the basement of the building with victim's services workers.

Jennifer Mason and Al Baxter had chosen to stay home in Winnipeg, still stung by the belief that many in Saskatchewan – including the Munroes – felt Kyle was more of a victimizer than a victim. They felt it would be best to keep their distance.

Plus, Kyle had been going through a rough time. As the anniversary of his abduction approached, his behaviour became more erratic, more concerning. He was having constant nightmares, flashbacks and cold sweats. His heart was racing, his moods would swing rapidly and he was suffering from chronic anxiety.

There were also bouts of violence in which he would begin destroying belongings or lashing out at those around him. He was under medical care and on prescription drugs, but any success seemed to be short-lived.

There was a noticeable hush as Peter Whitmore was shuffled into court and seated in the prisoner's box. He was wearing a blue plaid shirt, beige khaki pants. He was flanked by two uniformed RCMP officers, while another two were posted in the courtroom.

Security was tightened for the hearing, with a security checkpoint set up outside the courtroom door that included bag checks and a portable x-ray scanner. The public gallery was packed with members of the media, both local and national, along with some local Saskatchewan residents who wanted a first-hand glimpse at the process.

Everyone knew it wasn't going to be pleasant. The Crown, for the first time publicly, was going to have to read out all the facts of Whitmore's crimes. The Munroes had tried to brace themselves but knew it was going to be difficult, if not impossible.

The hearing began with lawyers announcing the resolution and Whitmore formally entering his pleas and saying he understood what was happening. As each charge was read aloud, he quietly responded with the world "guilty", keeping his eyes focused on the floor, his lawyer or the judge. He never looked towards the gallery, never met eyes with Larry or Paula Munroe.

Crown attorney Anthony Gerein began his submission by telling court that Whitmore's "evils unleashed a torrent of pain, loss and fear."

"What we have heard today is a tragedy. For these boys to end up as sex slaves...one can't imagine anything more grave. He was, and is, beyond control," he said. "He killed so much of who they were and where they lived."

The Crown described how Whitmore forced the boys to watch media coverage of the desperate 48-hour search for them and began laughing at the work of police, calling them "stupid".

How Whitmore forced the boys to walk around in front of him naked and demanded they call him "master."

How Whitmore forced Kyle Mason to shave his pubic hair so he would appear younger.

How Whitmore controlled Kyle with a walkie-talkie, instructing him on where to take Adam Munroe on the fateful bike ride before grabbing both boys.

How Whitmore kept Adam chained to a bed at various times while raping him, and also repeatedly raped Kyle.

How Whitmore threatened to go back and kidnap Adam's younger sister, and also threatened to take out other young relatives and his parents. Similar threats were made to Kyle.

How Whitmore put Adam on a dog leash at one point and also fed him dog food, along with water and crackers.

How Whitmore was armed with an Exacto knife which he told the Adam he'd use to cut all his skin off if he didn't have sex with him.

How Whitmore told the boys he was a former member of the Canadian military and an ex-Navy Seal who had access to all sorts of high-powered weaponry plus access to an aircraft carrier.

How Whitmore told the boys he had tortured many other prior victims and killed 13 other children whose bodies he had buried.

How Whitmore was armed at all times with a pellet gun, but told the boys it was a loaded .22 calibre handgun with hollow point bullets capable of shooting through body armour.

How Whitmore told the boys about a so-called "Night Mission" in which they were going to wait a few days and then kill an entire family in the Kipling area before stealing their vehicle and making a getaway.

How Whitmore willingly let Adam escape once he was cornered but pointed his gun at the head of Kyle and didn't allow him to escape.

How Whitmore repeatedly showed the boys pictures and movies of child pornography on a portable DVD player, telling them they should do what the kids in the images were doing.

Paula Munroe was weeping quietly while her husband comforted her and kept a stoic look on his face.

Crown and defence lawyers tried to do some public damage control by explaining how this deal was in the best interest of justice because it brought a quick resolution to the case and means the two victims won't have to relive their horror on the witness stand.

"He destroyed so much that can never be restored," said Gerein. "It ends here. It ends now, with life in prison....Society needs the maximum protection by law."

When asked if he had anything to say, Whitmore quietly said "I'm sorry."

Defence lawyer Merv Shaw offered a longer apology from his client by reading excerpts from some recent letters Whitmore had written him.

"I had no right to take either of the children from the love and safety of their families. I'm ashamed of what I've done to the children, their families, the community," Whitmore wrote.

Shaw also described Whitmore's troubled childhood. He also thanked the RCMP for the way they'd handled the case.

"There are none more vulnerable, none more valuable than children," he said.

Queen's Bench Justice Ian McLellan described Whitmore's actions as "repulsive and sickening." He also approved the decision to strike a deal with Whitmore and spare the victims from testifying while acknowledging there was controversy.

"This has come after careful deliberations between highly competent and skilled counsel," said McLellan.

The judge said a dangerous offender designation was "almost the same" sentence as a life term regardless.

The most dramatic part of the hearing came in the form of written victim impact statements from all involved in the case.

They were touching, poignant, heartbreaking.

• • • • •

## Paula Munroe

*There are issues at school with the kids picking on our children because of what happened. There is one particular bully who calls Adam "faggot" to his face all the time. We are withdrawing our children from school this coming year and will be home-schooling. Our family needs more time to heal without all the negative impact from school.*

*We had taken Adam off Ritalin in the spring before the abduction. We had to put him back on it at school so that he could settle down in school. We had to put him on sleeping pills for a while at night because he was afraid to go to sleep at night. Adam would struggle to get out of bed in the morning because sleep was a safe place. He had nightmares for quite a while and still wakes several times each night. We had to take his bed out of his room because he was afraid to sleep on a bed and it brought back too many memories. We had to put a futon couch in his bedroom so that he was able to get some rest.*

*Adam doesn't like to ride his bike anymore and has only left the yard once on his bike in the last year. He is easily scared when he encounters confrontations of any kind, i.e. fighting with his sisters, or violence on TV.*

*Adam was tested for AIDS and other communicable diseases. This was very stressful for us, knowing that our little boy may have been infected with a disease like AIDS. The waiting was unbearable and we waited for test results from Peter Whitmore and Kyle Mason.*

*We have been a family in crisis. So much has happened and we need to just put it to rest. We don't understand the criminal justice system and have been very frustrated with the delays. Neither Larry nor I have heard the whole story yet of Adam's abduction. He has just finished it with his counsellor, but I do not know the details. I don't want to know, but I have to know.*

*I feel that we need to get past the trial stage so that we can deal with it one more time and then put it to rest. We need to heal and carry on with our lives. I don't know what long term effects this will have on (my son). Hopefully with continued counselling he will have a bright future, grow up to be a loving husband and father. I pray this makes him a stronger person.*

• • • • •

### Jennifer Mason

*Not knowing if I would ever see my son again, or if I did would he still be alive was unbearable. Eating and sleeping did not exist during the days my son was missing. All I did was cry, pace the floor and always have the phone close to me.*

*My son has been terrified to sleep by himself for months after the incident and still continues to sleep in the living room. I would often sit and watch my son sleep to help him feel secure, and sometimes I would hear him whispering and stirring.*

*I have experienced nightmares that have kept me awake at night. In the last year I have also experienced depression and panic attacks.*

*My son has had emotional breakdowns where he would cry and say things like "I'm worthless, my life sucks." All I could do was hold him and tell him he was not worthless.*

*Since this has happened there is not a night that goes by that I don't check on him at least twice through the night.*

*My son will never be the same. Maybe he will learn to cope and find a place to carry it within himself through his therapy, but he will carry the memories every single day of his life.*

*My son did not deserve for these horrible things to happen to him, but as horrible as it is all we can do is stick together as a family and pray that he will come through this and be able to live a normal life.*

● ● ● ● ●

## Larry Munroe

*My wife phoned me at work and said Adam is missing and that she found the bikes in (a neighbour's) car garage, that Adam didn't come home for lunch. She said that Rob Summer (the alias used by Peter Whitmore) and Kyle have him. Life took a sharp and painful turn.*

*Who is this guy? The search is on. Police and more police. No Adam. Time stops. Adam is gone. Numb with pain. Who is this person? Police bring a picture. That's him, Rob Summer. Who is he? We can't tell you at this time.*

*On Canada AM — Peter Whitmore is a pedophile.*

*Morning comes. Good news, he doesn't kill his victims, just sexually assaults them. Sick with fear and a building rage for this could happen to us. Police explain the Amber Alert — child in harm's way. Police and media know Whitmore well. So mind-numbing and hard to* understand. Our family members so far away, a state of shock and bewilderment and major stress. Try to understand.

My wife blames herself for how Whitmore did this. Truly not her fault, just a cunning Whitmore I say to her. The rest of our lives to live with. We are strong but are we strong enough? For this we have to hope.

Prayers are answered with Adam being found. He is our Adam. But not the Adam we had. The battered body and the shattered look. A whole new life begins. AIDS cocktails, hepatitis drugs, and all the sexually transmitted disease products for our 10 year old boy. His innocence gone.

• • • • •

### Al Baxter

Ever since this happened to my family things haven't been the same. Emotional feelings all over the house. I feel that my wife hates me, somewhat. I can't talk to my wife about what she is feeling. I feel angry, mad, upset. Also feel that I let my family down as a father when this happened to Kyle.

I was looking day and night, not sleeping, not eating, and not stopping. When I came back from looking I couldn't look at my wife in the face. She was really mad. I don't feel loved sometimes from my family. I don't get respect sometimes; feelings are crazy at the house. I can't sleep.

*Sometimes it feels like it happened just yesterday. I cry when people from my family are around. I think of it every day and night. When I wake up until I go to bed. I feel lost, my heart hurts.*

*I feel like I did something wrong inside of me. My life changed on that day. Feelings are so hard. I lost my habits going out to work. I don't have the feel for it right now. It's hard trying to go to work.*

*I lost trust in everybody that I don't know. I've been feeling like this for about one year now. I cry inside thinking that it is my fault. Where did I go wrong? Why is this happening to me? It feels that I come to the end of the world.*

*A year's gone by and I still feel the same on that day when Kyle was gone. My marriage isn't the same, it's up and down. July is a good plus bad month for us. But more bad, hurting feelings. I feel scared, sad, lost, down, upset, angry my family also has to go through each day that goes by.*

*People know who I am all over Winnipeg. They ask how Kyle is. I say OK. I feel like crying. I feel that I let down everybody. Right now I'm feeling distressed, hopeless, worthless, and lost. I feel mad, also, too, I feel sick inside myself while I writing this letter.*

*Just like it happened yesterday. I wish God would take this pain away from our hearts and souls. If there's a God, I want to send him an SOS Call.*

•  •  •  •  •

# DEVIL AMONG US

**Adam's older sister.**

*I see a counsellor weekly. Adam does not talk about it at all. I found out he was chained to a bed post. I saw some marks on his wrist and ankles.*

*I think Whitmore is really mean.*

*As a family we didn't go anywhere. We got family to run to do errands. When Adam went missing my sister was watching us and she forgot something and had to leave. I thought Whitmore might come back so I was scared. I am still scared sometimes to stay home alone.*

*I just want to get this over with, because it keeps on bringing back the memories. I want to be in the courtroom when Whitmore is sentenced because I want to see what happens when a guy does something like that.*

• • • • •

**Adam's younger sister.**

*I really didn't like Peter Whitmore when I first saw him. He looked mean. He came and asked for eggs and when we didn't have any he got disappointed and that made me scared. I stayed in the house because I was scared while Adam showed them the pigs. Adam would be friends with everyone he knew. I found out after he got home that Peter Whitmore told Adam that if he didn't help him he would get me. I felt very very scared and I wanted to stay near everyone.*

*There is a bully at school and he beats on my brother because of what happened. It makes me feel mad and angry when he does that to him. My mom is going to home-school us in the fall of 07. My friend is home-schooled.*

*This tragic event has made our family closer together. I feel scared when me and my brother and sister are home alone and I like it when my Mom comes and picks us up to go to her work. I won't answer the door if I don't know the person and I know how to phone my sister and Mom and Dad.*

*I see a counsellor weekly to help me with what happened. I felt left out when all the attention and the presents and cards were for Adam. I felt that everyone forgot about me and my sister. So at the end of the month we are having a coming home party for Adam.*

• • • • •

Kyle Mason

*In the past year I've been feeling afraid and always looking over my shoulder. I don't trust anyone I don't know. And I don't like going outside alone. I'm always home or at my friend's.*

*The past year has been really hard. When I first got back I couldn't sleep, I was having nightmares. And I would cry inside every time I thought about it or I would wait till there was no one around.*

*Ever since I've been back I sleep in the living room. I don't know why but I feel really safe in the living room. Anytime I leave this city I feel like I'm going there again. I wish none of this ever happened then I would still be me.*

• • • • •

# DEVIL AMONG US

**Adam Munroe (as told to victim services worker)**

*I don't remember a lot about what happened. I don't want to remember. I was scared and mad when he stole me — when he took me away from my family. I was scared. I did not feel safe. I did not know what was going on. I was scared that he would kill me. When he took me I was quiet and confused. I was mad and afraid he was going to hurt me. I was unable to sleep when I was away. I was worried about dying.*

*My room at home looks much like the room I was kept in. This made me feel I was uncomfortable. I slept downstairs until I got the new futon in my room. My pet mice keep me company in my room. They make me feel more comfortable so I am sleeping in my room again.*

*I did not do as well at school this year. Most of the kids at school are good, but want to know what happened. Every time there is something in the media, the kids at school start to ask questions again and I do not feel that great. There is a bully at school that calls me names. My Mom is going to home-school me next year.*

*Sometimes what happened is on my mind. I am trying to forget what happened. I have a counsellor. She is helping me. I can talk to her. I wrote a story for her about what happened to me. It is three pages long.*

*I feel kinda safe now unless it storms. I had to take this really gross medicine. I am not sure what the medicine is for. Medicine is from a doctor in Regina. I was mad when he stole me. I was mad at (the 14-year-old Winnipeg victim) because he tricked me. I thought he was my friend, but he wasn't.*

*We went on a bike ride to the neighbours and that's when he took me. I was not given much food, just crackers and water and dog food stuff one day. I just about threw up. My tummy felt upset, like there were frogs in my tummy. I felt pretty shaky while I was gone.*

*When I came home I felt kinda better because I wasn't alone. I felt kinda safe with my family. I felt relieved because the police had got him. I did not have to look at him all the time.*

*I feel kinda good now. If I have to go to court it makes me feel good and bad. I want to see him sentenced for life. I feel nervous about going to court.*

*My family is different now. My Mom does not want me to go out by myself anymore. He threatened to take (his younger sister) if I tried to run away*

*I had marks on my leg. I told my sisters that I had fallen in a gopher hole. The truth is that I was chained to the bed. I did not feel good. I had to pee in a bucket. I heard sounds at night. There were mice in the walls. I like mice so I shared my food with the mice.*

# CHAPTER TWENTY-SEVEN

## KIPLING, SASKATCHEWAN

Pat Beaujot lay awake some nights wondering what might have been – but the Saskatchewan farmer was sleeping a lot easier these days knowing Peter Whitmore was behind bars for a very long time, if not forever.

Beaujot didn't think of himself as a hero, downplaying his pivotal role in rescuing Kyle Mason and Adam Munroe from Whitmore's clutches. He insisted he just did what anyone else would have done, despite all the local and national attention he's received.

"It was overwhelming and very appreciated. But a lot of people would have done the same."

Hearing all the details for the first time at Whitmore's sentencing hearing had only underscored the urgency of the search.

"There was going to be a major community search the next day so I'm sure they probably would have been found then. But a day can be a very big thing," he said. "To hear some of the things they went through is pretty tragic."

Beaujot was especially interested in the revelation Whitmore spoke of a plan to kill a neighbouring family and then steal their food and vehicle to escape with his prisoners. It is possible the family Whitmore had in mind was the Beaujots.

"You can see the house (where Whitmore was) quite easily from our place, so a lot of thoughts come to mind. It's very unnerving that this was so close and we have a little guy as well," Beaujot said. His family had become close with the Munroes in the year that had passed, with his son and Adam now forming a bond.

"Rural people like Pat are why we still have Adam," said Larry Munroe.

•  •  •  •  •

## JULY 25, 2007

Peter Whitmore may have struck a deal with justice officials – but his long-time lawyer saw no reason to celebrate.

Despite not raising the mental illness defence, Dan Brodsky still believed Whitmore should be wearing a hospital gown – not prison clothes.

In an interview following Whitmore's sentencing hearing, Brodsky said Canada would be a much safer country if dangerous predators such as Whitmore could get proper medical treatment rather than simply be warehoused behind bars before being returned to society.

He said it was clear Whitmore is suffering from mental illness based on the depravity of his crimes, his disturbing fantasies and an obsession with young boys that didn't waver.

And, Brodsky dismissed suggestions that there was no hope for someone like Whitmore because pedophilia is deemed an "incurable mental disorder" by many professionals.

"We don't refuse to treat cancer patients because there is no cure," Brodsky said.

He said the facts heard in court only showed how deep Whitmore's illness runs. "The facts are appalling. Normal or sane are not the descriptors that come to mind for me," Brodsky said.

He also noted that Whitmore had made at least three bizarre, half-hearted attempts to take his own life in the past year –swallowing a combination of tobacco and WD-40 just prior to his arrest and rubbing feces in a stomach wound and jamming a pen into his scrotum while behind bars.

Brodsky said Whitmore didn't end up pursuing a not-criminally-responsible finding at trial because the state of mental health care is so poor – and the chance of being released so slim – that he was better off taking his chances with a prison term and applying for parole in seven years.

Of course, Crown attorney Anthony Gerein told court Whitmore has often refused sex-offender treatment and counselling while in custody.

Whitmore spoke to Brodsky by telephone after his sentencing and said he was "relieved" the case was over. And Brodsky noted the plea bargain was exactly what Whitmore had agreed to when he had surrendered in August.

"I had offered to shut the case down in two weeks. It could have been done in that time," Brodsky said.

• • • • •

JULY 27, 2007

Was it a serious offer to change his ways or just the first step in trying to appease a parole board that would one day determine his fate?

Either way, Peter Whitmore's offer to be chemically castrated was certainly getting the public's attention.

Only days after being sentenced, Whitmore wrote a letter to prison officials seeking the procedure, which involves ingesting a cocktail of hormonal drugs designed to dramatically reduce his sexual urges. Taken over an extended time, the drugs can permanently remove a person's hormonal drives and his ability to create testosterone.

Whitmore's consent was a major development because Canadian criminals can't be ordered to undergo the treatment. Brodsky said Whitmore needs serious medical help to control his urges and appears serious about finally changing his ways.

Dr. Phil Klassen, a Toronto-based expert on pedophilia, vouched for chemical castration as an effective tool. He testified in a Winnipeg courtroom regarding a dangerous, high-risk pedophile who was branded a long-term offender that required him to be monitored in the community for a decade after his release from jail.

Klassen said the only way to seriously reduce the risk to the public is through chemical castration, which that offender wasn't agreeing to. "Unfortunately, it's rarely accepted by sexual offenders," he said.

Studies have shown the treatment isn't always effective. Some pedophiles who have received significant oral dosages of medication still reported regular sexual arousal and fantasies.

The American Civil Liberties Union has also spoken out against chemical castration in the United States, claiming it is "cruel and unusual punishment" and violates a man's right to "procreate".

Jake Goldenflame, a convicted California sex offender who had turned his life around and become a public speaker, author and advocate for tougher laws against pedophiles, had seen chemical castration work its magic before. One friend of his, who has struggled to control his sexual urges against children, told Goldenflame the drug has changed his life.

"He said to me 'Jake, do you know what it's like to have peace for once in my life. I'm gonna keep taking it," said Goldenflame.

Despite its success, Goldenflame isn't a fan of making it mandatory for all sex offenders as has been done in many American states.

"I think it should only be allowed when the professionals say it is worth doing. It should be solely in the hands of professionals," he said.

• • • • •

## JULY 30, 2007

Peter Whitmore may have been out of sight – but Dan Brodsky was doing his best to ensure he wasn't out of mind. Brodsky launched yet another offensive, calling on the federal government to launch a public inquiry that would study how to better protect society from high-risk sex offenders.

He said Whitmore's case has rocked public confidence in the justice system that can only be rectified through an "impartial, independent" study of what went wrong in the handling of his client and others like him.

"This government no longer has the capacity to protect its citizens from high-risk, high-needs offenders nor does it presently meet the assessment, treatment and management needs of the said group of offenders," Brodsky wrote in a letter sent to Prime Minister Stephen Harper.

"For the victims, their families and the community at large, the Peter Whitmore case will not be over until the serious lingering questions are answered and (preventive) measures are put into practice as a result. On that day, you should feel comfortable letting your own children go for a walk or bicycle ride anywhere in Canada without wondering if they are targets of the next sexually violent predator."

Brodsky said a commissioner should "immediately be appointed" with the mandate to inquire into what changes, if any, should be made in the law and especially the practice relating to the assessment, treatment and management of high-risk, high-needs offenders.

"It would give the proper forum to air all of the competing questions and opinions and look for answers. Do you feel that all of the 'what went wrong?' and 'what do we do?' questions have been answered to your satisfaction? To the victims, police, public...?"

Larry and Paula Munroe found themselves in the unusual position of agreeing with Brodsky that a serious national push for change was needed. They'd been spearheading a local petition calling for tougher penalties and better monitoring, and hoped to one day become more vocal on a national platform.

"We're not going to withdraw and hide. This never should have happened. But we can't change it. There needs to be better controls out there and we are going to go to town over it," said Larry Munroe.

Their future no longer included having to face the man who attacked them or worry about having to testify. But what was in store for Kyle Mason and Adam Munroe?

Not even their families knew. This was entirely new territory, with no textbook telling them what to do or say to ensure the best possible outcome. Experts said the key is to get help early – something both families had taken advantage of.

Billy Brodovsky is one of four full-time counsellors with a unique program in Winnipeg called Families Affected by Sexual Assault. It deals with child sexual assault, except incest. The program is run by New Directions, a non-profit private counselling group that is considered a leading Winnipeg therapy service agency.

The sexual assault program is the only one in Winnipeg that counsels families as well as child victims. It's tailored to crisis intervention and short-term therapy for children 18 years and younger who have been victimized by a sex offender who does not live in the home and who isn't related to the child. It treats about 300 children and their families each year.

"It's not like it never happened, but kids can and do recover from sexual assault and it doesn't have to leave a permanent scar," Brodovsky told the *Winnipeg Free Press*.

Children who suffer at the hands of a pedophile are now believed to be able to return to a normal life as they grow up.

In the past, families were told the odds of their children ever being completely normal were uncertain. Countless tales of self-destruction and suicides of former victims pointed to troubles down the road for child victims, depending on how bad the abuse was and how long it lasted.

Parents were told some children internalized the abuse and others externalized it. Internalizing meant the victim could fall prey to drugs or alcohol addiction or other self-abusive behaviours to mask feelings of insecurity, rage and emotional trauma. Externalizing the abuse meant the child could grow up to become an offender.

Now, counsellors tell families that doesn't have to happen. The key to a recovery is to make sure the victim feels the assault is a real crime and he or she is not to blame.

"The most important thing is that kids are believed by their parents and other family members. They can tell the child, 'We believe you. You're not guilty of anything and we're going to keep you safe,'" Brodovsky said

● ● ● ● ●

**FEBRUARY 11, 2008**
**KIPLING, SASKATCHEWAN**

More than six months after he called for a national inquiry, Dan Brodsky had finally gotten a reply from Canada's justice minister.

Thanks, but no thanks.

Rob Nicholson had written back to Brodsky, saying such a review wouldn't be "productive" because steps have already been taken to address the many legal flaws that allowed Whitmore to continue his sexual predation.

Nicholson apologized to Brodsky for his lengthy delay in responding but said the concerns raised by him were already being addressed through tougher legislation.

He outlined several key areas where changes were being made including the creation of Bill C-2 (the Tackling Violent

Crime Act) which he said was finally starting to make some progress in Ottawa.

• • • • •

OTTAWA, ONTARIO
FEBRUARY 28, 2008

It took nearly two years and the threat of a surprise election but federal politicians had just taken a major step towards offering greater protection to Canadian children. In a ceremony on Parliament Hill, Bill C-2 received Royal assent and was on its way to becoming law.

The bill proposes raising the age of consent and streamlining the process for getting a dangerous offender designation. There were also sections dealing with improved drug-impaired driving laws and introducing new firearms offences.

Prime Minister Stephen had threatened to call an election if the bill wasn't passed. He made the threat in the Commons last fall by making the bill a matter of confidence. That prompted all parties to quickly support the bill and send it to the Senate.

It stalled again. So Harper repeated his threat and brought in a motion telling the Liberal dominated Senate if it didn't pass the bill before March 1, he would take the country to the polls.

Liberal senators balked and said Harper's motion was unconstitutional because the House of Commons can't dictate what the senate does. But the threat of the election pushed the senate to fast-track its hearings and it passed the bill by a vote of 19 to 16. Thirty-one senators – all Liberals but one – abstained from the vote and another 27 senators didn't show up for the vote.

Manitoba senior cabinet minister Vic Toews – who was the justice minister when most of the provisions in C-2 were first introduced – told the *Winnipeg Free Press* it was satisfying to see them become law.

Toews said his government's decision to pressure the Liberals to pass the bill or go to the electorate was the right one. He said most of the measures in the legislation had Liberal support during the last election campaign, and it should never have taken this long to get them into law.

Roz Prober, founder of Winnipeg based Beyond Borders, said she is delighted the law finally got through. "Common sense has prevailed," said Prober.

She said people in other countries "were stunned" to see Canada's age of consent was only 14, and not 16. And she welcomed the beefed-up dangerous offender designations for those convicted three times of a sexual offence. She said before, the onus to convince a judge someone should be labelled a dangerous offender "was all on the shoulders of children."

An extensive *Maclean's* magazine investigation, published in January 2008, produced some alarming results.

Their findings – all of which can be found at www.macleans.ca – included the fact an estimated 1,270 of the 16,295 registered sex offenders in Canada were considered "non-compliant" and had gone missing.

And that wasn't even the worst news. *Maclean's* found that barely half of all convicted sex offenders in Canada had even been added to the registry in the first place.

That's because registration isn't mandatory and must be requested by a prosecutor – something which is only done in about half of all cases, according to *Maclean's*.

"A sex offender registry is only as effective as it is accurate—and Canada's system is certainly not complete," the magazine wrote in calling the registry both "dysfunctional" and a "national embarrassment."

• • • • •

The second anniversary of Kyle Mason's abduction proved to be every bit as harrowing as the first.

Now living with family in eastern Canada, the 16-year-old began having severe anxiety attacks in July 2008 that required him to be taken to hospital on several occasions.

"There were just so many thoughts going on in his head," said his mother, Jennifer Mason.

She would often sit with her son while he tried to fall asleep, stroking his hair as he was obviously struggling with nightmares reliving his horror.

"He'd often start yelling 'No, no' and wake up and be up all night," she said.

She hopes the symptoms will ease as the years pass. But she knows the future remains uncertain.

"We constantly tell him how much he's loved and cared for, that we're here for him," she said, adding Kyle remains reluctant to discuss what happened to him.

Mason doesn't regret the deal that was struck with Whitmore, believing it was best for her son.

"It would not have been good for Kyle to testify," she said. "I don't really care about the political process. I just don't want any other kid to go through this."

Her efforts to speak with members of the Munroe family have fallen through, a product of the lingering feeling from many in Saskatchewan that Kyle could have, and should have, done more to prevent Adam from being abducted and attacked.

"If only people could see what Kyle has been through, all those sleepless nights. If they would have experienced all that, they'd see he's just as much a victim as Adam," said Mason.

Her family still believes Winnipeg police should have taken their initial missing persons report more seriously, despite the circumstances of Al Baxter leaving the boy with "Robert Summer" and the fact Kyle had a history of running away.

She is no longer together with Baxter, the couple driven apart by her bitter feelings over the way he left Kyle with Whitmore. "I found myself always beating up on him for what he did," she said.

The Whitmore case also took an emotional toll on all the police officers who were involved.

Bernard Tremblay, the lead investigator, said there are no regrets about the way the investigation was handled. But officers wish they could have found the boys sooner. Still, he's thankful they found them alive.

"We did everything that we should have done," said Tremblay, who now speaks to other Canadian police agencies about the case as a teaching tool.

• • • • •

Peter Whitmore will be eligible to apply for parole as early as 2013. There is no limit on how many times he can continue to seek release if denied.

One would assume that Whitmore has virtually no chance of getting out based on his history. But to ignore the very real possibility of release is to ignore the reality of the Canadian justice system.

No matter how vile, no matter how dangerous, every criminal in this country can cling to the knowledge that they will always have a shot at freedom.

There are no pieces of legislation, either proposed or pending, which would metaphorically lock the prison door and have the keys thrown away. There is, however, a significant move underway to make early release more difficult.

The federal government commissioned a panel in 2007 to study the way parole in handled in Canada. The group's findings included doing away with statutory release after two-thirds of a sentence and replacing it with something called "earned parole."

Essentially, a prisoner would have to prove their worth behind bars and clearly demonstrate why they deserve to return to the community before their full sentence expires. There would also be greater emphasis on establishing effective, thorough release plans – the kind of thing often missing with Whitmore and so many others – so that criminals don't find themselves like fish out of water the moment they regain their freedom.

The recommendations are now in the hands of the federal government.

"A common frustration expressed to the panel was the lack of motivation displayed by a significant percentage of younger offenders. There seems to be a growing tendency by some offenders to wait out the parole system until they reach their statutory release date at two-thirds the sentence. Consequences seem to be relatively minor for adopting this attitude – living conditions are the same as those for offenders actively engaged in rehabilitation, and few are denied release at their statutory release date. Additionally, offenders not positively engaged while incarcerated pose threats to the safety of staff and other offenders, which in turn, hampers the positive efforts being made by other offenders," the panel wrote in its report.

"An arbitrary release that is not based on rehabilitation is counterproductive and when aggravated by shorter sentences, reduces public safety. This has been demonstrated by the fact the most violent reoffending by federal offenders is committed by those on statutory release. The one resounding theme, heard from both within the walls of the penitentiaries and in communities across Canada, was that statutory release is not working."

The panel found it is currently too difficult to override statutory release and keep someone locked up for their entire sentence.

"For example, an offender serving a sentence of three years will be automatically released at 24 months, unless CSC can present acceptable reasons to the National Parole Board to detain the offender because they are deemed likely to cause death or serious harm to another person or commit a sexual offence involving a child or a serious drug offence before the warrant expiry date. The bar to detain offenders is set very high and few cases meet that bar," they wrote.

"Although CSC has made some attempts to motivate disengaged offenders, the panel believes that more must be done in this area. Rehabilitation must be a shared accountability and the offender must work to address his or her risks and needs. To encourage the offender, different privileges should be afforded those offenders who are positively engaged than to those who are not. Life inside penitentiaries should mirror Canadian society, and the core concept should be the same: earn your own way."

• • • • •

Peter Whitmore's oldest brother gave up trying a long time ago. The man who once tasked himself with protecting a young Peter at all costs now rarely thinks about him.

"I moved to the U.S. in order to get away from the problems he has caused for the family and yet some of them still see him as a victim," said the brother.

"Maybe there was something that wasn't right in his head as a child and I do know that his mental capacity and learning ability was never right. I wanted to help him when he got into trouble and did help a few times. But when does one say no more? I have my own life to deal with and am finally getting on with it. I have met someone and we are planning on getting on with our lives. I have told her a few things about my family and that I don't speak with them anymore. She is very understanding," he said.

"Unfortunately we didn't have an easy life growing up but I look at what happened in my childhood and see the person I have become and notice that I am stronger and better for it. I only wish Peter could have done the same things in his life and could have made adjustments. But he didn't and he blames everyone else for his problems. "

• • • • •

Life has seemingly returned to normal in Whitewood. But locals admit their community will never truly be the same.

The same goes for the Munroe family, who face each day as it comes but never truly know what tomorrow might bring. They cite the overwhelming family and neighbourly support for helping them get through their worst days but know many challenges lay ahead.

Strangers still stop at their farm looking for gas or help fixing a tire. And the family usually doesn't hesitate to lend a helping hand.

"I still stop and help people. We still pretty much do what we've always done," said Larry Munroe. "It's a tragedy, but you've got to keep going. We're not going to withdraw and hide. We are a very strong family."

They continue to keep an observant eye on Ottawa, confident that what they experienced will ultimately make a change for the better.

But they know there are other Peter Whitmores out there today. And the system remains far from perfect as long as predators of his kind can continue to seek and obtain release from prison despite being untreated.

"What the hell is a peace bond to a pedophile?" Larry asks rhetorically. "I know everybody makes mistakes, but somebody made a major mistake by letting this guy loose."

He believes mandatory electronic monitoring should be required for every person who has proven they can't co-exist in society with children. And there is reason for optimism on that front.

The federal Conservative government dropped a bombshell in August 2008 by announcing a pilot project that will put ankle monitors on paroled prisoners to track them day and night.

Public Safety Minister Stockwell Day said the one-year project would involve about 30 prisoners. The devices will use GPS technology to report parolee movements to a monitoring network. The monitors will then alert Corrections Canada any time a parolee violates curfew or location restrictions.

Day said if the program is successful the government will look at extending it across the country. Nova Scotia already uses such a system to monitor offenders and will share its technology and expertise with the federal government. Day said the plan is to help correction officials and police prevent crimes and protect communities.

"We have listened to police and victims groups who have been requesting such a tool for years," he told the Canadian Press. "Compelling offenders to abide by the conditions of their release is a key aspect of our reform of Canada's prison system."

The Munroe family is thankful that some positive changes appear to be coming out of such a tragic situation. Still, their primary focus remains on Adam, his recovery and his future.

"What they do to Whitmore makes a lot of difference to me, Paula, the community. But it doesn't matter to Adam," said Larry.

"He's going to carry this with him the rest of his life."